Timothy George

Reading Scripture
with the Reformers

IVP Academic

An imprint of InterVarsity Press
Downers Grove, Illinois

InterVarsity Press
P.O. Box 1400, Downers Grove, IL 60515-1426
World Wide Web: www.ivpress.com
E-mail: email@ivpress.com

InterVarsity Press* is the book-publishing division of InterVarsity Christian Fellowship/USA*, a movement of
students and faculty active on campus at hundreds of universities, colleges and schools of nursing in the United
States of America, and a member movement of the International Fellowship of Evangelical Students. For
information about local and regional activities, write Public Relations Dept., InterVarsity Christian
Fellowship/USA, 6400 Schroeder Rd., P.O. Box 7895, Madison, WI 53707-7895, or visit the IVCF website
at <www.intervarsity.org>.

Design: Cindy Kiple

Images: The Protestant Church in Lyon, called "The Paradise" at Bibliotheque Publique et Universitaire,
Geneva, Switzerland. Erich Lessing/Art Resource, NY.

ISBN 978-0-8308-2949-1

Printed in the United States of America ∞

Library of Congress Cataloging-in-Publication Data

George, Timothy.
  Reading scripture with the reformers/Timothy George.
     p. cm.
  Includes bibliographical references and index.
  ISB 978-0-8308-2949-1 (pbk.: alk. paper)
  1. Bible—Criticism, interpretation, etc.—History—16th century. 2.
Reformation. 3. Church history—16th century.   I. Title.
  BS511.3.G46 2011
  220.6094'09031—dc22

                                                                2011013673

P	19	18	17	16	15	14	13	12	11	10	9	8	7	6	5	4	3	2	1
Y	27	26	25	24	23	22	21	20	19	18	17	16	15	14	13	12	11

For
The Honorable Albert P. Brewer
and
The Reverend Charles T. Carter

ἀλλήλων τὰ βάρη βαστάζετε, καὶ οὕτως
ἀναπληρώσετε τὸν νόμον τοῦ Χριστοῦ

GALATIANS 6:2

CONTENTS

Abbreviations

ANF   A. Roberts and J. Donaldson, eds. Ante-Nicene Fathers. 10 vols. Buffalo: Christian Literature, 1885-1896. Reprint, Grand Rapids: Eerdmans, 1951-1956. Reprint, Peabody, Mass.: Hendrickson, 1994.

ARG   *Archiv für Reformationsgeschichte.* Archive for Reformation History, Gütersloh, Westf; G. Mohn, 1904-.

CC   Calvin's Commentaries. 22 vols. Grand Rapids: Baker, 2003.

CNTC   Calvin's New Testament Commentaries. 12 vols. Edited by D. W. and T. F. Torrance. Grand Rapids: Eerdmans, 1959-1972.

CO   *Ioannis Calvini Opera Quae Supersunt Ommia.* 59 vols. Corpus Reformatorum 29-88. Edited by G. Baum, E. Cunitz and E. Reuss. Brunswich and Berlin, 1863-1900.

CR   Corpus Reformatorum. Edited by C. G. Bretsjchneider. Halle, 1834-1860.

CWE   Collected Works of Erasmus. 86 vols. planned. Toronto: University of Toronto Press, 1969-.

EE   P. S. Allen, ed. *Opus espistolarum Desiderii Erasmi Roterodami.* 12 vols. Oxford: Oxford University Press, 1906-1947.

HCC   Philip Schaff. *History of the Christian Church.* 8 vols. New York: Charles Scribner, 1882-1910.

JETS   *Journal of Evangelical Theological Society.* Published by the Evangelical Theological Society, Louisville, Ky. 1958-.

LB   J. Leclerc, ed. *Desiderii Erasmi Roterodami Opera Omnia.* 10 vols. Leiden [Lugduni Batavorum], 1703-1706.

LCC   J. Baillie et al., eds. The Library of Christian Classics. 26 vols. Philadelphia: Westminster, 1953-1966.

LCL   Loeb Classical Library. Cambridge, Mass.: Harvard University Press; London: Heinenmann, 1912-.

LW   *Luther's Works* ["American Edition"]. 55 vols. St. Louis: Concordia; Philadelphia: Fortress, 1955-1986.

MBW   *Melancthons Briefwechsel: Kritische und Kommentierte Gesamtausgabe.* Stuttgart-Bad Cannstatt: Frommann-Holzboog, 1977-.

OER   *Oxford Encyclopedia of the Reformation.* 4 vols. Edited by Hans J. Hillerbrand. New York: Oxford University Press, 1996.

PG   J. P. Migne, ed. Patrologia cursus completus. Series Graeca. 166 vols. Paris: Migne, 1857-1886.

PL   J. P. Migne, ed. Patrologia cursus completus. Series Latina. 221 vols. Paris: Migne, 1844-1864.

WA   D. Martin Luther Werke: Kritische Gesamtausgabe. 66 vols. Weimar: Hermann Böhlaus Nachfolger, 1883-1987.

WA, Br *D. Martin Luther Werke: Kritische Gesamtausgabe: Briefwechsel.* 18 vols. Weimar: Hermann Böhlaus Nachfolger, 1930-1985.

WA, DB *D. Martin Luther Werke: Kritische Gesamtausgabe: Deutsche Bibel.* 12 vols. Weimar: Hermann Böhlaus Nachfolger, 1906-1961.

WA, TR *D. Martin Luther Werke: Kritische Gesamtausgabe: Tischreden.* 6 vols. Weimar: Hermann Böhlaus Nachfolger, 1912-1921.

WLS   *What Luther Says: A Practical In-Home Anthology for the Active Christian.* 3 vols. St. Louis: Concordia Publishing House, 2006.

WML   Works of Martin Luther with Introductions and Notes. 6 vols. Philadelphia: A. J. Holman & Castle, 1915-1932.

Z   Emil Egli, George Finsler, et al., eds. *Huldreich Zwinglis Sämtliche Werke.* Corpus Reformatorum. Vols. 88-101. Berlin-Leipzig-Zürich, 1905-1956.

PREFACE

G. R. ELTON, AN ESTEEMED HISTORIAN OF AN EARLIER GENERATION, once wrote that "if there is a single thread running through the whole story of the Reformation, it is the explosive and renovating and often disintegrating effect of the Bible."[1] This book is the story, or at least part of the story, of how the Bible came to have a central role in the sixteenth-century movement for religious reform that we call the Protestant Reformation. There had been many Bible-based reform movements throughout the history of the church, beginning with monasticism, in which the Scriptures had a prominent place in the daily liturgy of the hours. Closer to the Reformation, the Bible had also been championed by late medieval movements of dissent—the Lollards in England, the Hussites in Bohemia and the Waldensians spreading from the Italian Alps to every corner of Europe. There were the Brothers and Sisters of the Common Life who copied, read and taught the Bible in their many communities throughout Germany and the Low Countries. The old myth that there was complete ignorance of the Bible between the death of Augustine and the birth of Luther has long been exploded.

And yet there was something unique in the way the Bible took

---

[1]G. R. Elton, *Reformation Europe, 1517-1559* (New York: Harper & Row, 1963), p. 52.

center stage at the time of the Reformation. Nearly a century after King Henry VIII allowed the first royally sanctioned Bible to be published in English, William Chillingworth, a Catholic who became a Protestant only to return later to the Church of Rome, declared in 1638: "The Bible, the Bible only I say, is the religion of Protestants." While much controversy would surround that little word *only*, it was manifestly true that the translation and dissemination of the Scriptures had profoundly shaped the spiritual lives of many people. John Foxe tells of a farmer who gave a wagonload of hay for a copy of the epistle of James. And John Knox relates the story of a believer in Scotland who was so excited to have the Bible in English that he left his wife alone in bed at night to read from his treasured volume. And there was the incomparable John Bunyan who asked, "Have you never a hill Mizar to remember? Have you forgot the close, the milk house, the stable, the barn, and the light, where God did visit your soul? Remember also the Word—the Word, I say, upon which the Lord hath caused you to hope."[2] These examples and many others speak of the transformative effect of the Bible on many who read it eagerly for the first time.

It would be easy to find similar testimonies of the Bible's power and influence from earlier periods in the history of the church. But two developments on the eve of the Reformation made the Protestant appropriation of the Bible more encompassing than anything that had happened in the previous fifteen hundred years. One was the advent of printing, which effected a communications revolution comparable to that brought about by the computer and the Internet in our day. Bibles had to be chained in the Middle Ages, not to prevent their being read but to keep them from being stolen. Bibles were expensive and rare, and it took many months for one copy to be made by hand. The printing press changed all of this almost

---

[2]John Bunyan, *Grace Abounding to the Chief of Sinners* (London: J. M. Dent and Sons, 1928), p. 5.

overnight. By the time of Luther's death in 1546, it is estimated that half a million copies of his Bible were in circulation. The other development was the product of the "new learning" brought about by the recovery of classical languages and the critical study of ancient sources. This made possible a new approach to biblical scholarship and exegesis.

In the following pages we touch on three recurring tensions that came to the fore in the Reformation understanding of the Bible. First, there is the question of Scripture and tradition. The reformers insisted that the Word took precedence over the church. Because of this all decisions, decrees and traditions had to be normed by "the proper touchstone" of Scripture. But it was never simply a question of Scripture *or* tradition, holy writ *or* holy church. The sufficiency of Scripture functioned in the context where the Bible was regarded as the book given to the church, gathered and guided by the Holy Spirit. In many ways, the Reformation was as much a struggle over the writings of the church fathers as it was over Scripture itself. Which Ambrose? Whose Augustine? Why Origen and not Chrysostom? The question of biblical authority and theological continuity helped to frame the issue of Protestant identity in the Reformation.

Another tension of the period grew out of the desire to make the Bible available to everyone in the common languages of the day. On this issue, Erasmus and Luther, and indeed some of the Catholic reformers, stood together. Early Reformation initiatives were driven by the call to translate the Bible into the vernacular so that farm boys at their ploughs and milkmaids at their pails could hold the Word of God in their hands and read it with their eyes. It soon became evident, however, that godly pastors and teachers were necessary to help interpret the Bible in responsible ways. The old joke was that down in Rome there was one pope sitting on seven hills while up in Germany there were a hundred popes sitting on every little ant hill, and the joke had enough truth behind it to make Protestants wince. The disaster of the Peasants' War and the later debacle of the Anabaptist kingdom of Münster prompted Protestant reformers to develop programs for pastoral training and theological resources for those charged with handling the Word of God.

A third issue related to how the Bible was used in the life and worship of the Protestant churches. For the Bible was meant to be not only read, studied, translated, memorized and meditated on. It was also to be embodied in preaching, baptism, the Lord's Supper, singing, praying and service in the world. The distinct traditions of the Protestant Reformation often grew out of the diverse ways the Word was embodied in what might be called the practicing of the Bible.

It is fitting that we open this book with a hymn that is also a prayer. Though written in modern times, these words breathe the spirit of the Reformation:

> Thanks to God whose word incarnate
> came to save our human race.
> Deeds and words and death and rising
> testify to heaven's grace.
> God has spoken:
> praise him for his open word.
>
> Thanks to God whose word was written
> in the Bible's sacred page,
> record of the revelation
> showing God to every age.
> God has spoken:
> praise him for his open word.
>
> Thanks to God whose word is published
> in the tongues of every race.

See its glory undiminished
by the change of time or place.
God has spoken:
praise him for his open word.[3]

[3]The words to this hymn were written by Reginald Thomas Brooks (1918-1985). "Thanks to God Whose Word Was Spoken," words: R. T. Brooks, ©1954, Ren. 1982 Hope Publishing Company, Carol Stream, IL 60188. All rights reserved. Used by permission.

ONE

WHY READ
THE REFORMERS?

Most of all, perhaps, we need intimate knowledge of the past.
Not that the past has any magic about it, but because we cannot study the future,
and yet need something to set against the present, to remind us that the basic
assumptions have been quite different in different periods. . . . A man who has lived in
many places is not likely to be deceived by the local errors of his native village:
the scholar has lived in many times and is therefore in some degree immune
from the great cataract of nonsense that pours from the press
and the microphone of his own age.

C. S. LEWIS

THE AGE OF THE REFORMATION WAS A TIME OF TRANSITION, vitality
and change that gave us the compass, the printing press, the telescope,
gunpowder, the first map of the New World, the revival of the visual
arts and letters (Michelangelo and Shakespeare), widespread infla-
tion, the rise of the modern nation-state, wars of religion—and a
word to describe all of this, revolution, from Nikolaus Copernicus's
famous work, *De revolutionibus orbium coelestium* (1543). The Protestant Reformation was a revolution in the original scientific sense of

that word: the return of a body in orbit to its original position. It was never the desire of Luther to start a new church from scratch. He and the other reformers who followed in his tracks wanted to re-form the one, holy, catholic and apostolic church on the basis of the Word of God and to do so by returning to the historic faith of the early church as they found it set forth in the pure teachings of the Scriptures. This led to a fundamental reorientation in Christian theology. Luther's rediscovery of justification by faith alone, Zwingli's insistence on the clarity and certainty of the Bible, Calvin's emphasis on the glory and sovereignty of God and the Anabaptist quest for a true visible church all found expression in numerous new confessions, catechisms, commentaries, liturgies, hymns, martyrologies and church orders. Like a great earthquake that continues to generate seismic aftereffects long after the first shock is over, the Reformation set in motion a revolution in religious life the effects of which are still being felt half a millennium later.

The reformers of the sixteenth century shared with ancient Christian writers and the medieval scholastics who came before them a high regard for the inspiration and authority of the Bible. Already in the New Testament the writings of the Hebrew Bible, which Christians would later come to know as the Old Testament, are regarded as divinely inspired, God-breathed (2 Tim 3:16). On more than one occasion, Paul identified the Scripture with God's own speaking (see Gal 3:8; Rom 9:17; 10:11). It is God who speaks in the Scripture, and for this reason it has an unassailable validity for the people of God. What J. N. D. Kelly wrote about the early church is equally true for biblical exegetes in the medieval and Reformation eras: "It goes without saying that the fathers envisaged the whole of the Bible as inspired."[1]

---

[1] J. N. D. Kelly, *Early Christian Doctrines* (San Francisco: Harper & Row, 1978), p. 61. On the medieval understanding of biblical authority, G. R. Evans has observed: "It was taken for granted by all students of scripture in the Middle Ages that the text of the Bible was literally

There were many debates about the Bible in the sixteenth century: Should it be translated and, if so, by whom and into which languages? What is the extent of the canon? How can one gauge the true sense and right interpretation of Scripture? How was the Bible to be used in the preaching and worship of the church? What is the relative authority of Scripture and church tradition? These and other questions about the Bible were debated not only between Catholics and Protestants but also among scholars and theologians within these two traditions. Such disputes should not be minimized, for some of them proved to be church-dividing. But it is also important to recognize that the exegetical debates of the sixteenth century were carried out within a common recognition of the Scriptures as divinely given. Referring to the books of the Old and New Testaments as "sacred and canonical," the First Vatican Council (1869-1870), looking perhaps backward more than forward, summarized the Catholic view of the Bible in words that would have been warmly embraced by both Protestant and Catholic reformers in the sixteenth century:

> These books are held by the Church as sacred and canonical, not as having been composed by merely human labour and afterwards approved by her authority, nor merely because they contain revelation without error, but because, written under the inspiration of the Holy Ghost, they have God for their author.[2]

It was a core conviction of the Reformation that the careful study and meditative listening to the Scriptures, what the monks called *lectio divina*, could yield a life-changing result. For the reformers the Bible was a treasure trove of divine wisdom to be heard, read, marked,

---

and directly inspired. The picture of an evangelist sitting writing with the Holy Spirit in the form of a dove with its beak in his ear is an iconographical commonplace. "The Middle Ages to the Reformation," in *The Oxford Illustrated History of the Bible*, ed. John Rogerson (Oxford: Oxford University Press, 2001), p. 188.

[2]Alfred Duran, "Inspiration of the Bible," in *Catholic Encyclopedia* (New York: Robert Appleton Company, 1910), 8:45-46.

learned and inwardly digested, as the Book of Common Prayer's collect for the second Sunday in Advent puts it, to the end that "we may embrace, and ever holdfast, the blessed hope of everlasting life, which thou has given us in our Savior Jesus Christ." In his commentary on Hebrews 4:12, "The Word of God is living and active, and sharper than any two-edged sword," Calvin declared, "Whenever the Lord accosts us by his Word, he is dealing seriously with us to affect all our inner senses. There is, therefore, no part of our soul which should not be influenced."[3] The study of the Bible was meant to be transformative at the most basic level of the human person, *coram deo*. It was meant to lead to communion with God.

But for the reformers the Bible had public as well as personal consequences. The Bible was not merely a text to be observed, analyzed and internalized. It was also an event, a "happening" of earth-shattering moment. In 1522, one year after his famous confession, "Here I stand, God help me," at Worms (April 18, 1521), Luther described, with a twinkle in his eyes no doubt, how the Reformation had been brought about solely by the Bible while he had been taking a snooze or having a drink with his friends.

> Take me, for example. I opposed indulgences and all papists, but never by force. I simply taught, preached, wrote God's Word; otherwise I did nothing. And then while I slept or drank Wittenberg beer with my Philip and my Amsdorf, the Word so greatly weakened the papacy that never a prince or emperor did such damage to it. I did nothing. The Word did it all.[4]

The reformers knew, of course, that the expression "Word of God" referred in its most basic sense to Jesus Christ. Jesus Christ is the substantial Word, the eternal Logos who was made flesh—*verbum*

---

[3]CNTC 12:50.
[4]WML 2:399-400; LW 51:77. This is from Luther's second Invocavit sermon, delivered on March 10, 1522.

incarnatum—for us and for our salvation. And Word of God was also
the spoken word, so that the preaching of the gospel is a sacramental
event, a means of grace. As Heinrich Bullinger put it boldly in the
Second Helvetic Confession (1566): "The preaching of the Word of
God *is* the Word of God."[5] Yet the Word of God was also a canon of
texts, a collection of books (*biblia*), something that could be written
down, copied, translated, edited, published, disseminated, commented on and taught. In the quotation cited above, when Luther
said that he "wrote God's Word," he was referring to his recently
completed translation of the New Testament from Greek into German. Soon William Tyndale would follow suit in English, and others
in French, Dutch, Swedish, Spanish, Italian, Czech, Hungarian, even
Arabic, so that the written Word of God resounded from the lecture
rooms, debate halls and pulpits of all parts of Europe.

IMPERIALISMS OF THE PRESENT

I first came to the study of the Reformation during my undergraduate
studies at a state university in Tennessee where I majored in history
and took many courses in philosophy and religion. I had wonderful
professors who taught me to think critically, to weigh historical sources
carefully, to appreciate the long sweep and complexity of what was
called in those days western civilization. I remain grateful for what I
learned in that institution, but the reigning paradigm was shaped by
the assumptions and icons of modernity whose works we read—Kant,
Schleiermacher, Hegel, Hume, Heidegger, Husserl, Tillich, Bult-
mann and (just a little snippet of) Barth. I still have my well-marked,
blue-backed copy of John Herman Randall's *The Making of the Modern Mind*, a major textbook in one of my courses. This book, first pub-

---

[5]*Praedicatio verbi Dei est verbum Dei*. See A. C. Cochrane, ed., *Reformed Confessions of the
Sixteenth Century* (Louisville, Ky.: Westminster John Knox, 2003), pp. 220-304. For the
Latin text, see W. Herrenbrück in *Bekenninisschriften und Kirchenordnungen der nach Gottes
Wort reformierten Kirche*, ed. Wilhelm Niesel (Zollikon-Zürich: Evangelischer Verlag,
1938), 3:223.

lished in 1940, offered a sweeping overview of the intellectual background of the modern world. The Reformation was presented as a form of medieval supernaturalism, a regressive reaction against the growing naturalism and humanism that was increasingly to mark the modern age. In this schema, Erasmus was a proto-modernist at once liberal and liberating in his appeal to reason and free will; Luther was a Fundamentalist with a capital F. The book closed with a quotation from Bertrand Russell extolling Thought, with a capital T (read "autonomous human reason"), in exalted religious tones: "Thought looks into the pit of hell and is not afraid. It sees man, a feeble speck, surrounded by unfathomable depths of silence; yet it bears itself proudly, as unmoved as if it were Lord of the universe. Thought is great and swift and free, the light of the world, and the chief glory of man."[6]

When I arrived at Harvard Divinity School in the 1970s, I met Harvey Cox, like me a former Baptist youth evangelist. Cox was then in his post-*Secular City*, pre-postmodern phase and was much enamored with Buddhism and spiritualities of the East. In 1977 he published a book titled *Turning East* in which he argued for what he called the "principle of genealogical selectivity."

> As late twentieth-century Christians trying to work out a viable spirituality, there are two principal historical sources to which we should look. They are the earliest period of our history and the most recent, the first Christian generations and the generation just before us . . . the ransacking of other periods for help in working out a contemporary spirituality soon becomes either antiquarian or downright misleading.[7]

Cox's counsel against "ransacking" the past reflects an attitude

---

[6]John Herman Randall, *The Making of the Modern Mind* (Cambridge, Mass.: Riverside Press, 1940), p. 680. The quotation is from Bertrand Russell, *Why Men Fight* (New York: A. C. Boni, 1916), pp. 178-79.
[7]Harvey Cox, *Turning East* (New York: Simon & Schuster, 1977), p. 157.

common in American culture in general, especially within evangelicalism. It reflects what might be called the heresy of contemporaneity or, in less theological terms, the imperialism of the present. What do I mean by this term? In the Middle Ages, everyone believed that the earth was at the center of reality, that the whole created cosmos was ordered in relation to what we now know, thanks to Copernicus, is a mere speck of dust among myriads of constellations and galaxies. The Copernican revolution was a paradigm shift. It radically altered our view of space. But we have yet to experience a similar revolution with respect to time. We still place ourselves, our values, our worldview at the center of history, relegating whole epochs to the Dark Ages or pre-Enlightenment culture. Thus the Christian past, including ways earlier generations of believers have understood the Bible, becomes not so much something to be studied and appropriated as something to be ignored or overcome.

Reading Scripture with the fathers, the scholastics and the reformers finds no place in the polarizing dialectic recommended by Cox. The dialectic of primitivism or presentism establishes two centers of scriptural engagement—the first Christian generation, which means the writings of the New Testament, and the most recent generations, notably my generation. This dichotomy governs the way Scripture is read in much of the Christian community today, both in liberal mainline churches and in conservative evangelical ones. There is, we might say, a presentist imperialism of the left and a presentist imperialism of the right.

Cox's statement clearly stands in continuity with the liberal Protestant theology of Friedrich Schleiermacher, the father of modern hermeneutics, who defined religion as the feeling of absolute dependence and understood Scripture as a detailed expression of that faith which was present in a feeling of need.[8] Schleiermacher displaced the

---

[8]Friedrich Schleiermacher, *The Christian Faith* (New York: Harper & Row, 1963), 2:593.

central teachings and dogmas of the church with Christian self-consciousness. This allowed him to relativize the doctrines of traditional orthodox belief by "entrusting them to history for safekeeping," as he once put it.[9] It is not surprising to find Schleiermacher's entire treatment of the doctrine of the Trinity relegated to a brief appendix at the end of his nearly eight-hundred-page textbook of systematic theology, *On the Christian Faith.*

If the reader's own religious self-consciousness and that of the immediately preceding generations form one pole of biblical interpretation, then the other consists in the experience of the first Christians, reconstrued by means of presumably objective and disinterested scholarship. At the heart of this enterprise is the effort to identify what we might call the Bible behind the Bible. In this critical approach, one part of Scripture is played off against another (most obviously, the two Testaments). Discrete units within the Bible are further dissected in terms of competing hypotheses of authorship, literary form, original context, source of origin, and so forth, so that any sense of Scripture as a coherent narrative unity is negated. Historical-critical exegesis arose as an effort to release the Bible from the shackles placed on it by the intervening two millennia of biblical interpretation. In his famous 1885 Bampton Lectures, Frederic W. Farrar so described the critical scholarly enterprise:

> And how often has the Bible thus been wronged! It has been imprisoned in the cells of alien dogma; it has been bound hand and foot in the grave clothes of human tradition; it has been entombed in a sepulcher by systems of theology, and the stone of human power has been rolled up to close its door. But now the stone has been rolled away from the door of the sepulcher,

---

[9]See Jaroslav Pelikan, *Historical Theology: Continuity and Change in Christian Doctrine* (Philadelphia: Westminster Press, 1971), p. 160. See also Timothy George, "Dogma Beyond Anathema: Historical Theology in the Service of the Church," *Review and Expositor* 84 (1987): 691-707.

and the enemies of the Bible can never shake its divine authority unless they be fatally strengthened by our hypocrisies, our errors, and our sins.[10]

The history of how the Bible has been interpreted throughout the history of the church thus becomes at best a distraction, a useless habit of ransacking the past for spiritual guidance to the neglect of the scientific analysis and reconstruction of the Bible itself. It was the aim of Farrar and his colleagues to liberate the Bible from its churchly bondage.

An imperialism of the present also thrives on the right within a populist evangelicalism shaped by the likes of the celebrated evangelist Billy Sunday, who once boasted, "I don't know any more about theology than a jackrabbit does about ping pong, but I'm on the way to glory."[11] A higher level of discourse is carried on in the Evangelical Theological Society, but even this august group of scholars has only recently amended its annually subscribed statement of faith to include, in addition to the affirmation of biblical inerrancy, a required belief in the doctrine of the Trinity. If, in Paul Tillich's terms, Protestant principle has swallowed up Catholic substance in much of contemporary evangelicalism, this is because evangelicals have paid too little attention to the sum total of the Christian heritage handed down from previous ages, including the practice of reading Scripture in the company of the whole people of God. It is ironic that the Reformation principle of *sola scriptura*, though much misunderstood, has led to the neglect among Protestants of the biblical commentaries of the reformers. We shall revisit the principle of *sola scriptura* throughout this volume as we consider how the reformers understood the Bible in relation to the tradition of the church. For now it is sufficient

---

[10]Frederic W. Farrar, *History of Interpretation* (New York: E. P. Dutton, 1886), pp. 17-18.
[11]W. T. Ellis, *"Billy" Sunday: The Man and His Message* (Philadelphia: Universal Book and Bible House, 1914), p. 147.

to recognize the danger of using *sola scriptura* as a slogan to cut our-selves off from reading along with the fathers and reformers of ages past. J. N. Darby, the founder of the Plymouth Brethren, tried to eliminate all vestiges of the Catholic tradition, including ministerial orders and the use of biblical commentaries, which he considered un-helpful intermediaries between the Scriptures and the individual soul. F. F. Bruce, the great evangelical New Testament scholar, re-lated a comment made about Darby: "He only wanted men 'to submit their understanding *to* God,' that is, to the Bible, that is, to his interpretation!"[12] Today Darby's disciples are legion and not only among the Brethren movement he inspired.

SUPERIOR EXEGESIS

The historical-critical interpretation of the Bible held sway during the latter part of the nineteenth and nearly all of the twentieth cen-tury, and it still informs much of the discourse within the secular academy and the academic guild of biblical scholars. Within the past generation, however, the dominance of the historical-critical para-digm has been challenged from two different yet converging sources. On the one hand, there is a growing appreciation for the history of exegesis and the theological interpretation of the Bible understood as the book of the church. On the other hand, postmodern interpreta-tions of the human self, language and textuality, while often couched in nonreligious terms, draw on themes and sensibilities of the pre-modern Christian tradition and call into question many assumptions of critical exegesis. Together these developments have created a new openness for a fresh engagement with the exegetical writings of the church fathers, scholastics and reformers.

In 1980, David C. Steinmetz published in *Theology Today* an essay with an edgy title, "The Superiority of Precritical Exegesis."[13] A lead-

---

[12]F. F. Bruce, *Tradition Old and New* (Exeter: Paternoster, 1970), p. 14.
[13]David C. Steinmetz, "The Superiority of Precritical Exegesis," *Theology Today* 37

ing scholar of the Reformation, Steinmetz does not deal directly with sixteenth-century exegesis in this article. Rather, he tackles what C. S. Lewis once called the "chronological snobbery" of scholarly methods that dismiss Reformation-era studies of the Bible, along with the interpretive tradition that preceded them, as antiquated, regressive and all but useless for understanding the Bible today. As an example of this approach, Steinmetz quotes Benjamin Jowett, Regius Professor of Greek in the University of Oxford, whose oft-cited 1859 essay, "On the Interpretation of Scripture," included this statement: "The true use of interpretation is to get rid of interpretation, and leave us alone in company with the author."[14] Jowett's jibe, though dressed in high Anglican garb, sounds strikingly similar to Alexander Campbell's advice to his disciples. The Restorationist leader encouraged his followers to "open the New Testament as if mortal man had never seen it before."[15]

Returning to Augustine and the early church, Steinmetz shows how the famous theory of the fourfold sense of Scripture that came to be widely used in the Middle Ages was a way of taking seriously the words and sayings of Scripture, including implicit meanings beyond the original intentions of the human authors. According to Steinmetz, this kind of exegesis did not mean the abandonment of the literal sense of the text, which was always taken as a given (the history in the Bible was understood as historical and the miracles as miraculous). Indeed, beginning with Thomas Aquinas and Nicholas of Lyra in the Middle Ages and continuing into the Reformation the literal sense became more prominent, even if more complex as it absorbed more and more of the content of the spiritual meanings. But the pre-

(1980-1981): 27-38.

[14]Benjamin Jowett, "On the Interpretation of Scripture," in *Essays and Reviews*, 7th ed. (London: Longman, Green, Longman & Roberts, 1861), p. 384.

[15]Cited in Nathan O. Hatch, "*Sola Scriptura* and *Novus Ordo Seclorum*," in *The Bible in America*, ed. Nathan O. Hatch and Mark A. Noll (New York: Oxford University Press, 1982), p. 72.

critical exegetical approach did not mean an "anything goes" method of interpretation. The Bible opened up a field of possible meanings that allowed for considerable exegetical creativity but also imposed limits on the interpreter. Exactly what those limits were and how they related to the magisterial authority of the church would become major issues of dispute in the Reformation.

Like his teacher, Heiko A. Oberman, Steinmetz has emphasized the importance of understanding the Reformation in medieval perspective. He has also pioneered the method of comparative exegesis showing both continuity and discontinuity between major Reformation figures and the preceding exegetical traditions (see especially his essays collected in *Luther in Context* and *Calvin in Context*).[16] The work of Steinmetz and his many students has contributed significantly to a renaissance in the theological interpretation of the Bible that has become one of the major and most encouraging developments in recent theology.

One of the best recent introductions to the theological interpretation of Scripture is J. Todd Billings's *The Word of God for the People of God*, in which the value of premodern biblical exegesis is affirmed and defended against popular objections.[17] Billings emphasizes the churchly context of reading Scripture—the Bible is the church's book and is meant to be a means of grace, an instrument of communion with God. The sterility of the historical-critical method resulted in part from the sequestration of biblical studies to the context of an increasingly secularized academy divorced from the life and faith of the people of God. The closing sentence in Steinmetz's programmatic essay points to the peril of such a dichotomy: "Until the historical-critical method becomes critical of its own theoretical foundations and develops a hermeneutical theory adequate to the nature of the

---

[16]David C. Steinmetz, *Luther in Context* (Bloomington: Indiana University Press, 1986); David C. Steinmetz, *Calvin in Context* (Oxford: Oxford University Press, 1995).
[17]J. Todd Billings, *The Word of God for the People of God* (Grand Rapids: Eerdmans, 2010).

text which it is interpreting, it will remain restricted—as it deserves to be—to the guild and the academy, where the question of truth can endlessly be deferred."

"The Superiority of Precritical Exegesis" has been reprinted several times and is frequently cited by scholars engaged in biblical interpretation. Also, an important volume of essays has been published to show how major themes in Steinmetz's essay have been applied in sixteenth-century exegesis and interpretation: *Biblical Interpretation in the Era of the Reformation*, edited by Richard A. Muller and John L. Thompson.[18] This volume includes an earlier statement by Steinmetz, his ten theses on theology and exegesis, which he first presented in the 1970s and which continues to inform studies in the history of biblical interpretation.

1. The meaning of a biblical text is not exhausted by the original intention of the author.

2. The most primitive layer of biblical tradition is not necessarily the most authoritative.

3. The importance of the Old Testament for the church is predicated upon the continuity of the people of God in history, a continuity which persists in spite of discontinuity between Israel and the church.

4. The Old Testament is the hermeneutical key which unlocks the meaning of the New Testament and apart from which it will be misunderstood.

5. The church and not human experience as such is the middle term between the Christian interpreter and the biblical text.

6. The gospel and not the law is the central message of the biblical text.

---

[18]Richard A. Muller and John L. Thompson, eds., *Biblical Interpretation in the Era of the Reformation: Essays Presented to David C. Steinmetz in Honor of His Sixtieth Birthday* (Grand Rapids: Eerdmans, 1996).

7. One cannot lose the tension between the gospel and the law without losing both law and gospel.

8. The church which is restricted in its preaching to the original intention of the author is a church which must reject the Old Testament as an exclusively Jewish book.

9. The church which is restricted in its preaching to the most primitive layer of biblical tradition as the most authoritative is a church
which can no longer preach from the New Testament.

10. Knowledge of the exegetical tradition of the church is an indis-
pensable aid for the interpretation of Scripture.[19]

A further note should be added about the loaded terms "precritical" and "superior." As Muller and Thompson pointed out, the concept of precritical exegesis is fraught with hubris and condescension.
A close reading of premodern exegesis will show that many of its
practitioners were keenly aware of the kind of issues that preoccupy
contemporary students of the Bible such as the authorship of the
Pentateuch, multiple versions of the same event, imprecision in quotations, the so-called synoptic problem, and so forth. Through the
work of Erasmus and other humanist scholars, these issues became
more prominent at the time of the Reformation, but they are pre-
saged in earlier commentaries as well. In other words, "precritical"
does not equal "uncritical." In what sense then, is pre-Enlightenment
study of the Bible superior to that practiced by Jowett, Farrar, and
their successors?

It must be admitted that the knowledge base for the study of the
Bible today is quantitatively much greater than it was in the sixteenth
century. To take only one example, the field of archeology (and its
related disciplines like epigraphy, numismatics, comparative philol-

[19]Originally published as "Theology and Exegesis: Ten Theses," in *Historie de l'exégèse au
XVIe siècle* (Geneva: Librarie Droz, 1978), p. 382.

ogy, and so on) was just emerging in the age of the Renaissance. Textual criticism of the Bible was also in its infant stages. No one had heard of the Dead Sea Scrolls or the Rosetta stone. The study of New Testament Greek remained uninformed by the discovery of additional manuscripts and Hellenistic papyri. It would be foolish to neglect these and many other advances that have been made in the study of the Bible over the past two centuries, and no responsible practitioner of theological exegesis advocates anything like that. The appeal to the superiority of premodern biblical exegesis is a protest against the reductionism inherent in the longstanding monopoly of the historical-critical method, not a rejection of rigorous historical study of the Bible. Biblical commentaries written in the sixteenth century are marked by diverse and sometimes clashing interpretations, to say nothing of the many centuries of Christian exegesis that preceded them. However, what this tradition shares in common, often in contrast to more recent critical approaches, are five principles that guide our reading and understanding of Scripture.

The Bible is the inspired and authoritative Word of God. Recent debates on biblical inspiration and inerrancy have obscured for some what has been the received wisdom for all orthodox Christians: Scripture is a divinely bestowed, Spirit-generated gift of the triune God and should thus be received with gratitude, humility and a sense of reverence. Christians do not worship the Bible, but the God they do worship—Father, Son and Holy Spirit—has revealed himself and his plans for them and for the world through the words and message of the Bible. This commitment has been expressed in various ways throughout the history of the church, but the great Methodist leader John Wesley put it in a way that would have been met with large approval by most of the biblical exegetes who preceded him: "The Scriptures, therefore, of the Old and New Testament are a most solid and precious system of divine truth. Every part is worthy of God and altogether are one entire body, wherein is no defect, no excess. It is the fountain of heavenly wisdom, which they who are able to taste, prefer to all writings of men, however wise or learned or holy."[20] Because this is true the Bible cannot be read just "like any other book" (Jowett's phrase) but must be received in faith, the kind of faith that is formed by love and leads to holiness.

The Bible is rightly read in light of the rule of faith. Some readers may have balked at the word *system* in the quotation from Wesley given above, thinking it a cipher for foundationalist epistemology or a doctrinal grid derived from a nonbiblical view of reality and imposed on Scripture from without. But Wesley was no systematic theologian. What he had in mind was the pattern of Christian truth found in the Bible and recognized by the church since the days of the apostles as the *regula fidei*, the rule of faith. What is the rule of faith? It is the apostolic summary of the Bible's storyline. It is the story of how the God of Israel created all that is, the drama of his redemptive mission in the life, death and resurrection (and coming again) of Jesus Christ, and the account of his sending the Spirit to gather to himself a people called by his name. The rule of faith is the plot of the biblical canon. Its earliest forms are found already in the hymns and creeds of the New Testament and in the first baptismal confession of faith: "Jesus is Lord!" As the early church confronted new threats from within and from without, the rule of faith found fuller expression in what we now call the Apostles' Creed and the Nicene-Constantinopolitan Creed of 381. The reformers of the sixteenth century were guided by this rule of faith in their interpretations of the Bible. Their catechisms, commentaries and longer theological works, such as Melanchthon's *Common Places* and Calvin's *Institutes*, they considered as but summaries of the basic Christian message found in the Bible and expressed in the rule of faith.

How does the rule of faith function for precritical exegetes of

---

[20]John Wesley, *Wesley's Notes on the Bible* (Grand Rapids: Francis Asbury, 1987), p. 403.

Christian Scripture? Perhaps Steinmetz can help us once again. Drawing on the genre of detective fiction, he points out that reading the Bible is sort of like reading a mystery story that has two narratives. The first narrative is the one the reader of the mystery story encounters as the tale unfolds: clues not fully revealed, false leads, shadowy characters who may or may not assume a larger part as the story goes on, unexplained encounters, altogether a haphazard and puzzling sequence of events. The second narrative is revealed by the master detective, a Miss Marple or a Sherlock Holmes, who near the end of the story brings the suspects and interested spectators all together into a room and reveals in short order what has been happening all along. Other possible interpretations of the story the reader may have entertained along the way are then once and for all dispelled. The unrecognized clues are now seen for what they really were. If the master detective performs his or her task well in presenting the second narrative, the whole story makes perfect sense, a kind of psychological closure takes place, and we are free to go on to the next novel. According to Steinmetz, the New Testament does what the second narrative in good detective fiction does: it discloses at the end the structure of the whole from the beginning.

Early Christians believed that what had occurred in the life, death and resurrection of Jesus Christ was of such importance that it had transformed the entire story of Israel and, through Israel, of the world. The long, ramshackle narrative of Israel with its promising starts and unexpected twists, with its ecstasies and its betrayals, its laws, its learning, its wisdom, its martyred prophets—this long narrative is retold and reevaluated in the light of what early Christians regarded as the concluding chapter God had written in Jesus Christ.[21]

---

[21]David C. Steinmetz, "Uncovering a Second Narrative: Detective Fiction and the Construction of Historical Method," in *The Art of Reading Scripture*, ed. Ellen F. Davis and Richard B. Hays (Grand Rapids: Eerdmans, 2003), p. 56.

Faithful interpretation of Scripture requires a trinitarian herme-neutics. The rule of faith demands that Scripture be read as a coherent dramatic narrative, the unity of which depends on its principal actor: the God who has forever known himself and who, in the history of redemption, has revealed himself to us as the Father, the Son and the Holy Spirit. Athanasius and the other fathers who struggled against the Arians for the Nicene doctrine of Trinity were embroiled in serious exegetical arguments. How could the Old Testament affirmation "God is one" be reconciled with the New Testament confession "Jesus is Lord"? What was the relationship of the eternal and unchanging God to the Logos who became flesh, Jesus Christ? Among many other things, the struggle for the doctrine of the Trinity was a debate over the meaning of the Bible, over texts such as John 1:1-14, Proverbs 8:22 and Hebrews 3:2.[22] At the time of the Reformation, the doctrine of the Trinity once again emerged as a major point of dispute, especially between the mainline reformers and certain evangelical rationalist leaders among the radicals. The doctrine of the Trinity could not be surrendered because it had to do with the nature and character of the God whom Christians worship. This God, the triune God of holiness and love, was not a generic deity who could be appeased by human striving, but rather the God of the Bible who had made himself known by grace alone through the sending of his Son, Jesus Christ, "for us and for our salvation." To enter into the mind of Scripture with a trinitarian hermeneutics is to come to know *this* God and not another. As Billings puts it, "The Bible is the instrument of the triune God to shape believers into the image of Christ, in word and deed, by the power of the Spirit, transforming a sinful and alienated people into children of a loving Father."[23]

---

[22]See the discussion in John J. O'Keefe and R. R. Reno, *Sanctified Vision: An Introduction to Early Christian Interpretation of the Bible* (Baltimore: Johns Hopkins University Press, 2005), pp. 56-63.

[23]Billings, *Word of God*, p. 199.

The Bible is front and center in the worship of the church. The reformers of the sixteenth century inherited a Christian tradition in which the Bible, for more than a thousand years in the Latin Vulgate edition, had been at the heart of the church's liturgy and life. They inherited manuscripts of the Bible painstakingly copied by Benedictine monks whose motto was *ora et labora*, pray and work. But the monk's engagement with Scripture did not end when the day's work of copying was done in the scriptorium. The monk continued to pray, sing and recite the Scriptures in the daily liturgy of the hours. This did not mean that the Bible was never read by an individual apart from corporate worship—think of Augustine and his encounter with Romans 13:11-14 in the garden in Milan. Yet Augustine had been prepared for that encounter with Paul's text by first hearing the Bible prayed and proclaimed by Bishop Ambrose in regular services of worship in the cathedral, and even earlier by the Scripture-soaked prayers and tears of his mother, Monica.

In the sixteenth century, the translation of the Bible was accompanied by the translation of the liturgy: Luther's German Mass and Order of Service was published in 1526, Calvin's Form of Prayers followed in 1542, and the Book of Common Prayer, overseen by Thomas Cranmer, appeared in the two versions of 1549 and 1552. The reading and preaching of the Bible was central to these and all other books of worship produced by the Protestant reformers. As part of their protest against clerical domination of the church, the reformers aimed at full participation in worship. Their reintroduction of the vernacular was jarring to some since it required that divine worship be offered to God in the same language used by businessmen in the marketplace and by husbands and wives in the privacy of their bedchambers. However, the intent of the reformers was not so much to secularize worship as to sanctify common life. For them, the Bible was not merely an object for academic scrutiny in the study or the library; it was meant to be practiced, enacted and embodied as the people of

God came together for prayer and praise and proclamation.

The study of the Bible is a means of grace. The post-Enlightenment split between the study of the Bible as an academic discipline and the reading of the Bible as spiritual nurture was foreign to the reformers. They all repudiated the idea that the Bible could be studied and understood with dispassionate objectivity, as a cold artifact from antiquity. When the Cambridge scholar Thomas Bilney discovered the meaning of salvation while reading Erasmus's new Latin translation of 1 Timothy 1:15, "Christ Jesus came into the world to save sinners," he tells us that "immediately I felt a marvelous comfort and quietness insomuch that my bruised bones leaped for joy."[24] The reformers practiced what Matthew Levering has called "participatory biblical exegesis" in which the intimate "vertical" presence of the Trinity's creative and redemptive action suffuses the "linear" or "horizontal" succession of moments. According to Levering, "to enter into the realities taught in the biblical text requires not only linear-historical tools (archeology, philology, and so forth), but also, and indeed primarily, participatory tools—doctrines and practices—by which the exegete enters fully into the biblical world."[25] Bilney's experience led to his becoming an evangelist, and this eventually resulted in his being put to death in 1531, one of the first martyrs of the English Reformation.

Reformers as Proto-Postmoderns?

The Enlightenment project, with its dogmatic rationalism and its scientistic epistemology, can be roughly dated from the fall of the Bastille in 1789 to the fall of the Twin Towers in 2001. Though its aftereffects still linger, today the Enlightenment is in trouble from a serious erosion from within: postmodernism. The postmodern moment privi-

---

[24]See A. G. Dickens, *The English Reformation* (New York: Schocken, 1974), p. 79.
[25]Matthew Levering, *Participatory Biblical Exegesis* (Notre Dame, Ind.: University of Notre Dame Press, 2008), pp. 1-2.

leges the visual, the ephemeral, the pleasurable, the immediate, the evanescent, the disconnected. Metanarratives with absolute or universal implications have been replaced by local stories, and principles by preferences. The mood of postmodernity is aptly captured in a comment made by the central character in Richard Ford's novel *The Sportswriter*: "I can't bear all the complications, and long for something that is facades only. All we really want is to get to the point where the past can explain nothing about us and we can get on with life."[26] Postmodern hermeneutics, left to itself, devolves into relativism, fragmentation and subjective perspectivism. The death of God in Nietzsche has led to the death of the author in Foucault and the death of the reader in Stanley Fish. The answer to the title of Kevin J. Vanhoozer's *Is There a Meaning in This Text?* is—No, not really.

Postmodernism challenges the historic Christian understanding of language as a reliable medium of truth. At the same time, we must recognize its importance in unmasking the pretentions of the kind of exaggerated individualism and overweening confidence in reason that has shaped the historical-critical method of studying the Bible. Postmodernism has emphasized the relational character of knowledge, the role of the community (for Christians the church) in interpretation and the situatedness (language, gender, culture and historical particularity) of every interpreter. This requires that all texts, including the Bible, be approached with humility from a posture of receptivity, not with the aim of mastering or dominating what is encountered. Postmodernism calls for us to recognize our limitations, our finitude. As it turns out, these are habits of reading already deeply embedded in the Christian tradition. They are found, among other places, in the hermeneutical legacy of the Protestant Reformation.

In a bold and important study, *Recovering Theological Hermeneutics*, Jens Zimmermann has argued that the postmodern critique of

---

[26]Richard Ford, *The Sportswriter* (London: Havril, 1996), pp. 37, 30.

the Enlightenment was anticipated by major themes in the biblical and theological work of the reformers. Among others, these three themes stand out.

The relational and correlative nature of knowledge. The famous opening lines of Calvin's *Institutes* declare that "nearly all the wisdom we possess, that is to say, true and sound wisdom, consists of two parts: the knowledge of God and of ourselves." There is no proper knowledge of God that does not involve self-understanding. These two kinds of knowledge are simultaneous and correlative. It is not as though one could gain a thorough knowledge of the self by earning a Ph.D., say, in psychology, and then transfer to a divinity school to pursue an advanced degree in the knowledge of God. No, at every step of the way and in every area of life, we are confronted by a seeming contradiction: The knowledge of ourselves drives us to look at God while it presupposes that we have already contemplated him. Calvin is a pre-Cartesian thinker. The act of knowledge involves more than a thinking subject and extended stuff. Calvin knew that the human mind, left to itself, would become a "factory of idols" producing self-made gods of darkness and delusion. Like later postmodern theorists, Calvin wrestled with the problem of understanding. He recognized the finitude of the human person and rejected naïve objectivism. The true interpretation of the Bible required the inward witness of the Holy Spirit: there is no independent epistemological platform on which we may stand and sovereignly survey our theological options. In every act of understanding, as in every moment of life, we all have "business with God" (*negotium cum deo*). As Zimmermann notes, for Calvin, "the whole purpose of reading Scripture is the restoration of our humanity to the fullness of the image of God in us as individuals and in society as a whole."[27]

---

[27]Jens Zimmermann, *Recovering Theological Hermeneutics* (Grand Rapids: Baker Academic, 2004), p. 33. See the appreciative but critical review of Zimmermann by Anthony C. Thiselton in *International Journal of Systematic Theology* 8 (2006): 224-26.

A trinitarian hermeneutics of the cross invites us to study the Bible with humility and conviction. The young Heidegger was drawn to the young Luther's strong critique of Aristotelian scholasticism, especially to his development of a theology of the cross in opposition to a theology of glory.[28] In his 1518 Heidelberg Disputation, Luther argued that the message of the cross destroyed (the Latin word is *destruere*), dismantled and reduced to nothing all abstract, speculative and objectified knowledge of God. The young Heidegger thought that later Reformation traditions had failed to build on Luther's radical insight, and he saw himself as "a kind of philosophical Luther of western metaphysics."[29] Heidegger proposed a "deconstruction" both of Aristotle and the subsequent foundationalist construals of Descartes and Hegel on which so much modernist thinking is based. Thus, according to Zimmermann, the postmodernist critique of autonomous reason, including the notion of deconstruction itself, was foreshadowed in an important strand of early Reformation theology.

Vanhoozer has transposed Luther's theology of glory/theology of the cross distinction into a contrast between a "hermeneutics of the cross" and a "hermeneutics of glory."[30]

> Those who read according to the hermeneutics of glory revel in their own interpretative skills, imposed their interpretive theories on texts, and eclipse the text's own meaning. Such "glory" is, of course, short-lived. According to the hermeneutics of humility, by contrast, we will only gain understanding—of God, texts, others, and ourselves—if we are willing to put ourselves second and our interpretive theories to the test of the text.[31]

---

[28]See John Van Buren, "Martin Heidegger, Martin Luther," in *Reading Heidegger from the Start: Essays in His Earliest Thought* (Albany: State University of New York Press, 1994), pp. 159-74.

[29]Ibid., p. 172.

[30]Kevin J. Vanhoozer, *Is There a Meaning in This Text? The Bible, the Reader, and the Mortality of Literary Knowledge* (Grand Rapids: Zondervan, 1998), p. 465.

[31]Ibid.

Humility is a corrective to the temptation to idolatry, the post-modern penchant for making of the human mind a factory of idols. Yet, as Vanhoozer rightly argues, a genuine hermeneutics of the cross also involves a hermeneutics of conviction, the conviction that

> God has already staked his truth claim in the cross of Christ. He has already redeemed his claim in resurrection. . . . While there may be more light on the Bible's meaning to come, we have a firm enough grasp of the overall storyline as to encourage boldness in our witness. Only such confidence, commitment, and conviction about what can be known can serve as the corrective to interpretive skepticism and sloth. The uncommitted interpretation is not worth hearing.[32]

Scripture and the community of saints. Jacques Maritain's famous book *Three Reformers* presents the story of Luther as the "advent of the self." Luther was the supreme individualist, Maritain claimed, a rebellious monk pulling down the pillars of Mother Church by placing his own subjectivist interpretation of the Bible above that of fifteen hundred years of ecclesial tradition. In this view, Luther and the reformers who followed him were early advocates of what Wilhelm Dilthey called "the autocracy of the believing person."[33] Yet the "deconstruction" that Heidegger rightly noted in Luther's approach was not carried out in lonely isolation from the church, the body of Christ extended throughout time as well as space. The reformers read, translated and interpreted the Bible as part of an extended centuries-old conversation between the holy page of God's Word and the company of God's people. While in many cases they broke with the received interpretations of the fathers and the scholastics who came before them, theirs was nonetheless a churchly hermeneutics. One of

---

[32]Ibid.

[33]Steven E. Ozment, *The Age of the Reform, 1250-1550* (New Haven: Yale University Press, 1980), p. 260.

the most lyrical expressions of this robust ecclesiology at the time of the Reformation comes from Johannes Oecolampadius, the reformer of Basel, in an address he gave shortly before his death in 1531.

> The Church is the vineyard of the Lord, his heritage, his temple and his bride; even more she is his body, for which he has shed his precious blood and outside which there is no salvation. If one is not concerned for the church then martyrdom has no crown, charity is no longer a good work, and religious knowledge brings no wisdom. The person who does not love the Church does not love Jesus Christ.[34]

Thus, by emphasizing the correlative and communitarian character of knowledge and by following an incarnational, cross-centered hermeneutics, the reformers of the sixteenth century did anticipate major themes of postmodern theories of interpretation. At the same time, Reformation exegesis resisted the disintegrating impulse of deconstruction, affirming of God (with Francis Schaeffer) that "he is there and he is not silent." The reformers refused to isolate the knowing subject from the God of creation—for them there is no genuine epistemology without revelation. They also read Scripture as a coherent story, a nontotalizing but still all-encompassing metanarrative in the light of which everything else has to be understood. In the words of Richard Bauckham, the biblical story is about nothing less than the whole of reality and thus it cannot be "reduced to an unpretentious local language game in the pluralism of postmodernity."[35]

---

[34]Cited in E. G. Léonard, *A History of Protestantism* (Indianapolis: Bobbs-Merrill, 1968), 1:160.

[35]Richard Bauckham, "Reading Scripture as a Coherent Story," in *The Art of Reading Scripture*, ed. Ellen F. Davis and Richard B. Hays (Grand Rapids: Eerdmans, 2003), p. 48. Michael Cahill has noted that "to read a history of exegesis is to open oneself to what might be termed an experience of postmodernism. What postmodernism talks about, the history of exegesis illustrates and effects. The postmodern climate provides a window of opportunity for the history of exegesis." Cahill welcomes those scholars who have engaged the history of exegesis to the roundtable of academic biblical scholarship, though he proposes a model in

We read the reformers for the same reason that we pay attention to the church fathers: we share with them a common patrimony in the sacred Scriptures. We listen to their struggles, musings and debates about the written Word of God as a way of better attending to the thing itself. From the reformers we learn that the true purpose of biblical scholarship is not to show how relevant the Bible is to the modern world, but rather how irrelevant the modern and postmodern world—and we as persons enmeshed in it—have become in our self-centered preoccupations and sinful rebellion against the God who spoke and still speaks by his Spirit through his chosen prophets and apostles.

If in some ways we privilege the reformers within the company of the whole people of God throughout the ages, it is not because they were more learned or more holy than others who came before or after them, but rather that the decisive theological conflict of their age so closely paralleled what Tillich named as the three deepest anxieties of our own: the mystery of death, the persistence of guilt and the loss of ultimate meaning in an ordered and benevolent reality beyond ourselves.[36] The world of the reformers, like our own, was an age of adversity and flux. The God of the Bible whom they heard speaking in the pages of Holy Writ still speaks by his Word and through his Spirit into the stress and emptiness of our lives. This hymn text by Nikolai F. S. Grundtvig, set to the music of Luther's "Ein feste Burg," extols God's Word in confession and prayer:

> God's Word is our great heritage
> And shall be ours forever;

---

which the historical-critical method retains "the post of chairperson," albeit a chairperson who faces new challenges. Cahill's model seems to reflect the condescension of an unreconstructed modernism, one still captivated by the "imperialism of the present." See Michael Cahill, "The History of Exegesis and Our Theological Future," *Theological Studies* 61 (2000): 337, 346.

[36]For further reading on the three deepest anxieties, see Paul Tillich, *The Courage to Be* (New Haven: Yale University Press, 1952), pp. 57-63.

To spread its light from age to age
Shall be our chief endeavor.
Through life it guides our way;
In death it is our stay.
Lord, grant, while time shall last
Your church may hold it fast
Throughout all generations.[37]

---

[37]"God's Word Is Our Great Heritage," in *Lutheran Book of Worship* (Minneapolis: Augsburg, 1990), p. 239.

Two

Ad Fontes!

Scrutamini Scripturas: Search the Scriptures.
These two words have undone the world. Because Christ spake it
to his disciples, therefore we must also, men, women, and children,
read and interpret the Scriptures.

JOHN SELDEN

THE REFORMATION WAS ABOUT THE WORD OF GOD, but it was also about words, millions of them, human utterances from pulpit, pen and press. Sermons, lectures, disputations, catechisms and commentaries poured forth from the presses of Europe along with a flood of Bibles both in traditional Latin and in the emerging vernaculars of the time. The study of the Bible in the Reformation era was both a scholarly and a popular phenomenon. In recent decades, much attention has been given to what is called reforming from below, that is, the shaping of religious beliefs and devotional practices that marked the popular culture of the majority of the population in the age of the Reformation. Social historians have taught us to examine the diverse pieties of townspeople and city folk, of rural religion and village life, the emergence of lay theologies and the experiences of women in the religious tumults of Reformation Europe.[1]

Formal commentaries by their nature are artifacts of learned culture. Almost all of them were written in Latin, the lingua franca of learned discourse well past the age of the Reformation. Biblical commentaries were important in the work of pastors and in the training of theological students, but they were not the primary means by which the Protestant message spread so rapidly across wide sectors of sixteenth-century society. Small pamphlets and broadsheets, later called *Flugschriften* ("flying writings"), with their graphic woodcuts and cartoon-like depictions of Reformation personalities and events, became the means of choice for mass communication in the early age of printing. Sermons and works of devotion were also printed with appealing visual aids. Luther's early writings were often accompanied by drawings and sketches supplied by Lucas Cranach and other artists. This was done "above all for the sake of children and simple folk," as Luther put it, "who are more easily moved by pictures and images to recall divine history than through mere words or doctrines."[2]

We should be cautious, however, in drawing too sharp a distinction between learned and lay culture in this period. The phenomenon of preaching was a kind of verbal bridge between scholars at their desks and the thousands of illiterate or semi-literate listeners whose views were shaped by the results of Reformation exegesis. Theodore Beza reported in 1561 that more than one thousand persons were crowding into the Cathedral of Saint Pierre in Geneva to hear Calvin expound the Scriptures every day. Bucer in Strasbourg, Zwingli and Bullinger in Zurich, Urbanus Rhegius in Augsburg, Oecolampadius in Basel, Johann Brenz in Württemberg, Hugh Latimer and William Perkins in England and Menno Simons and

---

[1]See Peter Matheson, ed., *Reformation Christianity* (Minneapolis: Fortress, 2007).
[2]Luther, *Passional* (1522). See R. W. Scribner, *For the Sake of Simple Folk: Popular Propaganda for the German Reformation* (Cambridge: Cambridge University Press, 1981), p. xi.

Dirk Phillips among the scattered Anabaptist conventicles in the Low Countries were all superb preachers. Their sermons were interlaced with numerous references to the Scriptures: they preached not only about the Bible but also from it. Biblical exegesis in the sixteenth century was not limited to full-length commentaries written by learned scholars, or even to sermons delivered by effective preachers. Citations from the Bible and expositions of its meaning permeate the extant literature of letters, court depositions, records of public disputations, hymns and popular songs, even last wills and testaments.

The impact of the Bible as a shaping force in Reformation Europe was accelerated by two developments in the fifteenth century: the rediscovery of a vast store of ancient learning that included new methods of studying the Bible as well as other classical texts from the past; and the invention and rapid development of printing. Before turning to these developments, however, let us look at three scenes from the Reformation, one from Switzerland, one from Germany and one from England. Each of them shows how in these different contexts the Bible had a transforming effect on lay persons with no university training but with an eager readiness to appeal to the Scriptures.

THREE SCENES

Platter and his Testament. Thomas Platter was born in 1499 in a remote region of Switzerland called the Valais, high in the Alps near the Matterhorn. His early life was one of abject poverty. After working as a goatherd, he joined a group of wandering students, *bacchants*, as they were called, who moved from place to place singing, begging and sometimes stealing for their food, hoping along the way to take in a lecture or find a teacher to instruct them in some subject of interest. In this way, Platter taught himself to read and write, and eventually he became proficient in Latin, Greek and Hebrew. In the 1520s he moved to Zurich, where he met Oswald Myconius, a leading educator and teacher in the city. Myconius took Platter into his home and made him custodian for the cathedral choir. One cold winter morning when the reformer Zwingli was scheduled to preach at an early service, Platter, whose job it was to make the daily fire, seized a statue of Saint John from one of the altars and threw it into the stove for kindling. He later recalled this event:

> As the bells rang for the service, I thought: "You have no wood, yet there are so many idols in this church." So I went to the nearest altar, seized the statue of St. John, and put it in the stove. "Johnny," I said to him, "Bend yourself, because you have to go into the stove even though you may be St. John." During the sermon, Myconius said, "You surely had wood today," and I thought: "St. John has done his best."[3]

Platter's action shows how much he had imbibed of the theology he was hearing from Zwingli and the other pastors. When he returned to his home village in the Valais, he was accosted by a local priest who condemned the new religious ideas he had picked up from the heretics of Zurich. "Why are they heretics?" demanded Platter. "Because they do not consider the Pope the head of the Christian Church." "Why" continued Platter, "is the Pope the head of the Christian Church?" "Because St. Peter was the pope at Rome." Whereupon, as Platter recalled, "I drew my Testament out of my little sack" and proved to the priest that "St. Peter had never once been in Rome."[4] We do not know which version of the New Testament he had packed in his travel sack, though it was likely the 1524 Zurich imprint of Luther's German New Testament. It would also be interesting to know the priest's reaction to Platter's use of the Bible

---

[3]Platter recalled this incident in his autobiography, which is the basis for Theodore K. Rabb's vivid account, *Renaissance Lives: Portraits of an Age* (New York: Pantheon, 1993), pp. 82-83. The full text of Platter's autobiography is found in Alfred Hartmann, ed., *Thomas Platter: Lebenbeschreibung* (Basel: Benno Schwabe, 1944).

[4]Rabb, *Renaissance Lives*, p. 83.

as an arsenal in a theological argument. He must have been surprised at the ability of a local yokel to read and argue from the sacred text in so bold a manner. We do know that a few decades later, in 1556, the authorities of the Swiss town of Zug required the townspeople there to deliver all their Bibles to the city hall, where they were publicly burned.[5] The Swiss authorities rightly understood that there was something subversive about the printing and dissemination of the Bible. Thomas Platter later became a printer and schoolmaster in the reformed city of Basel. His life reads like a sixteenth-century version of Horatio Alger, a case study of social mobility in early modern Europe—from goatherd to student beggar to church custodian to rope maker (a skill he acquired along the way) to printer to schoolmaster to respected burgher with houses and lands to his credit when he died at the ripe age of eighty-three. As a printer, his great claim to fame came from 1536, when he set to type the first edition of John Calvin's *Institutes of the Christian Religion*.

Argula's arguments. Argula von Grumbach was born around 1492 in the Regensburg region of Bavaria. At the age of ten, she received a special gift from her father: a copy of the Bible in German, likely the beautifully printed *Biblia deutsch* published by Anton Koberger at Nuremberg in 1483. This was one of fourteen German Bibles published prior to Luther's New Testament in 1522. Though her husband was less than fully supportive of her activities, Argula became a strong supporter of Luther, whom she met once during his visit to Coburg in 1530. She was also a confidant of Andreas Osiander, the reformer of Nuremberg. Her range of contacts and correspondents is remarkable for anyone in Reformation Germany: Philipp Melanchthon, Martin Bucer, Johann Eck, Urbanus Rhegius, and even the prince of electoral Saxony, Frederick the Wise.

Argula is best remembered because of her defense of Arsacius

---

[5]See Jane O. Newman, "The Word Made Print: Luther's 1522 *New Testament* in an Age of Mechanical Reproduction," *Representations* 11 (1985): 95-133.

Figure 2.1. Argula von Grumbach, a Bavarian noblewoman, challenges theologians at the University of Ingolstadt by appealing to the Scriptures.

Seehofer, an eighteen-year-old student at the University of Ingolstadt who was brought to tears and forced to renounce his evangelical faith under threat of torture. On September 20, 1523, Argula addressed the professors of the University of Ingolstadt. Her public letter created a sensation at the time and went through fourteen editions in less than two months. She challenged the Ingolstadt theologians to debate publicly the issues at stake. Her appeal reveals a deep knowledge of both the Old and New Testaments, which she quoted liberally in demanding an answer from the Bible. "I can find no word in the Bible about this Roman church," she said. "I'd be glad if you could show me what God has said about the Roman church." Again, "I hear nothing about any of you refuting a single article [the authorities at Ingolstadt had drawn up seventeen "heretical" articles by Arsacius] from Scripture." "Ah, but what a joy it is when the Spirit of God teaches us and gives us understanding, flitting from one text to the next—God be praised—so that I came to see the true, genuine light shining out."[6] Frequently appealing to the words of Jesus in her favorite verse, "Whoever confesses me before another, I too will confess before my heavenly Father" (Mt 10:32), Argula claimed that she was "compelled as a Christian" to speak out on behalf of the young student. She also warned the "high and mighty teachers" (*hohen meister*) that "God will not put up with your ways much longer."[7]

Argula was well acquainted with the writings of Luther and Melanchthon, but she appealed not to their authority but to the Bible itself. "What do Luther or Melanchthon teach you but the Word of God? You condemn them without having refuted them. Did Christ teach you so, or his apostles, prophets, or evangelists? Show me where this is written!"[8] Unlike Thomas Platter, Argula von Grumbach had no knowledge of Latin but made good use of her native tongue: "I, too, can ask questions, hear answers, and read in German," she said.[9] She acknowledged Paul's statements in 1 Timothy 2 and 1 Corinthians 14 about women not teaching and keeping silent in church but claimed that she was constrained to speak out in this case because no man has stepped forward to do so. Argula's arguments did not carry the day at Ingolstadt, and she was sharply condemned as too uppity for her own good, a "silly bag" and a "female devil." But her case reveals that even in the male-dominated world of the Reformation, a biblically literate and well-read woman could gain a hearing and have an effect by appealing to the Scriptures.

Elizabethan separatists. Our third scene takes place in early Elizabethan London, where, in June 1567, a meeting of an underground church was disrupted by the sheriff. This group of dissenters had gathered for worship in the Plumber's Hall, a building they had

---

[6]Peter Matheson, ed., *Argula von Grumbach: A Woman's Voice in the Reformation* (Edinburgh: T & T Clark, 1995), pp. 75-95. See also Susan C. Karant-Nunn, "Argula von Grumbach," *OER* 2:198-99.

[7]Matheson, *Argula*, pp. 75, 84.

[8]Ibid., p. 76.

[9]Ibid., p. 89.

rented under the pretext of holding a wedding. About twenty of their leaders were arrested, seven of whom were summoned to appear before Edmund Grindal, the bishop of London, and his ecclesiastical commission. We know little about this group, but evidently they had separated from the official established church, which they found deficient in discipline. They, like many Anabaptists and some Reformed leaders on the Continent, regarded discipline as a necessary mark of a true church.

In their interview with Grindal and his inquisitors, the separatist leaders claimed to find in Scripture a warrant and mandate for immediate and specific reforms that they found lacking in the Elizabethan Settlement. After the event, the dissenters wrote "The true report of our examination and conference," which was later printed in 1593 and circulated within the underground Puritan network in London.[10] Throughout the examination the commissioners sought to isolate the separatists from the wider Reformation consensus: "All the learned men in Europe are against you. . . . Will you be judged by the learned in Geneva? They are against you. . . . The entire learned are against you!" to which the separatists replied with single-minded persistence—"We will be tried with the Word of God. . . . We will be judged by the Word of God. . . . We hold nothing that is not warranted by the Word of God. . . . If you can reprove . . . anything we hold by the Word of God, we will yield to you, and do open penance at Paul's Cross, if not, we will stand to it." When Bishop Grindal tried to persuade his prisoners of the necessity of accepting the regulation of "things indifferent" (such as church discipline) by those in authority, the dissenters demanded a text: "Prove that, said one, where find you that, said another."[11] The separatists of Plumber's

---

[10]*A Parte of a register*, as this document was called, is reprinted in the *Remains of Edmund Grindal*, ed. William Nicholson (Cambridge: Cambridge University Press, 1863), pp. 201-16. See also Patrick Collinson, *Archbishop Grindal, 1519-1583: The Struggle for a Reformed Church* (Berkley: University of California Press, 1979), pp. 177-83.

[11]See Timothy George, *John Robinson and the English Separatist Tradition* (Macon, Ga.: Mer-

Hall had learned from the Bible that the scriptural pattern of discipline, as set forth by Jesus in Matthew 18, was no trifling matter but one that was related to the role of Christ in his kingly office. As they told the bishop, "You preach Christ to be priest and prophet, but you preach him not to be king, neither will you suffer him to reign with the scepter of his Word in his church alone."[12]

The story of the Plumber's Hall separatists was often retold among the hot-gospel protestants who formed the core of the Elizabethan puritan movement. Their appeal to the scriptural norm was only one manifestation of the much wider cultural transformation effected by the translation and dissemination of the Bible in the sixteenth century. Like Thomas Platter and Argula von Grumbach, these radical protestants discovered in the Bible both a mirror of their own lives and a call to action. In time their spiritual progeny would produce what Christopher Hill has called "a world turned upside down."[13]

RENAISSANCE HUMANISM

Thomas Platter, Argula von Grumbach and the underground separatists in London were all self-taught individuals, yet their encounter with the Scriptures would not have taken place apart from the painstaking scholarship devoted to the study of biblical texts during the Renaissance. Originally a term in the history of art, the word *Renaissance* (French for "rebirth") has come to define an entire cultural epoch in the history of Europe. It marks the age of transition from Dante and Petrarch in fourteenth-century Italy to Shakespeare and Milton in early modern England. This period witnessed at once the death throes of the Middle Ages and the birth pangs of the modern world. Feudalism was on the wane as a new economy based on capi-

---

cer University Press, 1982), pp. 28-29.

[12]Ibid.

[13]See Christopher Hill, *The World Turned Upside Down: Radical Ideas During the English Revolution* (London: Penguin, 1975).

talism emerged. The once powerful Holy Roman Empire gave way to new communal structures, bustling city-states in Italy and centralized nation-states in England, France and Spain. In an age of great artistic achievement (think of Raphael, Brunelleschi and Leonardo da Vinci), the Renaissance also saw the rise of vernacular literatures and a new interest in the classics that was called (after Cicero) *studia humanistica*: humanism. The word *humanist* (*humanista*) was coined in the fifteenth century to refer to persons, often laypersons, who devoted their lives to such scholarly pursuits. The word *humanista* corresponded to other recognizable types and professions of the time such as *jurista, canonista* and *artista*.

In the nineteenth century, the Swiss historian Jacob Burckhardt published *The Civilization of the Renaissance in Italy* (1860). In this important work Burckhardt defined humanism as an anthropocentric philosophy of life geared toward "the development of the individual."[14] Burckhardt saw the Renaissance as the gateway to modernity and humanism as an early stage of secularism. While Burckhardt's work is still influential in the study of the Renaissance, his view of humanism has been challenged by Paul Oskar Kristeller, who portrayed humanism as a particular method of learning based on the recovery and study of the classical texts, not so much an all-embracing philosophy of life. Humanism, Kristeller claimed, was more about pedagogy than ideology; it was something closer to what we mean by the humanities today. Humanist scholars emphasized three major themes that were to influence the course of the Reformation itself: history, rhetoric and social ethics.

The Renaissance is said to have begun with Francesco Petrarch, a remarkable scholar and poet who was born at Arresto in Italy in 1304. Petrarch fell in love with a woman named Laura when he was quite young, but she was a married lady and did not return his affec-

---

[14]See James Michael Weiss, "Renaissance," *OER* 3:418-21.

tion. He seems to have transferred his passion to the distant past, to ancient Greece and Rome. He thought that his own time, ravaged by war and plague, could possibly be renewed by a fresh encounter with the likes of Homer, Cicero, Livy, Seneca, Virgil and especially Augustine. Petrarch wrote letters to these characters as though they were his contemporaries. To Livy, he wrote:

> I would wish either that I had been born in your age, or you in ours. I should thank you, though, that you have so often caused me to forget present evils and have transported me to happier times. As I read, I seem to be living amidst Scipio, Brutus, and Cato. It is with these men that I live at such times and not with the thievish company of today, among whom I was born under an evil star.[15]

Petrarch's love for both pagan and Christian antiquity inspired him to collect valuable relics from the past—ancient coins, inscriptions, and above all, manuscripts of classical texts. Petrarch brought to his study of the past two perspectives that still influence historians: a sense of anachronism and periodization. Only by recognizing the past as the past did Petrarch realize a sense of contemporaneity with it. History was more than a chronicle of "one damn thing after another," as Henry Ford defined it. Understanding the past required the development of a historical imagination, a sympathetic entering into times and places perhaps radically different from one's own. Following in the tracks of Petrarch, later Renaissance scholars such as Francesco Guicciardini and Niccolò Machiavelli would lay the foundations of modern historiography. But it was Petrarch who gave us the term "Dark Ages" to refer to the intervening centuries between "the glory that was Greece and the grandeur that was Rome" and his own age, so conscious of making a new beginning in the human story.[16]

---

[15]Quoted in Rabb, *Renaissance Lives*, p. 13.
[16]See Theodore E. Mommsen, "Petrarch's Conception of the 'Dark Ages,'" *Speculum* 17

The pattern of golden age-fall-renewal would also shape the way biblical humanists and reformers understood the significance of their times. The division of Christian history into three ages was common among the reformers. There had been an age of primitive purity in the early church followed by a calamitous fall, variously identified with the conversion of Constantine, the pontificate of Gregory I or the enforcement of clerical celibacy and other changes made by Pope Gregory VII in the eleventh century. Their own age was a new epoch, the daybreak at the end of the Middle Ages. The motto of the Genevan Reformation, *post tenebras lux* ("after the darkness, light"), was a typical motif among the humanists. The reformers made the academic study of history a staple in their new academies and universities, next in importance to the study of the classics and biblical languages. When Melanchthon arrived at the University of Wittenberg in 1518, he presented an inaugural lecture "On Improving the Studies of Youth" in which he extolled the value of history in the new curriculum: "And I do not know if our world would suffer less harm without the sun, its soul as it were, than without history, the principle of all civil activities."[17]

One studied the past, however, with an eye to the present, especially the public presentation of words and arguments in persuasive speech. As one teacher of rhetoric put it in 1576, "Pay attention not only to the brilliant greenery of words, but more to the ripe fruit of meaning and reasoning . . . unite dialectic and knowledge with rhet-

---

(1942): 226-42. Mommsen points out the ambiguity in the imagery of darkness and light. The fathers of the early church referred to the pre-Christian past as one of darkness before the coming of Jesus, the light of the world. Petrarch and his fellow humanists introduce a new chronological demarcation into history: seeing the pre-Christian pagan past as an era resplendent with light followed by the obscurity of the centuries after the fall of the Roman Empire, an era of *tenebrae*, of darkness, to be dispelled by the radiance of the new learning in their own day.

[17]Philipp Melanchthon, "On Improving the Studies of Youth," quoted in Lewis W. Spitz, "Humanism and the Reformation," in *Transition and Revolution*, ed. Robert M. Kingdon (Minneapolis: Burgess, 1974), p. 169.

oric. Keep your tongue in step with your mind."[18] But where could one find models of such effective eloquence? Answer: *ad fontes!* Thus Calvin did not hesitate to recommend the study of the classics as a preparatory discipline for reading the Bible: "Read Demosthenes or Cicero," he recommended. "Read Plato, Aristotle, or others of that crew: they will, I admit, allure you, delight you, move you, enrapture you in wonderful measure. Then betake yourself to that sacred reading."[19]

Both the study of history and the attainment of eloquence had a practical output: the moral betterment of society through civic activism and social reform. The humanists were doers as well as thinkers. They would have recoiled from the word *academic* as it is sometimes used today to mean not practical enough, too speculative, purely theoretical. The reformers too found in their study of the Bible a basis for social and political engagement, though there was great divergence on how this worked out in practical terms. Some followed Luther's colleague Andreas Bodenstein von Karlstadt, who withdrew from the fray and became for a while a village farmer and preacher. Luther himself saw a greater disjunction between salvation and civilization than some of his fellow reformers and developed a theory of the state in relation to his doctrine of the two kingdoms. In the Reformed tradition, the world was seen as "the theater of God's glory," while the Anabaptist ethic stressed radical discipleship and the need for the church to confront and resist the culture.

What was the relationship between humanism and scholasticism? To hear the humanists tell it, it was the difference between freedom and enlightenment on the one hand and bondage and barbarism on the other. Sir Thomas More, who could turn a phrase, declared that

---

[18]Peter Mac, "Humanist Rhetoric and Dialectic," in *Renaissance Humanism*, ed. Jill Kraye (Cambridge: Cambridge University Press, 1996), p. 82.

[19]*Institutes* 1.8.1. On the importance of rhetoric for Calvin, see William J. Bouwsma, *John Calvin: A Sixteenth-Century Portrait* (Oxford: Oxford University Press, 1988).

the study of scholastic syllogisms and subtleties was "as profitable as milking a he-goat into a sieve."[20] The early reformers echoed More's disdain of the petty views of the "sophists," Calvin's favorite term of abuse for the scholastic masters.

When it came to the study of the Bible, however, the early reformers did not start with a *tabula rasa*. They built on and often cited the earlier works of medieval commentators and monastic teachers of Scripture. Erasmus could heap ridicule on the scholastic hairsplitters for pursuing questions such as whether it was possible for God to have become incarnate as a donkey, and whether, if he had become incarnate in that way, he could have been nailed to the cross, and other subtle refinements of scholastic disputes—but even Erasmus could say that his critique of scholasticism had been meant to clear away the underbrush, to make it better, not to destroy it. In fact, many scholastic teachers welcomed the reform-minded efforts of the humanist scholars, just as many of the early reformers drew from the well of scholastic wisdom while using humanist tools to frame their restatement of Christian doctrine.

Sacred Philology

It is hard to exaggerate the importance of Lorenzo Valla as a catalyst in the development of critical philology. Valla has been called the "most brash and least compromising of the Italian humanists," because he dared to rush in where others, including Petrarch, had feared to tread.[21] Valla applied to the Latin Bible the same tools of literary analysis he had used in proving that the so-called Donation of Constantine was an eighth-century forgery rather than an authentic document of the early church. According to the Donation, the emperor

---

[20]Quoted in William Manchester, *A World Lit Only by Fire* (Boston: Little, Brown, 1992), p. 107.

[21]Jerry H. Bentley, *Humanists and Holy Writ: New Testament Scholarship in the Renaissance* (Princeton: Princeton University Press, 1983), p. 32.

Constantine had granted to Pope Sylvester I temporal sovereignty over his lands in exchange for having been cured of leprosy. Valla's demythologizing of the story had obvious implications for papal politics in his own day, but it was his tampering with the text of the Vulgate that led some to accuse him of heresy.

Valla compared the extant version of the Vulgate with certain Greek manuscripts he had acquired. His aim was not to produce a better Greek text of the New Testament, but rather to improve the Latin of the Vulgate by comparing it with these Greek sources. Valla's *Collatio* ("comparison") *novi testamenti* was a comparative analysis of Greek and Latin versions of many verses and particular texts of the New Testament. Valla was able to show in this way how the received Vulgate version was frequently inadequate, or downright wrong, in light of the Greek manuscripts. Many of Valla's emendations were minor points of grammar or style, but others involved larger issues of doctrine. For example, his comparison of the Latin and Greek at 1 Corinthians 15:51 unearthed a major mistranslation. The traditional Vulgate reading was, "We shall all rise, but we shall not all be changed." However, the original Greek reads, "We shall not all sleep, but we shall all be changed." Valla argued that a scribe had likely altered the meaning of the Greek at 1 Corinthians 15:51 in order to make it harmonize with John 5:29, which seems to imply, in contrast to the text in 1 Corinthians, that all persons will experience death and then be raised into eternal life or eternal judgment. Valla offered a more accurate Latin translation of the Greek text: *Non omnes quidem dormiemus, omnes autem immutabimur*—"We shall not all sleep, but we shall all be changed." Jerry Bentley has said that "Valla's attention to the Greek text . . . led to a vastly improved understanding of New Testament teachings on resurrection."[22]

Valla's evaluation of the Vulgate and his correction of it at many

---

[22]Ibid., p. 56.

points elicited a firestorm of criticism. How dare he criticize the translation of Jerome? In response, Valla denied that Jerome was responsible for the received text of the Vulgate then in circulation. We know that in the centuries following Jerome's death (420), the Latin translation of the Bible he had undertaken at the behest of Pope Damasus underwent many changes. The text Jerome produced (scholars now believe that he emended but did not translate afresh the Latin New Testament) proceeded along several lines of transmission down to the ninth century. At that point two Carolingian scholars, Alcuin and Theodulf, stabilized the text of Jerome's Bible and provided a version of the Vulgate that remained essentially unchanged until the masters and scholars of the Paris schools reworked this version in the twelfth century. They in turn made several important changes that have survived to our day, such as arranging the books in a standard canonical order and dividing the text into chapters. (Verse divisions would not be added until the Reformation.)

Valla, imbued with the humanist sense of history, denied that he had shown any dishonor to Scripture by trying to establish a better text based on the original languages. We must make a distinction, he argued, between the Bible as originally inspired and given by God and its later renderings, which were subject to the accidents of time.

> If Jerome came back to life, he would correct what has been vitiated and corrupted in some places. . . . To say it briefly: if I emend the text, I do not emend Scripture but a translation of it. In doing so, I am not scornful, but rather biased, and I merely offer a better version than the previous translator, so that my version should be called authentic rather than his. And if Holy Writ is, properly speaking, what the saints themselves wrote in Hebrew or Greek, the Latin text is nothing of this sort.[23]

---

[23]*Antidotum Primum*, ed. Ari Wesseling (Amsterdam: Van Gorcum, 1978), par. 135-36. Quoted in Erika Rummel, "Voices of Reform from Hus to Erasmus," in *Handbook of Euro-*

It is not hard to see why Valla walked on a razor's edge in a fragile age of adversity and conflict. Look at what he had done. He criticized and emended a sacred text regarded as inviolable for nearly a millennium. He knocked the props out from under a major premise of the papacy's claim to power. He went even further to deny that the Apostles' Creed had been written by the twelve disciples of Jesus. He also claimed that the popular writings of Dionysius the Areopagite, identified by tradition with the convert of Paul at Athens (Acts 17:34), had been written by an unknown author five hundred years later, and he gave them the prefix by which they have been known ever since—pseudo.

Valla was a rare horizontal figure whose life's work pointed forward to an age of new beginnings. He was, we might say, ahead of his time. Erasmus's discovery and publication of Valla's *Collatio* in 1505 was a major turning point in his own career as a biblical scholar. Luther and Calvin praised Valla, and the Catholic Index prohibited him. His views on free will and predestination were closer to those of Luther than of Erasmus, though his spiritualist understanding of the Eucharist resonated more with the Dutchman than with the prophet of Wittenberg. The Protestants cited with relish his exposé of the Donation of Constantine, for it seemed to support their own critique of papal authority. Charles Trinkaus has argued that Valla's approach to the study of sacred texts was destabilizing and subversive of the established doctrines of the church.[24] It is true that Valla barely escaped an encounter with the Inquisition at Naples. But, at the end of the day, he settled for inner faith over open conflict with the church. In words that would surely have pleased Erasmus, he wrote, "It is not

---

pean History, 1400-1600: Late Middle Ages, Renaissance and Reformation, ed. Thomas A. Brady, Heiko A. Oberman and James D. Tracy (Grand Rapids: Eerdmans, 1996), p. 66. It should be noted that Jerome made this same argument in defending his "new" translation of the Scriptures against critics who charged him with corrupting the inspired Word of God.
[24]Charles Trinkhaus, *In Our Image and Likeness* (Chicago: University of Chicago Press, 1970), 2:571-78.

the external man but the inner one who pleases God."[25] Valla was not Hus at Constance, or Savonarola in Florence or Luther at Worms. He spent his last days at Rome in the arms of Mother Church, warmly embraced by the humanist-friendly Pope Nicholas V, founder of the Vatican Library. There Valla died in 1457 still preoccupied with his manuscripts and texts.

PRINTING THE WORD

The English philosopher Francis Bacon, who lived from 1561 until 1626, said that the three greatest inventions of recent history were gunpowder, the mariner's compass and printing.[26] Gunpowder changed forever the nature of armed conflict and introduced an era of savage warfare that is with us still. The compass enabled Columbus and other navigators to discover the New World and map it with precision. The printing press brought about an explosion of knowledge, the expansion of literacy and a revolution in learning that touched every aspect of European civilization, not least the church. One of the leaders of the church who was duly impressed by the advent of printing was the scholar-bishop Aeneas Silvius Piccolomini, who in 1458 would become Pope Pius II. In October of 1454, Aeneas Silvius found himself at the famous Frankfurt book fair, no doubt on the hunt for special treasures for his great library. Soon after the fair, he wrote to a friend about his meeting there a "marvelous man" (*vir mirabilis*) who had with him a perfectly produced book, one that was exceedingly clean and correct in all of its lettering, with beautiful characters that could be read "effortlessly without glasses." Some scholars think that the wondrous man Aeneas Silvius encountered at the fair was Johann Gutenberg and that the spotless book he

---

[25]Lorenzo Valla, *The Profession of the Religious and the Principal Argument from the Falsely Believed and Forged Donation of Constantine*, trans. Olga Pugliese (Toronto: Centre for Reformation and Renaissance Studies, 1985), p. 46.

[26]Francis Bacon, *The New Organon*, ed. Lisa Jardine and Michael Silversthorne (Cambridge: Cambridge University Press, 2000), pp. 98-100.

saw was Gutenberg's masterpiece, the forty-two-line Bible (so called because it had forty-two lines per page) hot off the press from his workshop at Mainz.[27]

Gutenberg was a goldsmith by trade. While living in Strasbourg, he had experimented with a metal alloy suitable for type and a machine that would allow printed characters to be cast with relative ease, placed in even lines of composition and then manipulated again and again to make possible the mass production of an unbelievable number of texts. Moving down the Rhine to the city of Mainz, he perfected his experiment with the press and was soon able to produce the world's first printed Bible. The printing press was an amazing ditto device that seemed to work like magic. Printing by woodcuts was known before the time of Gutenberg. This was a laborious process that involved carving letters or pictures onto a block of wood, inking the finished product and pressing it onto vellum (a surface made from calfskin) or paper (invented in China and introduced to Europe by Arab traders in the thirteenth century). However, wooden blocks wore out easily, were smudge-prone and could not be manipulated to vary the text from one printing to the next. This was hardly an improvement over the slow work of the scribe who might take up to a year to copy a long book by hand. Originally, printed books were designed to look like manuscripts. They had special abbreviations, ligatures and a style of lettering developed by scribes in the Middle Ages—the first Bibles were printed in gothic font. A vestige of the manuscript tradition still survives in the enlarged initial capital with which new chapters often begin.

What began at Gutenberg's print shop in Mainz in the 1450s soon spread, like McDonald's or Starbucks in our day, into every

---

[27]For the full Latin text of the letter by Aeneas Silvius, see Erich Meuthen, "Ein newes frühes Quellenzeugnis für den ältesten Bibeldruck," *Gutenberg-Jahrbuch* (1982): 108-18. See also Paul Needham, "*Haec sancta ars*: Gutenberg's Invention as a Divine Gift," *Gazette of the Grolier Club* 42 (1990): 101-21.

nook and cranny of the European world. Printing presses sprang up in Rome (1464), Venice (1469), Paris (1470), the Netherlands (1471), Switzerland (1472), Spain (1474), England (1476), Sweden (1483) and Constantinople (1490). By 1500 there were nearly 250 printing establishments across Europe. They had published some twenty-seven thousand titles, most of them in Latin. Erasmus once compared himself with an obscure preacher whose sermons were heard only by a few people in one or two churches while his books were read in every country in the world. Erasmus was not well known for his humility, but in this case he was simply telling the truth.[28]

Since Elizabeth Eisenstein's two-volume study of the printing press as "an agent of change" (1979), many studies have analyzed the connection between the advent of printing and the rise of the Protestant movement. That Protestants themselves saw printing as a divine gift bestowed from above to spur on the work of Reformation is beyond doubt. John Foxe spoke for many others when he wrote:

> The Lord began to work for his church not with sword and target to subdue his exalted adversary, but with printing, writing and reading . . . how many presses there be in the world, so many block-houses there be against the high castle of St. Angelo, so that either the Pope must abolish knowledge in printing or printing must at length root him out.[29]

However, the history of printing in the sixteenth century does not lend itself to a neat Protestant versus Catholic interpretation. In the first place, Catholics themselves became purveyors of the printed word. Luther's New Testament of 1522 was answered by

---

[28]See E. Harris Harbison, *The Christian Scholar in the Age of the Reformation* (New York: Charles Scribner's Sons, 1956), p. 80.
[29]See William Haller, *The Elect Nation* (New York: Harper & Row, 1963), p. 110.

Hieronymus Emser of Dresden, who in a brief period of time was able to produce a counter-Bible in German shorn of Luther's evangelical marginalia. In 1539, Jacopo Cardinal Sadoleto wrote a public letter to the magistrates and citizens of Geneva entreating them to return to the Catholic faith, to which Calvin responded later in the same year with a stout defense of the Protestant position. In 1516, the Fifth Lateran Council forbade the printing of any new volume without the explicit approval and imprimatur of Rome, but this decree could not be enforced. Just so, Sebastian Castellio's interpretation of the Song of Songs did not please the ministers of Geneva, but he fled to Basel, where he was appointed professor of Greek and published many works, including some against Calvin and Beza, with relative impunity, which added to the tension between the two cities. Censorship was interconfessional in the age of the Reformation. At the same time, the Frankfurt book fair continued to be a popular meeting place for publishers and book agents of all kinds, Catholic and Protestant alike, a notable case of capitalism trumping theology.

It is hard to deny Eisenstein's basic point: that Protestantism was the first religious movement to take full advantage of the new powers of the press.[30] The fact that between 1517 and 1520 the thirty publications of Luther in print at that time sold more than 300,000 copies suggests a groundswell of interest in the message he was preaching. With some exceptions, Catholic authorities were hesitant to permit

---

[30]Elizabeth L. Eisenstein, "The Advent of Printing and the Protestant Revolt: A New Approach to the Disruption of Western Christendom," in *Transition and Revolution: Problems and Issues of European Renaissance and Reformation History*, ed. Robert M. Kingdon (Minneapolis: Burgess, 1974), pp. 235-36. Of the many studies of the Reformation as a print event, two of the most helpful are Jean-François Gilmont, ed., *The Reformation and the Book*, trans. Karin Maag (Aldershot: Ashgate, 1998), and Mark U. Edwards Jr., *Printing, Propaganda and Martin Luther* (Minneapolis: Fortress, 1994). Edwards's nuanced study ends with this conclusion: "The printed word played a crucial role in the early Reformation, and when multiplied by the effects of preaching and conversation, can be said to be a major factor in spreading a relatively coherent message throughout the German-speaking lands" (p. 172).

Figure 2.2. This is the earliest known picture of a printing press, from La Grant Danse Maca-bre, *published at Lyon in 1499. The grisly figures of death disrupt the work of the print shop to seize a typesetter and pressmen on the job, shattering the illusion of the "immortality by print."*

vernacular translations of the Bible among the people in the parishes, especially after the Council of Trent, at its fourth session in 1546, ratified the Latin Vulgate as the official Catholic version of choice. By making the writings of the Old and New Testament available to an expanding reading public, the Protestant reformers ensured that the Bible and its interpretation would become a concern for the Thomas Platters and Argula von Grumbachs of the age no less than for the Bucers, Bezas and Bugenhagens.

TRILINGUALISM

The desire of biblical humanists to have complete and reliable texts of the Bible required the study of Greek and Hebrew as well as Latin. The idea of trilingual education was not new. The Council of Vienne in 1312 had called for the establishment of chairs of Greek and Hebrew in the major universities of Christendom, though this was a short-lived experiment at the time. The growing appreciation of Jerome as a paragon of Christian scholarship, as seen in Albrecht Dürer's engraving of *Saint Jerome in His Study* (1514), led Renaissance scholars to emulate the trilingual translator of the early church. A convenient New Testament proof text for this new approach was the *titulus* placed above the head of Jesus on the cross. According to John 19:20, the words "Jesus of Nazareth, the King of the Jews," were inscribed in Hebrew, Latin and Greek, indicating, as some said, the lordship of Jesus over the worlds of religion, law and culture.

It is sometimes thought that the appearance of vernacular Scriptures during the Reformation relegated the Latin Bible to the rare book room. But this is not true. The work Valla had done to achieve a more reliable text of the Vulgate continued and was accelerated during the sixteenth century. In 1522, Andreas Osiander brought out an updated version of the Vulgate corrected by a study of the biblical text in the original languages. Robert Estienne was a French biblical scholar and one of the great printer-publishers of his time. He is best remembered for his 1550 edition of the Greek New Testament, which was a significant improvement on the earlier work of Erasmus and provided the basis for the *Textus Receptus*, the standard basis for New Testament study until the pioneering work of Westcott and Hort in the nineteenth century. However, Estienne also published the first critical edition of the Vulgate (1527-1528), the first of five editions of the Latin Bible to come from his press in Paris. When King Henri II placed a ban on the sale of Estienne's Bibles in 1548, he moved to Geneva, where he embraced the Calvinist reform and continued his prodigious work of printing editions of the Bible, including the first one with a critical apparatus and numbered verses for each chapter.

The need for a definitive Latin text became urgent for the Catholic Reformation after the Council of Trent approved the Vulgate and called for it to be printed anew after a thorough revision. After several starts and stops, including the withdrawal of one edition because of its defects, the Sixto-Clementine edition of 1592-1593 became the authorized version of the Bible for Roman Catholics and retained its normative status until the twentieth century. The Second Vatican Council, while honoring both the Latin Vulgate and the Greek Septuagint, called for vernacular translations of the Bible based on the best critical Greek and Hebrew texts. Jaroslov Pelikan has seen in this affirmation

> an ultimate vindication, more than four centuries later, of the sacred philology of the Renaissance and the Reformation. For although the humanists did urge that the corruptions of the Vulgate text, which had occurred through its transmission from one medieval copyist to another, made the production of a critical edition of the Latin text mandatory, their chief criticism was directed against the inadequacies, indeed the inaccuracies, of the Vulgate as such, which no collation of Latin manuscripts, however thorough, could be expected to set straight.[31]

Both Catholic and Protestant reformers made fresh Latin translations of the Bible during the Reformation era. Erasmus's 1516 Greek New Testament was printed side by side with his own elegant Latin translation. Sante Pagnini, an Italian Dominican friar, published a Latin translation at Lyon in 1527-1528. The Protestant Hebraist Sebastian Münster published both a Hebrew-Greek-Latin

---

[31]Jaroslav Pelikan, *The Reformation of the Bible/The Bible of the Reformation* (New Haven: Yale University Press, 1996), p. 15.

dictionary (1530) and a fresh translation of the Old Testament into Latin (1534-1535).

Before we leave the world of sixteenth-century Latin Bibles, let us take note of yet another one, that of Sebastian Castellio which first appeared in Basel in 1551. Castellio was converted to the Protestant faith by reading Calvin's *Institutes* and lived for a while in his home. This made all the more painful their later separation and enmity. Calvin refused to ordain Castellio to the ministry but did give him a good letter of recommendation when he moved from Geneva to Basel in 1545. However, Castellio's role in protesting the execution of Servetus, his critique of the doctrine of predestination and his personal attacks against Calvin made the breach irreparable.

Just as today there are heated disputes between scholars who prefer to translate the Bible with precise attention to every word (formal equivalence) and others who aim for a more contextual rendering of the thought patterns of the biblical writers (dynamic equivalence), so also there were similar strategies at play in the sixteenth century. Castellio belonged to the radical wing of the dynamic equivalence party. A linguist of great ability, Castellio wanted to produce a Latin Bible in the fanciest classical style; one scholar has said that in Castellio's Old Testament, "Jonah was made to quote Cicero in the belly of the whale!"[32] He justified taking such liberties by claiming that had Moses lived in the time of the Roman Empire, he would have sounded like Julius Caesar. The result was a translation more Ciceronian than that of Erasmus. For example, Castellio turned *ecclesia* into *respublica, fides* into *confidentia* and *angelus* into *genius*. Instead of *baptismus*, he has *lavacrum*. Even God (*Deus*) is called Jove, the name of the supreme Roman deity![33] Calvin and Beza were shocked

[32]Roland H. Bainton, *Studies on the Reformation* (Boston: Beacon, 1963), p. 150.
[33]See Basil Hall, "Biblical Scholarship: Editions and Commentaries," in *Cambridge History of the Bible* (Cambridge: Cambridge University Press, 1963-1970), 3:72-73, and Lowell C. Green, "The Bible in Sixteenth-Century Humanist Education," *Studies in the Renaissance* 19 (1972): 112-34.

at what they considered Castellio's flippant handling of Scripture. In the annotations of his own Latin New Testament (1557), Beza criticized Castellio's work as ambiguous, violent, absurd and inept. Beza may have had a case for the first three epithets, but hardly for the last one. Still estranged, Castellio and Calvin died within one year of each other. "Inside a year," Bruce Gordon has said, "the French reformation lost its two greatest literary figures, freed to reconcile in the next world."[34]

Of the two original biblical languages there was less knowledge of Greek than Hebrew in the centuries leading up to the Reformation. From the fall of Rome in the fifth century until the fall of Constantinople in 1453, the ability to read and understand the Greek language was virtually unknown. (The ninth-century scholar John Scotus Erigenia was an exception. He translated into Latin the very difficult Greek of Pseudo-Dionysius.) The definitive schism of the eastern and western churches in 1054 left so great a scholar as Thomas Aquinas without a knowledge of the original language of the New Testament and the early church fathers of the east, though he commissioned some Latin translations of the latter. Petrarch once received as a gift a Greek manuscript of the epic poems of Homer but lamented that he was not able to read them. During the fourteenth and fifteenth centuries, a series of church councils (Basel-Ferrara-Florence-Rome) brought together leaders of the eastern and western churches in the hope of healing the schism. While this did not happen, important channels of communication were established. Then, in 1453, the armies of the Ottoman Empire scaled the walls of Constantinople. Christendom's second Rome became a Muslim city, and its largest church, the Hagia Sophia, was turned into a mosque. The conquest of Constantinople accelerated what had been going on for some years. Greek scholars fled to the west bringing with them

---

[34]Bruce Gordon, *Calvin* (New Haven: Yale University Press, 2009), p. 232.

the treasures of classical and Christian antiquity, including many precious manuscripts. Among Plato's writings, for example, only the *Timaeus* had been known in the medieval west. Now, with a much larger body of Plato's works rediscovered, a Renaissance revival of Platonic philosophy began in Florence and spread to other centers of learning.

The science of New Testament textual criticism, launched by Valla, went forward in the sixteenth century, especially with the work of Erasmus, the Estiennes (Robert and his son Henri) and Theodore Beza, whose Greek Testament was published in 1565. One of the major New Testament manuscripts bears his name, the Codex Bezae Cantabrigiensis. This manuscript came into the possession of Beza when the city of Lyon fell to the Huguenots during the French wars of religion. In 1581, Beza donated it to the University of Cambridge where it still resides.

One of the most important decisions of the early church took place in the second century when, against the heretic Marcion, the Old Testament was fully embraced as Christian Scripture. Yet how the Old Testament was to be understood in the light of Jesus Christ provoked controversy not only between the church and the synagogue (for Jews, of course, also continued to revere the Hebrew Scriptures as the Word of God) but also among Christians. These issues surfaced again at the Reformation with the Christian rediscovery of the Hebrew Bible. The first Hebrew Bible was printed in 1488 by Jewish scholars. This was followed by a series of other projects culminating in the great rabbinical Bible of Daniel Bomberg published at Venice in 1516-1517. Bomberg was a Christian scholar from Antwerp who moved to Italy, where he compiled his Bible in consultation with Felice da Prato, the son of a rabbi who had converted to Christianity. Bomberg's Bible, which was used by Luther in his translation of the Old Testament into German, was the basis for subsequent printings of the Hebrew Bible into modern times.

In 1501, Konrad Pellikan, a Franciscan friar who later taught Old Testament in Zurich, published the first Hebrew grammar, but this was superceded by Johannes Reuchlin's *On the Rudiments of Hebrew* (1506). Reuchlin never left the Roman Catholic Church, but he had a great influence on early Protestant reformers including Luther, who first learned Hebrew with Reuchlin's grammar in hand. Reuchlin's effort to help Christians read the Old Testament in its original language landed him in the midst of a swirling controversy that brought together the revival of sacred letters and the rising tide of anti-Semitism. A Dominican scholar named Johannes Pfefferkorn, who was a converted Jew from Moravia, called for all Jewish books, including the Talmud, to be confiscated and destroyed as part of an aggressive campaign for Jewish conversion. Reuchlin was a lawyer by training and opposed Pfefferkorn's initiative on two grounds. Jews, he said, were fellow citizens with Christians and should enjoy the same rights as others to read and study their own books. He also argued that Christians should have free access to both the Hebrew Bible and rabbinic commentaries as well as the Kabbalah, a Jewish book of mystical wisdom, because a careful study of these works would only confirm Christian teachings about Jesus the Messiah. Reuchlin certainly believed that Jews should be converted to Christ, but he argued that Jewish evangelization should be carried out by means of persuasion rather than compulsion. While we should not turn Reuchlin into a modern apostle of religious toleration, we should recognize, as Sophie Mesguich has said, that "he was still the first, and for many years the only humanist, as a jurist and as a Hebrew scholar, to defend the books of the Jews."[35]

---

[35]Sophie Mesguich, "Early Christian Hebraists," in *Hebrew Bible/Old Testament: The History of Its Interpretation*, vol. 2: *From the Renaissance to the Enlightenment*, ed. Magne Saebo (Göttingen: Vandenhoeck & Ruprecht, 2008), p. 263. Heiko A. Oberman has argued that, despite Reuchlin's defense of Jewish writings and his plea for the civil emancipation of the Jews, he also embodied anti-Semitic attitudes of social discrimination and religious ostracism. "Three Sixteenth-Century Attitudes to Judaism: Reuchlin, Erasmus and Luther," in

Despite the retrograde maneuvers of Pfefferkorn and his allies, trilingualism triumphed in the sixteenth century among scholars committed to the serious study of the Scriptures. Its victory was marked by two monumental Bible projects that resulted in multilingual versions of the biblical texts published in parallel columns: the six-volume Complutensian Polyglot brought together in 1520 by Cardinal Francisco Jiménez at Alcalá in Spain, and the even larger polyglot Bible Christopher Plantin published at Antwerp from 1568 to 1572. Trilingual biblical education became a part of the curriculum through new academic programs at the University of Alcalá (1508), Oxford (1518), Louvain (1518), the University of Wittenberg (1518) and Paris (1530). In the later sixteenth century, the same pattern of instruction was carried forward in the newly established Protestant academies, where it was made a necessary part of theological education for ordained ministry.

It is sometimes said that the reason why faculty politics is so intense is because so little is at stake. This is often true, but sometimes faculty politics are about things that really do matter. Such was the case when Hebrew and Greek studies were incorporated into the curriculum at the University of Paris in the early 1530s. The king, Francis I, had appointed four lecturers to teach Greek and Hebrew, and they duly posted a listing of their courses:

On Monday at seven, Guidacerius would be reading Psalm 20, while on Tuesday at two one of his students would study the Hebrew alphabet and the grammar of Moses Rinitius; on Monday at one, Vatable would be continuing his interpretation of the Psalms; Danés planned to teach Aristotle on Monday at

Jewish Thought in the Sixteenth Century, ed. D. B. Coperman (Cambridge, Mass.: Harvard University Press, 1983), pp. 326-64. See also Oberman's "Discovery of Hebrew and Discrimination Against the Jews: *Veritas Hebraica* as Double-Edged Sword in Renaissance and Reformation," in *Germania Illustrata*, ed. Andrew C. Fix and Susan C. Karant-Nunn (Kirksville, Mo.: Sixteenth Century Journal Publishers, 1992), pp, 19-34.

two; and, finally, Paul Paradis would be teaching Sante Pagninus's newly published Hebrew grammar and giving a commentary on Proverbs on Monday at ten.[36]

Without delay, the faculty of theology brought suit. The leader of the opposition was Noel Beda, the evil genius of the old school, as one scholar called him. He wanted to know "What good this Greek and Hebrew would do. The Church had used the Vulgate Latin for 1100 years, so why change? Moreover, the editions which the *lecteurs* prescribed had all been printed in Germany, sure proof that they were infected by heresy, whether of the Jewish or the Lutheran kind."[37] Because the advocates of the new learning at Paris had the support of the king at the time, Beda and his allies on the theological faculty did not prevail in their assault on the trilingual approach. But echoes of this skirmish along the Seine can still be heard today in faculty discussions of whether Greek and Hebrew should be required of theological students preparing for the ministry.

---

[36]Arjo Vanderjagt, "*Ad Fontes!* The Early Humanist Concern for the *Hebraica veritas*," in *Hebrew Bible/Old Testament: The History of Its Interpretation*, vol. 2: *From the Renaissance to the Enlightenment*, ed. Magne Saebo (Göttingen: Vandenhoeck & Ruprecht, 2008), p. 184. One of these "royal lecturers," François Vatable, was a disciple of Lefèvre d'Étaples and introduced Calvin to the study of Hebrew. See Henry Heller, "François Vatable," in *Contemporaries of Erasmus: A Biographical Register of the Renaissance and Reformation*, ed. Peter C. Bientenholz (Toronto: University of Toronto Press, 1987), 3:379.

[37]Vanderjagt, "*Ad Fontes!*"

THREE

THE ERASMIAN MOMENT

*It is I, as cannot be denied, who have aroused the study of languages
and good letters. I have brought academic theology, too much
subjected to sophistic contrivances, back to the sources of the
holy books and the study of the ancient orthodox authors;
I have exerted myself to awaken a world slumbering
in pharisaic ceremonies to true piety.*

DESIDERIUS ERASMUS

THE LIFE OF DESIDERIUS ERASMUS (1466-1536) STRADDLED, almost
evenly, the fifteenth and sixteenth centuries. More than anyone else
in his age, Erasmus embodied the ideals of biblical humanism. At the
same time, he represented the tensions inherent in both Renaissance
and Reformation. Born the illegitimate son of a Dutch priest, Erasmus always seemed to be running away from something—from his
murky past, from warring popes and imperial armies, from iconoclastic Protestants and stuck-in-the-mud Catholics, from dirty inns
with their flea-bitten beds, from bad cooks with their suppers of
moldy wine and smelly fish he could not stomach, and always from
the recurring plague that had carried away both of his parents. He
was always on the move. He once said that he had the most learned

horse in the world since he had ridden him to all the universities of Europe searching for manuscripts. His books, he said, were his children, and "my home is where I have my library."[1]

Despite the vast literature devoted to the prince of the humanists, Erasmus remains an enigma. He was an expert in dissimulation and self-promotion; one wants to ask, with many of his contemporaries, "Will the real Erasmus please stand up?" Luther found him as slippery as an eel that only Christ could catch.[2] He had a point. Nonetheless, there is a common theme running through the twists and turns of Erasmus's long and interesting life. He called it the *philosophia Christi*: a program of educational and moral reform for both the individual and society based on the recovery of classical letters and biblical wisdom and centered around personal devotion to Jesus. At the heart of this philosophy was a disdain for things external. This is how he put it in his 1505 treatise, *Enchiridion militis christiani* (*The Handbook of the Christian Soldier*):

> Do not tell me therefore that charity consists in being frequently in church, in prostrating oneself before signs of the saints, in burning tapers, in repeating such and such a number of prayers. God has no need of this. Paul defines love as: to edify one's neighbor, to lead all to become members of the same body, to consider all one in Christ, to rejoice concerning a brother's good fortune in the Lord just as concerning your own, to heal his hurt just as your own.[3]

In his early years, Erasmus had had jaded experiences with monasticism and scholasticism, and he was withering in his criticism of

---

[1]F. N. Nichols, ed., *The Epistles of Erasmus* (London: Russell & Russell, 1901), 2:163, 327.

[2]*WA, TR* 1 (no. 131): *Erasmus est Anguilla. Niemand kan yhn ergreiffen denn Christus allein. Est vir duplex: LW* 54:19, "Erasmus is an eel. Nobody can grasp him except Christ alone. He is a double-dealing man."

[3]Matthew Spinka, ed., *Advocates of Reform from Wycliffe to Erasmus* (Philadelphia: Westminster Press, 1953), p. 378.

both, sometimes attacking the "monks and the theologians" in the same breath.[4] With an eye to his own past, Erasmus said that in the monasteries "men with heaven-sent gifts and born for better things were often buried by ceremonies."[5]

And, recalling his days as a student of scholastic theology at the University of Paris, Erasmus compared his teachers there with Epimenides, a character of Greek legend who fell asleep in a cave for forty-seven years, although (unlike his professors, Erasmus said), Epimenides did eventually wake up.[6] Despite many such comments, Erasmus never renounced his own monastic vows, though he did get a papal dispensation that exempted him from wearing the ornate habit of his order, the Augustinian canons regular. He was also exempted from residing in his home monastery at Steyn in Holland, an exemption that allowed him to travel at will and become a kind of freelance celebrity scholar known to everyone. On the academic front, he did not refuse a doctor's degree when it was offered to him (with no coursework and no residence requirements) by the University of Turin. Not exactly a Th.D. from Paris, but at least he was Dr. Erasmus.

Although he spent many hours in his books, Erasmus was no antiquarian. His "philosophy of Christ" aimed for practical and social results. His scholarship was always in the service of the church, though his vision of the church was not limited to the Roman hierarchy from which nonetheless he was never willing to separate. A pacifist in an age of war and violence and an ecumenist in a time of confessional hostility and division, Erasmus tried to apply the principles of peace and love to the fractious world in which he lived. Through erudition and persuasion he aimed for Christian unity and moral betterment. One of his young admirers referred to Erasmus as "the first

---

[4]See Bejczy, *Erasmus and the Middle Ages*, pp. 96-101.
[5]CWE 8:227; EE 4:508 (no. 1211).
[6]EE 1:190-93 (no. 64); CWE 1:136-37.

author in this age of the rebirth of theology."[7] He was also the first public intellectual of early modern times.

JEROME AND THE FATHERS

Basel was a medium-sized city of some twelve thousand people in the early sixteenth century, larger than its Swiss neighbors, Zurich and Bern, but half the size of Strasbourg and Nuremberg. However, Basel was both a university town and the center of a thriving, international book trade. Here, in 1516, Johann Froben, the greatest printer north of the Alps, brought out two major publications, both landmarks of Erasmian humanism: Erasmus's *Novum Instrumentum*, the first critical edition of the Greek New Testament ever published, and the nine-volume *Opera omnia* of Jerome, which included four folio volumes of the saint's letters carefully edited by Erasmus.[8]

Erasmus had long been a champion of Jerome going back to his school days in Holland when he studied with the Brethren of the Common Life, an order of lay teachers known for their devotion to the great scholar-translator of the early church. The Basel edition of Jerome's works was part of a larger project begun by Johannes Amerbach, Froben's predecessor, to publish new critical editions of the four principal teachers of the Latin church. Ambrose came out in 1492, followed by Augustine in 1506. Work on the edition of Jerome's works had already begun when Erasmus arrived in Basel in 1514 to become the general editor of the project. The first edition of the works of Gregory the Great appeared in 1518, but they were printed by another publisher in Paris.

Erasmus had lectured on Jerome at Cambridge prior to coming to Basel, where the tedious work of collating ancient manuscripts and ferreting out the correct readings accelerated. He complained that he

---

[7]John C. Olin, *Six Essays on Erasmus* (New York: Fordham University Press, 1979), p. 33.
[8]See Eileen Bloch, "Erasmus and the Froben Press: The Making of an Editor," *The Library Quarterly* 35 (1965): 109-20.

had put more work into reading Jerome's letters than the saint had exerted in writing them.

> Often too I had to work with volumes which it was no easy business to read, the forms of the script being either obscured by decay and neglect, or half eaten away and mutilated by worm and beetle, or written in the fashion of Goths or Lombards, so that even to learn the letter-forms, I had to go back to school; not to mention for the moment that the actual task of detecting, of smelling out as it were, anything that does not sound like a true and genuine reading. This requires a man in my opinion who is well informed, quick-witted, and alert. But on top of this, far the most difficult thing is either to conjecture from corruptions of different kinds which the author wrote, or to guess the original reading on the basis of such fragments and vestiges of the shapes of the script as may survive.[9]

This was the hard labor of textual criticism that Erasmus had learned while serving as an apprentice in the printshop-cum-research institute run by Aldo Manuzio in Venice, the greatest publisher of classical texts in Europe. The same kind of intensive labors Erasmus exerted on the edition of Jerome's works he would expend on the collected works of other fathers of the early church: Cyprian (1520), Arnobius (1522), Hilary of Poitiers (1523), Irenaeus (1526), Ambrose and Athanasius (1527), Augustine (1528-1529), John Chrysostom (1530), Basil the Great (1532) and Origen (1536). Next to Jerome, Origen was Erasmus's favorite church father. The edition of Origen's works was Erasmus's swan song, released just two months after his funeral in the Basel Cathedral.

Reading Scripture with the church fathers was part of the ecumenical bequest of Erasmus to the church of the sixteenth century.

---

[9]CWE 3:260-61; EE 2:216 (no. 396). See the discussion in Eugene F. Rice Jr., *Saint Jerome in the Renaissance* (Baltimore: Johns Hopkins University Press, 1985), pp. 116-36.

Protestant and Catholic scholars alike appealed to the patristic tradition to corroborate their interpretations of the Bible and to defend their positions in the widening church disputes. Erasmus proceeded on the assumption that if only the writings of the church fathers could be made available in good reliable editions, with the accretions and corruptions of the text cleared away and the faulty interpretations of the scholastics brushed aside, then serious scholars would be led by the best minds of the early church to the pure teaching of Scripture. Alas, it was not to be! Erasmus bequeathed patrology to the Reformation, but rather than producing an armistice between the warring parties, better editions of the church fathers merely extended the battlefield. Only in recent years, through scholarly projects such as the Ancient Christian Commentary on Scripture, have both evangelical and Catholic heirs of the Reformation struggles found a common meeting place in the writings of the early church. Still, the groundwork for this development was laid during the Reformation by Erasmus and those who followed him in providing an accessible library of patristic sources.

Luther once said that the main difference between him and Erasmus was that he gave pride of place to Augustine while Erasmus preferred Jerome over the doctor of grace. On the crucial doctrine of justification by faith, which Luther called "the head and cornerstone which alone constitutes the church of God," Luther had to admit that not even Augustine had followed Paul as closely as he should have. "Let me not put my trust in Augustine—let us listen to the Scriptures."[10] Even so, by Luther's lights, Jerome had missed far more in Paul than Augustine because he read law where he should have seen gospel. Yet even Jerome contained golden nuggets worth retriev-

---

[10]*WA* 7, 142: *Sed Augustino non credam. Scripturas audiamus.* Quoted by Manfred Schulze, "Martin Luther and the Church Fathers," in *The Reception of the Church Fathers in the West*, ed. Irena Backus (Leiden: Brill, 1997), 2:621. For a similar concession by Calvin, see his *Institutes* 3.11.15.

ing. Luther found in Jerome this "really splendid" statement that seemed to corroborate his own view: "The believer does not live because of righteousness but the righteous person lives because of faith, and this means that he does not believe because of his righteousness but is righteous because of faith."[11]

The fact that the major patristic writings were available for the first time in published form during the lifetime of the reformers meant that their exegetical writings were interlaced with citations from the church fathers. For example, in his 1535 commentary on Galatians, Luther quoted many patristic and scholastic writers and carried on a running dialogue with Augustine and Jerome, always to the detriment of the latter.

An old genre, the patristic anthology, appeared in a new form in the sixteenth century. Anthony N. S. Lane has identified eighty different anthologies that were published in several hundred different editions down to the year 1566. Most of these were produced by Protestant scholars and were organized in a variety of ways reflecting different interpretive patterns and diverse ways of studying the Bible—some anthologies contained extracts from a single father on a variety of topics. Others covered a number of early Christian writers on ethical topics and doctrinal issues. Still others offered comments on a particular book or section of the Scriptures. Some of the anthologies also included selections by medieval writers such as Bernard of Clairvaux and Thomas Aquinas. Most of these source collec-

---

[11]In his lectures on Genesis, in the context of discussing the foreshadowing of the Trinity in the appearance of the three visitors to Abraham (Gen 18), Luther makes this parenthetical comment about the fathers and the doctrine of justification by faith: "After I know that we are justified by faith alone—for, like a dialectical argument, this has been abundantly proved and set forth in Holy Scripture—it pleases me very much that Augustine, Hilary, Cyril and Ambrose say the same thing, even though they do not stress the foundations so much and at times express themselves less properly. I do not charge that this is an error on their part. It is enough for me that they say the same thing, even though they say it less properly; and I am strengthened by their testimony, in spite of the fact that it is more rhetorical than dialectical" (LW 3:194-95).

tions were published in Latin, but some appeared in vernaculars, including one in German by Andreas Musculus and another in French by the Flemish reformer Guy de Brès.

Such collections served two purposes. In an age when scholarly books were still relatively expensive, these handy anthologies made available a library of patristic comment to ordinary pastors and theological students, most of whom could not afford to purchase the multivolume sets produced by Erasmus and others. Further, by connecting Reformation exegesis to patristic tradition, the Protestant anthologists provided a counterweight to the charge that the reformers were purveyors of novelty in religion. On the contrary, they asserted, if the fathers came back to life today, they would surely be no less persecuted by the Roman authorities than the Protestants were. Luther, Melanchthon, Zwingli, Bucer, Oecolampadius, Bullinger, Capito, Peter Martyr, these were the true successors of the church fathers, not the Roman party, which venerated their names but did not follow their doctrine.[12] For all their claiming of the fathers, however, the anthologists warned against their undue exaltation. Their writings should always be judged by the touchstone of Scripture, a standard the fathers themselves heartily approved.

Thus, for the Protestant reformers, the fathers were important if subsidiary authorities. In the context of the English Reformation, Bishop John Jewel in *A Treatise of the Holy Scriptures* (1570) spoke of the ancient Christian writers with the kind of critical reverence that was to mark the Protestant theological tradition as a whole:

They be interpreters of the Word of God. They were learned

---

[12]On sixteenth-century patristic anthologies, see the following studies by Anthony N. S. Lane: "Early Printed Patristic Anthologies to 1566: A Progress Report," *Studia Patristica* 18 (1990): 365-70; "Justification in Sixteenth-Century Patristics," in *Auctoritas Patrum* (Mainz: Verlag Phillipp von Zabern, 1993), pp. 69-93; *John Calvin: Student of the Church Fathers* (Grand Rapids: Baker, 1999).

men, and learned fathers; the instruments of the mercy of God, and vessels full of grace. We despise them not, we reverence them, and give thanks unto God for them. They were witnesses unto the truth, they were worthy pillars and ornaments in the church of God. Yet may they not be compared with the Word of God. We may not build upon them: we may not make them the foundation and warrant of our conscience: we may not put our trust in them. Our trust is in the name of the Lord. . . . I weigh them not as holy and canonical scriptures. Cyprian was a doctor of the church, yet he was deceived: Augustine was a doctor of the church, yet he wrote a book of Retractations; he acknowledged that he was deceived. . . . They are our fathers, but not fathers unto God; they are the stars, fair, and beautiful, and bright; yet they are not the sun. They bear witness of the light, they are not the light. Christ is the Son of Righteousness, Christ is the Light which lighteth every man that cometh into this world. His word is the Word of Truth.[13]

JEROME'S DREAM

It is not hard to see why Erasmus saw himself as a new Jerome come back to life again, *Hieronymus redivivus*. Jerome was the patron saint of sacred letters. In his preface to the works of Jerome, Erasmus called him eloquent, a great linguist, knowledgeable in the classics and history, adept in the study of Scripture—all items that might have been listed on Erasmus's own curriculum vitae. Like Jerome, Erasmus had also gone through a "conversion" from classical literature to sacred letters. The tension between these two poles was a persistent theme in his life and work.

Erasmus was well acquainted with the famous story of Jerome's

---

[13]John Ayre, ed., *Works of John Jewel* (Cambridge: Cambridge University Press, 1845-1850), 4:1173-74.

dream in which Christ had confronted the newly converted classicist about his inordinate love for secular writers such as Cicero and Vergil. He much preferred these grand authors to the uncouth style of the biblical writers. He could hardly put down their books in order to pray. Eugene F. Rice recounts Jerome's appearance before an angry Christ in his dream:

> One night, during Lent (probably in 374), when his body was so weakened by fever that death seemed near, he was suddenly caught up in the spirit, *subito raptus in spiritu*. He dreamed that he was called before the supreme Judge. "What condition of man are you?" asked Christ the Judge. "I am a Christian," replied Jerome. "You lie," thundered the Judge. "*Ciceronianus es, non Christianus*: you are a Ciceronian, a disciple of Cicero, not a Christian. Where your treasure is, there your heart is also." The Judge ordered him to be flogged. Smarting from the blows and even more from the burning of his own conscience, he cried out, "Have pity, Lord, have pity." Even the bystanders now fell on their knees and asked the Judge to forgive Jerome's youthful errors and allow him to do penance. Jerome himself swore a solemn oath: "Lord, if ever again I possess worldly books, if ever again I read them, I shall have denied you." He woke up, his eyes wet with tears and his shoulders bruised and swollen from the divine chastisement, clear physical evidence of the objective reality of his experience.[14]

What has Athens to do with Jerusalem? Or the church with the Academy? What has Horace to do with Paul? Or Cicero with the Gospels? Can one be both a Ciceronian and a Christian? Such questions had been asked by Tertullian even before Jerome was born. Indeed, the tension between Christianity and classical culture is inher-

---

[14]Rice, *Saint Jerome in the Renaissance*, p. 3.

ent in the words of Jesus, which do not come to us in his mother tongue of Aramaic (with few exceptions such as the familial term of address for God, *Abba* [Mk 14:36], and his cry of dereliction from the cross, *Eli, Eli, lema sabachthani* [Mt 27:46]). The Gospels, along with the entire New Testament, were written in the common idiom of Hellenistic Greek. Paul warned against the allurements of vain philosophy, but he also quoted the Greek poets at will and argued with the rhetorical skill of a Quintilian.

Neither Jerome nor Erasmus could leave the classics alone. On his first visit to England in 1499, Erasmus was charmed by John Colet and heard him lecture on Paul's letters at Oxford. The two maintained a close friendship until Colet's death in 1519. Erasmus resonated with Colet's piety and his rejection of scholastic methods, but he could not accept his counsel to abstain from reading pagan literature. In his *Lectures on Corinthians*, Colet warned:

> Those books alone ought to be read in which there is a salutary flavor of Christ, in which Christ is set forth for us to feast upon. Those books in which Christ is not found are but a table of devils. Do not become readers of philosophers, companions of devils. In the choice and well-stored table of Holy Scripture all things are contained that belong to the truth.[15]

Erasmus knew that Jerome, despite his dream, continued to quote from pagan authors and that Augustine too had recommended such literature for Christians to read. But why study the Greek and Latin classics? Erasmus answered: in order to understand better the meaning of the Bible itself. Drawing on an analogy used by Augustine in his treatise *On Christian Doctrine*, Erasmus asserted that just as the

---

[15]John Colet, *An Exposition of St. Paul's First Epistle to the Corinthians*, ed. J. H. Lupton (Ridgewood, N.J.: Gregg Press, 1965), pp. 110-11, 238-39. See Werner Schwarz, *Principles and Problems of Biblical Translation: Some Reformation Controversies and Their Background* (Cambridge: Cambridge University Press, 1955), p. 113.

children of Israel carried with them the "spoils of the Egyptians"
when they left their land of captivity, so too Christian scholars may
"steal" the riches of pagan learning in order to adorn the temple of the
Lord.[16] In other words, classical literature can and should be appropriated for Christian purposes. This became an important plank in
the program of biblical humanism as well as in the Protestant ap-
proach to the study of the Bible. Thus, when twenty-one-year-old
Philipp Melanchthon came to the University of Wittenberg in 1518,
his teaching assignment included the Greek classics (starting with
Plato and Homer) as well as New Testament Greek. Just so, when
Luther found himself sequestered in the Castle of Coburg during the
Diet of Augsburg in 1530, he translated the book of Ezekiel from
Hebrew to German in the morning and the fables of Aesop from
Greek to German in the afternoon: the winged seraphim and the tor-
toise and the hare on the same day.[17]

Despite his enthusiasm for Jerome, however, Erasmus fell far behind his hero in one crucial aspect of sacred learning. While Jerome
was the greatest Hebrew scholar of the early church, surpassing
even Origen, Erasmus considered Hebrew too strange and difficult
for him to learn and only "nibbled" at the language.[18] Colet once
urged Erasmus to lecture on the Pentateuch and the book of Isaiah
at Oxford, but he declined acknowledging his lack of Hebrew learning. Eventually Erasmus did publish commentaries on eleven of the
psalms, although they are more sermonic than textual or exegetical

---

[16]The idea of "spoiling the Egyptians" was bequeathed to Augustine by Origen (PG 11.88-
   89). Augustine refers to the use by the children of Israel of the spoils of Egypt in adorning
   the Lord's temple in *On Christian Doctrine* 2.40.61.

[17]See Jaroslav Pelikan, *The Reformation of the Bible/The Bible of the Reformation* (New Haven:
   Yale University Press, 1996), p. 3.

[18]On Erasmus's knowledge of Hebrew, see Erika Rummel, "The Textual and Hermeneutic
   Work of Desiderius Erasmus of Rotterdam," in *Hebrew Bible/Old Testament: The History of
   Its Interpretation*, vol. 2: *From the Renaissance to the Enlightenment*, ed. Magne Saebo (Göt-
   tingen: Vandenhoeck & Ruprecht, 2008), 219-21. For "nibbled," see LB 5, 78C-79A.

in style.[19] With other humanist scholars, Erasmus defended Reuchlin against his detractors who not only defamed the greatest Hebraist in Europe but also tried to destroy Jewish writings. Erasmus also continued to push for the ideal of trilingual education in the study of the Scriptures, but his own expertise in only two of the three sacred tongues left him less than fully sympathetic to the study of the Old Testament.

Wolfgang Capito, a reformer in both Basel and Strasbourg, was an outstanding scholar of Hebrew who published a Hebrew grammar (1525) and wrote commentaries on Habakkuk, Hosea and Genesis. As part of the humanist brain trust in Basel, he assisted Erasmus on textual matters related to Hebrew when the critical edition of the Greek New Testament was being prepared for the press in 1516. In that same year, Capito, together with Konrad Pellikan and Sebastian Münster, brought out the first edition of the Hebrew Psalter printed north of the Alps. While appreciative of the help Capito had given him, Erasmus spoke slightingly of his devotion to "the Hebrew truth." In words not meant for publication but laced with anti-Semitic sentiment, he wrote:

> I wish you were more intent on Greek rather than on those Hebrew studies, although I do not reprehend them. I see that that race is full of the most inane fables and succeeds only in bringing forth a kind of fog. . . . I wish the Christian church did not

---

[19]See Michael J. Heath's remark about Erasmus's commentary on Psalm 2: "Erasmus's enforced preference for rhetorical effect over textual accuracy, which shocked some contemporary critics, even led him to conclude, with a touch of bravado, that the Greek and Latin versions of the Psalms provided all the information and, especially, all the inspiration required by the exegete. It also made him indifferent to Hebrew itself; considering the different meanings of the word *bar* (a son? purity? wheat?) in Syriac and Hebrew, he cuts the discussion short with a dismissive pun: 'There is no need to cudgel our brains with complexities of these barbaric languages.' This is his only contribution to Jerome's erudite discussion of Psalm 2:12." Michael J. Heath, "Erasmus and the Psalms," in *The Bible and the Renaissance: Essays on Biblical Commentary and Translation in the Fifteenth and Sixteenth Centuries*, ed. Richard Griffiths (Aldershot: Ashgate, 2001), pp. 38-39.

give such weight to the Old Testament! It was given for a time only and consists of shadows, yet it is almost preferred to Christian writings.[20]

The reluctance of a middle-aged scholar to learn a new language does not fully explain Erasmus's relegation of Hebrew to the place of third rank among the three holy tongues or his degrading comments about the Jews and their language. Some scholars have found in this attitude a sign of his favor toward a Hellenic rather than a Hebraic worldview. His bent toward Platonism, with its disparagement of the earthly and the physical, made him more congenial with New Testament piety than Old Testament history. As the debates of the Reformation heated up, Erasmus kept looking over his shoulder at the group of first-rate Hebrew scholars Luther had gathered around him in Wittenberg—his "Sanhedrin," Luther called them—and he seems to have postulated a guilt-by-association theory of Reformation origins. Luther's positive approach to the Jews in his early career (as opposed to his brutal attacks on them later on) made Erasmus suspicious of Jewish collusion in the Reformation tumults. From his base at Basel, Erasmus could hear the violent noises of the Peasants' War across the Rhine in southern Germany. While he deplored the bloody conflict, he could not help passing along the rumor that the whole

---

[20]Ibid., p. 220. On the question of whether or to what extent Erasmus exhibited the traits of anti-Semitism, see Shimon Markish, *Erasmus and the Jews* (Chicago: University of Chicago Press, 1986), and especially the rejoinder by Arthur A. Cohen published in the same volume. Heiko A. Oberman places the views of Erasmus in the wider context of Reformation attitudes toward the Jews in *The Roots of Anti-Semitism* (Philadelphia: Fortress, 1981). See also Erika Rummel, "Humanists, Jews and Judaism," in *Jews, Judaism and the Reformation in Sixteenth-Century Germany*, ed. Dean Phillip Bell and Stephen G. Burnett (Leiden: Brill, 2006), pp. 3-32. Roland H. Bainton goes too far when he declares that "Erasmus would not have found it difficult to be a Marcionite" (Roland H. Bainton, *Erasmus of Christendom* [New York: Scribner, 1969], p. 143). In his 1533 treatise, *De sarcienda ecclesiae concordia* ("On Restoring the Unity of the Church"), Erasmus excoriates the "Manichaeans" for their Marcionite-like belief that the entire Old Testament should be rejected as "something handed down not by God but by the Prince of Darkness." See Raymond Himelick, trans., *Erasmus and the Seamless Coat of Jesus* (Lafayette: Purdue University Press, 1971), p. 13.

upheaval had been instigated by the Jews. Erasmus's exchange with
Capito before all hell broke loose points to a scholarly pattern that
would emerge among his disciples who embraced the Reformation:
devotion to the Erasmian way with respect to the New Testament
and Greek, but a far warmer embrace of the first three-fourths of the
Bible than their master could affirm.

THE GREEK NEW TESTAMENT

In the summer of 1504, Erasmus found himself in the library of the
Premonstratensian Abbey of Parc near Louvain. He was doing what
he always did in such places: rummaging through the collection,
searching in the corners, hunting for some unknown book or long-
forgotten manuscript. "In no forest is hunting a greater delight," he
once said of such pursuits.[21] This time he struck gold when he stum-
bled onto a manuscript of Lorenzo Valla's annotations on the Greek
New Testament. Valla died in 1457, in the early dawn of the age of
printing, and his controversial work correcting the Latin Vulgate by
comparison with the Greek original had never been published. Erasmus seized the manuscript, presumably with the permission of the
abbot, and carried it with him to Paris, where he saw it through the
press in March 1505. He appended a preface of his own justifying
Valla's approach to the sacred text and signaling his own desire to
make the Bible the primary focus of his own scholarship.

For the next ten years Erasmus immersed himself in the study of
Greek. He perfected his text-critical skills, scoured older manuscripts
of the Bible that came into his hands and began his own Latin translation of the New Testament. The result was the *Novum Instrumentum* published by Froben in 1516. Erasmus later complained that this
first edition had been rushed into print, "precipitated rather than ed-

---

[21]See Johann Huizinga, *Erasmus and the Age of Reformation* (New York: Harper & Row,
1924), p. 57.

ited," for fear that someone else would beat him to the punch.[22] In fact, we now know what the publisher Froben perhaps surmised: that the New Testament had already been printed in Greek in 1514 as part of the Complutensian Polyglot in Spain. But this edition would be "published" only after 1520, when the entire polyglot project received papal approval. Aware of the defects in the 1516 edition, Erasmus began at once to work on a second revised edition that came out in 1519 and that he called, more familiarly, *Novum Testamentum*. The process of clarifying textual variants, acquiring better manuscripts and improving his Latin translation proved to be an ongoing task. Eventually Erasmus brought out five editions of the Greek New Testament during his life (1516, 1519, 1522, 1527 and 1535).

To cite just one of the embarrassing gaffes that Erasmus had to correct in later editions: the last five verses of the book of Revelation had been omitted by the copyist Erasmus had hired to prepare the final transcription of the text for the printer in 1516. In haste to see the project through the press, Erasmus promptly and extemporaneously translated the missing verses back into Greek from the Latin! He had always claimed, with Jerome, that a translator was the servant of the inspired text, not a conduit of fresh revelations. Erasmus's ad hoc solution to the problem of the missing verses, while showing his facility with Greek, betrayed his philological principles and added unnecessary fuel to the fire of his critics. For all the flaws of the first edition, however, its significance in the history of New Testament studies can hardly be overstated. Roland Bainton described the importance of having the Greek New Testament in print for the first time:

> The mere fact alone that the New Testament in Greek was available in book form, whatever the text, was of immense significance, because thereby the task of collation was expedited. Manuscripts could not be transported from country to country

---

[22]EE 3:117 (no. 694); CWE 5:167.

without grave risks. Printed copies could be sent to the manuscripts and variant readings recorded in the margins. Then the books could be gathered and the evidence assembled. If in the process a book were lost, it was not irreplaceable.[23]

In addition to providing the Greek and Latin texts side by side on opposing columns on the same page, the 1516 edition also contained a set of annotations, printed at the back of the volume, and several items of significant front matter. In subsequent editions the annotations would grow larger than the New Testament text itself, eventually requiring a second volume. The annotations included philological comments, variant readings and textual analysis, but some of them were also content notes in which Erasmus responded to his growing chorus of critics.[24] Erasmus prudently dedicated the volume to Pope Leo X, whom he had met at Rome in 1509 as Giovanni de Medici. The edition of 1519 also included an approving letter of commendation from the pope, which Erasmus found a helpful feature in fending off charges of heterodoxy from his conservative Catholic critics. There was also an apology defending his efforts to restore the original text and a brief statement on hermeneutics that would be greatly expanded in the second edition—and later printed as a separate treatise, the *Ratio verae theologiae*. The *Ratio* contained Erasmus's recommendations for a proper theological education and a summary of his hermeneutics.

Erasmus's Greek New Testament also included a preface that he called *Paraclesis*. This is a Greek word that means summons or exhortation, a word closely related to Jesus' depiction of the Holy Spirit

---

[23]Bainton, *Erasmus*, p. 134.
[24]Erika Rummel has catalogued some of these controversies and described Erasmus's response in *Erasmus's Annotations on the New Testament from Philologist to Theologian* (Toronto: University of Toronto Press, 1986). See also Jerry H. Bentley, *Humanists and Holy Writ: New Testament Scholarship in the Renaissance* (Princeton: Princeton University Press, 1983), pp. 112-93.

as the Paraclete or Counselor (Jn 15:26). The *Paraclesis* was a passionate plea for the philosophy of Christ. The life of faith, Erasmus argued, is available to everyone regardless of age, gender, fortune or position in life. No one is excluded, unless a person deliberately keeps himself away. In this vein, Erasmus called for the translation of the Bible into the vernacular languages so that the mysteries of Christ could be accessible to all:

> I would that even the lowliest women read the Gospels and the Pauline epistles. And I would that they were translated into all languages so that they could be read and understood not only by Scots and Irish, but also by Turks and Saracens. . . . Would that, as a result, the farmer sings some portion of them at the plow, the weaver hums some parts of them to the movement of his shuttle, the traveler lighten the weariness of the journey with stories of this kind![25]

Erasmus's oft-quoted plea for vernacular translations of the Bible anticipates the Reformation doctrine of the spiritual priesthood of all believers. However, it is worth pondering why Erasmus himself never published a single page of Scripture in the vernacular, not even in his native Dutch. H. J. De Jonge has cogently argued that Erasmus was far more interested in his elegant Latin translation of the New Testament than in his edition of the Greek text that lay behind it.[26] Greek was acknowledged as the language of the learned few while the vernacular languages were just coming of age in the sixteenth century. Latin was still the common bond across the various national and language groups in Europe, and Erasmus, like everyone else, thought of the Bible primarily as a Latin book. He believed that the philosophy

[25]John C. Olin, ed., *Christian Humanism and the Reformation* (New York: Fordham University Press, 1987), p. 101.

[26]H. J. De Jonge, "*Novum Testamentum a Nobis Versum*: The Essence of Erasmus's Edition of the New Testament," *Journal of Theological Studies* 35 (1984): 394-413.

of Christ could provide the basis for a Christendom-wide harmony within the empire, the church and the multilingual cities and nation-states of Europe. Still, however great his expectations for a Bible freshly dressed in polished Latin, he genuinely welcomed efforts to place the Word of God in the hands of the common people. "Do you think," Erasmus asked, "that the Scriptures are fit only for the perfumed?"[27]

Erasmus closed the *Paraclesis* with an exhortation for everyone to love, read and listen to the Bible from earliest childhood until the very hour of death. "These writings bring you the living image of [Christ's] holy mind and the speaking, healing, dying, rising Christ himself, and thus they render him so fully present that you would see less if you gazed upon him with your very eyes."[28]

Erasmus next turned his attention to another project: publishing paraphrases of the New Testament. Starting with Romans in 1517 and concluding with Acts in 1524, he covered every book except Revelation—he was neither the first nor the last to find the last book in the Bible resistant to comprehensible summary. The paraphrase was neither a translation nor a commentary, though Erasmus did call it "a kind of commentary." A translation aims to render faithfully an original text from one language into another, if not word for word, at least with close attention to the base text. The commentary is an exegetical explanation or exposition of a given book or treatise, often divided into discrete units corresponding to verses or pericopes in the text being commented on. In style, the paraphrase is something in between these two genres. As he put it, the purpose of a paraphrase is to "say things differently without saying different things."[29]

In the *Paraphrases*, Erasmus sought to fulfill what he had promised in the *Paraclesis*. Through his own smooth, eloquent restating or

---

[27]Bainton, *Erasmus*, p. 141.
[28]John C. Olin, *Humanism and the Reformation* (New York: Harper & Row, 1965), p. 108.
[29]CWE 5:196; EE 3:138 (no. 710).

paraphrasing of the New Testament, he would inculcate the "love of divine books through the beauty of language." Like all theologians including "grammarians," as his scholastic critics called him, Erasmus wrote with an agenda, even when he protested that he had no agenda. The *Paraphrases* reveal a distinctively Erasmian pattern of biblical interpretation. Uppermost in his mind is the moral sense of the text, for ethics rather than doctrine was his main concern. As a disciple of Origen, he is drawn toward allegorical interpretations even when the plain reading of the text does not require such. For example, in his paraphrase of the story of Jesus asleep in the boat in the midst of the storm, Erasmus surmises that there must have been many other boats on the Sea of Galilee at the time, though the body of Jesus was present in only one of them. Just so, he claims, "there is one Catholic Church but there are many churches. Christ is in all of them equally and when all adhere to him as the one head, then the church is one. No ship is wrecked which follows Christ."[30] Erasmus does not tell us which other churches he has in mind. Perhaps the churches of the east? The emerging Protestant communities? The invisible church of pious souls moved by inward piety but distrustful of all ecclesial structures? In any event, Erasmus finds in this Gospel story a wider ecclesiology than that allowed by the traditional interpretation of "outside the church there is no salvation."

Through the *Paraphrases*, Erasmus spread the philosophy of Christ among Europe's pastors and literate laity from Leiden to Lithuania. Erasmus wrote the *Paraphrases* in Latin, but they were soon translated into the vernaculars. The reception of Erasmus's *Paraphrases* in England was a special case. Katherine Parr, the sixth wife of Henry VIII, and the only one to outlive her husband, was a major figure in turning the Reformation in England in an explicitly Protestant direc-

---

[30]LB 7, 192E. Quoted by Roland H. Bainton, "The Paraphrases of Erasmus," *ARG* 57 (1966): 72.

tion.[31] An author of several devotional works, she extended patron-
age to such high-profile reformers as Hugh Latimer and Nicholas
Ridley. Katherine arranged for the *Paraphrases* to be translated into
English. In 1547, King Edward VI issued a royal injunction requiring
that the *Paraphrases*, along with a copy of the English Bible, be publicly displayed in every parish in the Church of England. The same
requirement was reinstituted at the accession of Elizabeth in 1559.
While some have questioned the real impact of the *Paraphrases* on the
course of the English Reformation, John Craig's study of their reception has led him to a different conclusion: the *Paraphrases* were "widely
purchased and used; they helped to make the New Testament in
English available and known to clergy and people; and they were the
chief means by which Erasmus was claimed for the English reformed
church."[32] Nicholas Udall, a Tudor playwright who supervised the
English paraphrase project, portrayed Erasmus as a true proto-
Protestant, "the chief leader and shower of light and the principal
opener of a way unto the evangelical truth now in these last times by
God's goodness shining forth into the world."[33]

THE FORERUNNER?

"Erasmus laid the egg that Luther hatched." This old saw was
coined in the 1520s by some of Erasmus's detractors within the
Franciscan community at Cologne. Soon it was on the lips of everyone. When someone asked Erasmus what he thought about this
saying, he admitted to having laid the egg but quipped that Luther's
chicks were a different kind of bird.[34] Using the metaphor of bread

---

[31]On Parr, see Janel Mueller, "Katherine Parr," *OER* 3:221-22.
[32]Ibid., p. 335.
[33]Quoted in John Craig, "Forming a Protestant Consciousness? Erasmus' *Paraphases* in English Parishes, 1547-1666," in *Holy Scripture Speaks: The Production and Reception of Erasmus' Paraphrases on the New Testament*, ed. Hilmar M. Pabel and Mark Vessey (Toronto:
University of Toronto Press, 2002), p. 320.
[34]CWE 10:464; EE 5:609 (no. 1528): *Ego posui ouum gallinaceum, Lutherus exclusit pullum
longe dissimillimum.*

making, a popular broadsheet called "The Divine Mill" (1521) depicted Erasmus and Luther working side by side to produce the harvest of the gospel.

Figure 3.1. In "The Divine Mill" (1521), Erasmus and Luther
are shown working side by side in the harvest of the Gospel. The
threatening figure of the peasant with scythe in hand foreshadows
the violent upheaval of the Peasants' War that threatens to undo
the entire Reformation program.

This image was a revamping of an earlier fifteenth-century woodcut, called the Host Mill, which visually portrayed the Catholic doctrine of transubstantiation. In the Reformation version of the image, Christ pours into the hopper the four Evangelists represented by their traditional symbols. As Erasmus supervises the milling process, the flour comes forth in little cakes called faith, hope, love and the church. Standing next to Erasmus, Luther distributes the bread of life in the form of Gospel books to the pope, a bishop, a monk and a nun, all of whom refuse to receive Luther's offerings and allow the books to fall to the ground. Above this scene stands the peasant Karsthans, with scythe in hand, threatening to wreak divine vengeance on those who refuse to heed the Reformation message. Here, humanism and reformation are allies in a common cause; Erasmus mills the flour that Luther bakes.[35]

In traditional Reformation historiography, Erasmus often appears at the end of a long line of forerunners, precursors who anticipated the teachings of the sixteenth-century reformers and even prepared the way for their advent. Among these *Reformers before the Reformation*, to use the title of a famous book by Karl Heinrich Ullmann published in the nineteenth century, Erasmus stands with the likes of John Wycliffe, John Hus, Wesel Gansfort, Savonarola, and others. Apart from the fact that this interpretation turns such characters into stage props for the main show, Erasmus hardly fits the pattern because he was a participant observer of the events he helped to precipitate.[36]

For a while it seemed to almost everyone that Erasmus and Luther were rowing on the same team. When the Greek New Testament was published in March 1516, Luther was lecturing on the epistle to the Romans in Wittenberg. The manuscript of his lectures reveals that from Romans 9 forward he was drawing insights from the Greek text and annotations of Erasmus, which he frequently cites. He shows re-

---

[35]On "The Divine Mill," see Andrew Pettegree, *Reformation in the Culture of Persuasion* (Cambridge: Cambridge University Press, 2005), pp. 111-17.

[36]Heiko A. Oberman includes a chapter on Erasmus in *Forerunners of the Reformation* (Philadelphia: Fortress, 1966). Oberman defends the concept of the forerunner of the Reformation as "a valid and indispensible tool for historical interpretation" but qualifies the concept in three important ways: (1) that forerunners have explanatory but not causative connections to the Reformation; (2) that the concept of forerunner be broadened beyond Luther and the doctrine of justification by faith to include figures such as Zwingli, Bucer and later reformers; (3) that the reform programs of pre-Reformation forerunners have multiple outcomes in both the Protestant and the Catholic Reformation.

spect for the opinions "of Erasmus and of those who agree with him" even when his own studies lead to different exegetical conclusions.[37] Clearly Luther appreciated the philological prowess of Erasmus, but already he chided the great humanist for failing to grasp the gravity of sin and the true dilemma of the human before God. The knowledge of the biblical languages was important but not sufficient for grasping the true meaning of Scripture. No one is a wise Christian just because he knows Greek and Hebrew, Luther said.

Albert Rabil Jr. has compared Luther's lectures on Romans in 1516 with Erasmus's paraphrases on Romans published in the following year. He sees in their respective approaches to Romans a contrast of theological vision that would lead to their great debate over the bondage and freedom of the will in 1524-1525.

> Erasmus and Luther are very much alike and at the same time very different. For Erasmus, man is basically good, though finite, and the question is how man acts; for Luther, man is a sinner, and the question is the conditions under which he can act. It follows that for Erasmus there is continuity between the old and the new man, as there is between Christ and Moses and between nature and grace. For Luther there is a radical discontinuity: the new man is a man for the first time, Christ abrogates the Mosaic covenant, and grace annuls rather than perfects nature. Further, for Erasmus, God is a kind Father and Christ the perfect exemplification and pattern of the virtues derived from a kind Father. For Luther, God is a Father who shows his kindness only through his wrath but once we have passed through the fire of God's wrath we find Christ who is indeed the perfect exemplification of the kindness of God. For Erasmus, faith in Christ renders us righteous or potentially so,

---

[37]Wilhelm Pauck, ed., *Luther: Lectures on Romans* (Philadelphia: Westminster Press, 1961), p. 419.

given this faith, the choice of action is up to us. For Luther, faith
in Christ *is* our righteousness and there is nothing we can do
either before or after that righteousness to make it manifest.
Nonetheless, we will do so, for a man *does* as he *is*. The sign of
his doing will be suffering in the world, for the man of grace is
so unlike nature that he can only relate to it by opposition.[38]

The differences between Luther and Erasmus were indeed deep
and wide, as the events of the Reformation were to prove. Still,
Erasmus is rightly portrayed as the miller who provided the flour
for Luther's evangelical bakery. In the first of his Ninety-five Theses, Luther declared, "When our Lord and Master Jesus Christ
said, 'Repent,' he willed the entire life of believers to be one of
repentance."[39] The true understanding of *poenitentia* ("repentance,"
"penitence") had been at the center of Luther's tortured conscience
in the monastery. He knew that without true *poenitentia* there could
be no reconciliation with God, and yet his own struggles in the confessional left him mired in desperation for he realized that he could
never adequately fulfill requirements of the sacrament of penance.
It was Johann von Staupitz, his confessor and spiritual father, who
helped him to overcome his servile fear about his lack of a right
standing before God by pointing him to the cross and "the wounds
of the sweetest Savior." It was Staupitz who "started the doctrine,"
Luther said.[40]

Luther's evangelical breakthrough was followed by an exegetical
one when he realized that the traditional Vulgate rendering of Matthew 3:2 as *poenitentium agite*, "do penance," was a mistranslation of
the Greek. Luther learned from Erasmus that the Greek word
metanoia was derived from *meta* and *noein*, meaning "afterward" and

---

[38]Albert Rabil Jr., *Erasmus and the New Testament: The Mind of a Christian Humanist* (San
   Antonio: Trinity University Press, 1972), pp. 178-79.
[39]*LW* 31:83.
[40]*LW* 48:66.

"mind," "so that *poenitentia* or *metanoia* means a coming to one's senses . . . the emphasis on works of penance had come from the misleading [Vulgate] translation, which indicates an action rather than a change of heart and in no way corresponds to Greek *metanoia*."[41] In his note on Matthew 3:2, Erasmus criticized those theologians who connected this text with the works of satisfaction in the sacrament of penance. "Our people think that *poenitentium agite* means to wash away one's sins with some prescribed penalty . . . yet *metanoia* is derived from *metanoein*, that is, to come to one's senses afterwards when someone who sinned, finally after the fact, recognizes his error."[42] What Jesus and John the Baptist preached in the Gospel of Matthew was not penance but penitence, that is, repentance. And repentance was the habit of a lifetime, not a series of one-off responses or prescribed acts intended to assuage a guilty conscience. Erasmus never drew the radical conclusions Luther came to concerning the sacrament of penance. In his 1522 edition of the New Testament, under pressure from his Catholic critics, Erasmus reverted to the traditional Latin translation of *metanoeite, poenitentiam agite*. But by then the damage had been done.

As lines began to be drawn in the sand, Erasmus chose to be, as he put it, "a spectator rather than an actor."[43] At the behest of Melanchthon, Luther wrote a fawning letter in March 1518: "Who is there in whose heart Erasmus does not occupy a central place, to whom Erasmus is not the teacher who holds him enthralled . . . and so, dear Erasmus, accept this younger brother of yours in Christ." Recognizing Luther's flattery for what it was, Erasmus responded with a polite but curt note of thanks.[44] Luther's true sentiment came out in a letter he wrote to his friend Johann Lang on March 1, 1517: "I am reading

---

[41]*WA* 1/1 525:24-27. Quoted in Rummel, *Erasmus's Annotations*, 153.

[42]Ibid., 152.

[43]CWE 8:78; EE 4:371 (no. 1155). *Ego huius fabulae spectator esse malim quam histrio.* This letter was addressed to Reuchlin in 1520.

[44]EE 3:516-19, 605-7 (nos. 933 and 980); CWE 6:281-83, 391-93.

our Erasmus but daily I dislike him more and more. . . . Human
things weigh more with him than the divine."[45]

For his part, Erasmus called for fair treatment for Luther in the
wake of his excommunication and hearing before the Diet of Worms in
1521. If Luther were to be crushed, he reasoned, then the bloodhounds
would soon be on his own tracks and everything for which he had given
his life, the whole project of *bonae litterae*, could go up in flames. Pri-
vately, Erasmus spoke either favorably or disapprovingly about Luther
depending on the person to whom he wrote. The pressure mounted for
him to cease playing Mr. Facing-Both-Ways and to attack Luther in
print. The pressures came from the emperor, Charles V; from Duke
George of Saxony; from Henry VIII in England; and from Pope
Adrian VI, Erasmus's fellow Dutchman and the last non-Italian pope
until John Paul II. The result was Erasmus's blast on free will and Luther's counterblast on the will's thralldom. The rest is history.

If Erasmus thought his diatribe against Luther would quell his
critics within the old church, he was mistaken. In the summer of
1526, he reported that he had just received from the presses in Paris
"five volumes full of rabid accusations against me."[46] Erasmus never
became a gung-ho partisan on either side and remained under suspi-
cion in both camps. He hated the verbal violence that, he rightly saw,
was a likely prelude to religious war. He would not become a *carnifex*,
a cannibal, he said. But neither would he volunteer for the martyr's
pyre. Nothing pleased Erasmus more than a cozy dinner by a warm
fire with good conversation and a flask of well-aged wine from Crete
(his favorite). "Let others court martyrdom," he remarked. "I don't
consider myself worthy of this distinction."[47]

As late as 1518, Erasmus said that he thought he could see a golden

---

[45]*WA, Br* 1, 90, 15; *LW* 48:40.
[46]CWE 12:326; EE 6:399 (no. 1743). One of these volumes was by Noel Beda, opponent of
the new trilingual course of studies at Paris and Erasmus's *bête noir*.
[47]CWE 8:120-21; EE 4:410 (no. 1167).

age dawning in the near future.[48] The events into which he was invariably if reluctantly drawn dampened his optimism. A few years later, he was referring to his time as "the worst century since Jesus Christ."[49] From Basel, he wrote to his old friend Willibald Pirckheimer, a fellow humanist and patron of letters, "Peace is perishing, and love and faith and learning and morality and civilized behavior. What is left?"[50]

But the Erasmian moment outlasted Erasmus. Both Luther and Tyndale had copies of his 1519 Greek New Testament at hand as they labored to "verdeutschen" and "english" God's Word for the farmers, ploughboys, pimps and prostitutes of Germany and England. The debate between Erasmus and Luther on the bondage of the will did not result in the divorce of humanism and the Reformation, though it did serve to define the fronts in later theological battles. But the torch had been passed to a new generation of reformers for whom *studia humanitatis* and *theologia crucis* were both central in the renewal of the church.

---

[48]CWE 27:48.
[49]CWE 8:315; EE 4:594-95 (no. 1239): *Non arbitror a Christo nato seculum fuisse hoc maliciosius.*
[50]CWE 13:401; EE 7:216-17 (no. 1893): *Perit concordia, charitas, fides, disciplinae, mores, ciuilitas. Quid superset?*

Four

Whose Bible?
Which Tradition?

Ye interpret the Scriptures (said she) in one manner, and they interpret
it in another; whom shall I believe? And who shall be judge?

Ye shall believe (said he) God, that plainly speaketh in his Word:
and farther than the Word teaches you, ye neither shall believe one or the other.
The Word of God is plain in the self; and if there appear any obscurity in one place,
the Holy Ghost, which, is never contrarious to himself, explains the same
more clearly in other places: so that there can remain no doubt,
but unto such as obstinately remain ignorant.

Conversation between John Knox and Mary, Queen of Scots (1561)

There is enough clarity in the Bible to enlighten the elect
and enough obscurity to humble them.[1]

Blaise Pascal

---

[1]David Laing, ed., *The Works of John Knox* (Edinburgh: Bannatyne Club, 1846-1864), 2:284.
The quotation from Paschal is from *Fragment 578*, quoted in H. F. Stewart, *Pascal's Apology
for Religion* (Cambridge: Cambridge University Press, 1942), p. 190. The French text reads:
Il y a assez de clarté pour éclairer les élus et assez d'obscurité pour les humilier. Blaise Pascal,
Pensées, ed. Leon Brunschvicg (Paris: Hachette, 1897), p. 155.

In 1588, THE YEAR OF THE SPANISH ARMADA, William Weston, an English-born, Oxford-educated Jesuit priest, found himself imprisoned in Wisbech Castle, not far from the town of Ely in the Fenlands region of Cambridgeshire. Weston was a zealous Catholic missionary in Elizabeth's Protestant England. He could boast some notable success in winning for the Church of Rome several converts from the nobility, including Philip Howard, the Earl of Arundel. For his proselytism, Weston had been arrested and placed in strict confinement at Wisbech Castle along with more than thirty other Catholic recusants. As he looked out from his prison cell one day in 1588, Weston witnessed a remarkable gathering of puritan believers who had assembled on a large, level stretch of ground within the precincts of the prison for a kind of open-air Bible conference. During his eleven years of imprisonment, Weston had seen this sort of thing before, and he described, with some amusement, the scene before him:

> Each of them had his own Bible, and seduously turned the pages and looked up the texts cited by the preachers, discussing the passages among themselves to see whether they had quoted them to the point, and accurately, and in harmony with their tenets. Also they would start arguing among themselves about the meaning of passages from the Scriptures—men, women, boys, girls, rustics, laborers and idiots—and more often than not, it ended in violence and fisticuffs. . . . Here, over a thousand of them sometimes assembled, their horses and pack animals burdened with a multitude of Bibles. It was a wretched and truly pitiful sight, but in some ways it was comic and laughable for the onlookers.[2]

One of the major arguments against making the Bible available in

---

[2]William Weston, *An Autobiography from the Jesuit Underground*, trans. Philip Caraman (New York: Farrar, Straus & Cudahy, 1955), pp. 164-65.

the common languages of the people was that it would undermine the normative authority of the church and lead to the kind of mass confusion and conflict witnessed by Weston. Thomas Hobbes was born in the year Weston wrote his description of the gathering at Wisbech Castle. Though Hobbes was no Jesuit—he was a halfhearted Protestant with leanings toward atheism—he shared Weston's concern about giving unfiltered access to the Scriptures to just anybody. In his famous book, *Behemoth* (1682), he argued for political absolutism against the populist and libertarian trends of the Renaissance and Reformation. Looking back on the cultural transformation effected by the translation and dissemination of the Bible in the sixteenth century, Hobbes lamented that after the Bible was translated "every man, nay, every boy and wench, that could read English thought they spoke with God Almighty and understood what he said, when by certain number of chapters a day they had read the Scriptures once or twice over."[3]

It has been suggested that Henry VIII permitted the 1539 Great Bible to be published in England not because he was keen for the common people to have the Scriptures in their native tongue but as a prudential response to a growing Bible-based popular reformation from below. In this view, Henry needed the support of the emerging Protestant movement for his assertion of royal supremacy against the pope, and this was one way to get it. This may be true enough, but by 1545 the king was having second thoughts about giving the Bible so freely to the laity. As Margo Todd explains, the Bible "had become *too* popular, unleashing individual lay interpretation in an age that valued conformity and hierarchy."[4] Addressing himself to the leaders of Parliament, Henry warned them about the dangers of an unleashed

---

[3]Thomas Hobbes, *Behemoth*, or *The Long Parliament*, ed. Ferdinand Tönnies (London: Simpkin, Marshall and Company, 1889), pp. 21-22.
[4]Margo Todd, "A People's Reformation?" in *Reformation Christianity*, ed. Peter Matheson (Minneapolis: Fortress, 2007), p. 73.

Bible and instructed them "not to dispute and make Scripture a railing and a taunting stock against priests and preachers (as many like persons do). I am very sorry to know and hear how unreverently that most precious jewel, the Word of God, is disputed, rhymed, sung and jangled in every ale house and tavern, contrary to the true meaning and doctrine of the same."[5] Before Henry's death in 1547, English translations of the Bible, including those of William Tyndale and Miles Coverdale, were once again being collected and burned at Saint Paul's Cross in London.

A Nose of Wax?

Weston, Hobbes and Henry VIII all seemed to blame the exegetical anarchy they observed on the widespread distribution of the Bible among the common people. But while the advent of printing may have accelerated controversies over the proper interpretation of Scripture, such disputes were nothing new in the sixteenth century. Wrangling over holy texts is endemic to any religion that takes seriously a fixed canon of sacred writings: witness, among many other disputes, the debates over the resurrection between Pharisees and Sadducees during Second Temple Judaism, or the differences among Sunnis, Shias and Sufis over the correct interpretation of the Quran today. Because the Christian faith is so deeply tied to the story of Israel, it is not surprising that the role of the Old Testament law became a matter of great controversy within the apostolic church. Paul addressed this issue in his letters but, as we know, his writings generated even further controversy. The New Testament itself claimed that they contain "some things that are hard to understand, which the ignorant and unstable twist to their own destruction, as they do the other Scriptures" (2 Pet 3:16).

The debate over Paul's letters intensified in the second century,

---

[5]Ibid. See Edward Hall, *Henry VIII*, ed. C. Whibley (London: T. E. and E. C. Jack, 1904), 2:356-57.

when Marcion touted them as normative Scripture for Christians to the exclusion of the entire Old Testament and most of the rest of the New. The gnostics also appealed to the Scriptures. While they cherished their own spurious gospels and secret Jesus sayings, they also cited the texts of the Old and New Testaments, which they interpreted by means of extreme allegory to suit their preconceived schemes of salvation. Irenaeus accused the Valentinians of distorting the Scriptures in the manner of someone who took a beautiful mosaic image of a king, shattered it into pieces and then rearranged the gems into the shape of a dog or a fox. The villain would then parade before the ignorant this reconstructed parody of the genuine likeness in order to make them think that the real image of the king resembled that of a four-footed animal. "In like manner," Irenaeus wrote, "do these persons patch together old wives' fables, and then endeavor, by violently drawing away from their proper connection, words, expressions, and parables whenever found, to adapt the oracles of God to their baseless fictions."[6] Tertullian also challenged the gnostic exegesis of the Bible that allegorized away the historicity of the birth and crucifixion and resurrection of Jesus. "And, indeed, if all are figures," he asked, "where will be that of which they are the figures? How can you hold up a mirror for your face, if the face nowhere exists? But, in truth, all are not figures, but there are also literal statements; nor are all shadows, but there are bodies also. . . . It was not figuratively that the Virgin conceived in her womb; nor in a trope did she bear Emmanuel, that is, Jesus, God with us."[7] Through the work of Origen and Augustine, the use of allegory became a standard feature in the Christian understanding of the Bible in the Middle Ages, but the early struggles against the gnostics showed the danger of interpretive schemes not governed by the rule of faith.

In the sixteenth century, the reformers found another image to

---

[6]Irenaeus *Against Heresies* 1.8.1 (ANF 1:326).
[7]Tertullian *On the Resurrection of the Flesh* 20 (ANF 3:559).

show how the Bible could be malleably twisted this way or that to suit the predilections of the interpreter—a nose of wax. This image can be traced back to the twelfth century when Alan of Lille referred to the competing "authorities" used by scholastic theologians to construct an argument as a *cereus nasus*, a waxen nose capable of being turned one way or another to fit the argument. On the eve of the Reformation, Johannes Geiler of Kaisersberg, a famous cathedral preacher at Strasbourg, applied the image of the waxen nose directly to the Bible.[8] The first complete German Bible had been published at Strasbourg in 1466 and went through seventeen reprintings prior to the publication of Luther's German New Testament in 1522. Geiler opposed the dissemination of the Bible in German for fear of its being misinterpreted by the unlatined laity. In the Reformation debates that followed, Catholics and Protestants alike accused one another of abusing the Scriptures by turning it into a nose of wax.

The sixteenth century was not short of vivid verbal images. Thomas More came up with a graphic one in 1532 when he compared Bible translator William Tyndale with "a butterfly fallen on a lime twig, which the more it striveth and fluttereth, ever the faster it hangeth."[9] Tyndale was not long in responding, and he charged that More and all the "papists" make Scripture a "nose of wax, and wrest it this way and that way, til it agree."[10] The Dutch scholar Albert Pighius, the first Catholic theologian to write against Calvin's *Institutes*, hurled the charge right back. To the reformers, he said, "the Scripture is like a nose of wax, that easily suffereth itself to be drawn backward and forward, and to be molded in fashion this way and that

---

[8]M.-D. Chenu, *La Théologie au douzième siècle* (Paris: J. Vrin, 1957), p. 361. Geiler of Kaisersberg's comment (*Die heilige geschrift ist wie ein wachserne nase, man bügt es war man will*) is found in Samuel Berger, *La Bible au XVIe siècle* (Geneva: Slatkine, 1879), p. 32.
[9]Thomas More, *Confutation of Tyndale's Answer* (London, 1532), p. ccxlv. Quoted by H. C. Porter, "The Nose of Wax: Scripture and the Spirit from Erasmus to Milton," *Transactions of the Royal Historical Society* 14 (1964): 155.
[10]Ibid.

way, and howsoever ye list."[11] Roger Hutchison, an English Protestant, quoted Pighius's comment in 1550 not forgetting to return the compliment in kind while expanding the image with a metaphor from sports. The Catholics, he said, "make the Scriptures a nose of wax, and a tennis ball."[12] Back and forth it went.

AGAINST ROME

The Protestant reformers faced a battle on two fronts in their struggles for a proper interpretation of the Bible. On the one hand, they denied that the institutional church, its hierarchy, prelates and scholars could sit in judgment over the Scriptures. In March 1542, the dean and faculty of theology at the Sorbonne in Paris set forth a series of articles that all teachers and theological students were required to subscribe on penalty of banishment from the community. The articles prescribed "what doctors and preachers ought to teach, and the rest of the faithful, with the whole church, believe." Calvin's "antidote" to the Paris articles drips with sarcasm as he places in the mouths of his opponents these words: "Although our masters are deficient in proofs from Scripture, they compensate the defect by another authority which they have, viz., that of the church, which is equivalent to Scripture, or even (according to the doctors) surpasses it in certainty."[13]

In 1520, Luther responded to an attack against him by the Franciscan monk Augustine Alved of Leipzig. He accused Alved and his religious cohorts of making of the Scripture "whatever they want out of it, as if it were a wax nose to be pulled to and fro."[14] They have done this, he alleged, by throwing many passages together helter-skelter

---

[11]Ibid.

[12]Ibid., p. 156.

[13]"Articles agreed upon by the Faculty of Sacred Theology of Paris, with the Antidote," in *Selected Works of John Calvin: Tracts and Letters*, ed. Jules Bonnet (1844; reprint, Grand Rapids: Baker, 1983), 1:71-72.

[14]*LW* 39:81.

whether they fit or not. If I were to follow such a procedure in interpreting the Bible, Luther continued, I could prove from the Bible that "Rastrum beer is better than Malmsey wine."[15] Rastrum was the name of a local Leipzig beer known to turn the stomach inside out because of its bitterness, whereas Malmsey was a sweet Greek wine known today as Madeira. One example of such exegetical legerdemain was the effort of Catholic scholars to draw a direct parallel between the high priesthood of Aaron in the Old Testament and the office of the pope in the church today. In equating these two, Luther says, they jumble together figure and fulfillment. The figure of Aaron in the Old Testament is physical and external, whereas the fulfillment is spiritual and internal. Arguing from the letter to the Hebrews, he claimed that it was Christ, not Peter or the pope, who fulfilled the priestly office prefigured in Aaron. "Let Aaron be just Aaron in the simplest sense," Luther wrote, "unless the Spirit interprets him in a new literal sense—as when St. Paul makes Christ out of Aaron for the Hebrews (Hebrews 9:10)."[16]

Luther found another example of Scripture twisting by his Roman opponents in the way that Jesus' interpretation of the fifth commandment in the Sermon on the Mount was understood. Jesus had made clear that "when a man leers at a woman or cracks shady jokes or even thinks about her lustfully, this is an adultery of the eyes, or the ears, or the mouth, and above all, an adultery of the heart." But the plain meaning of this text (Mt 5:27-28) has been so twisted that various interpreters have drawn ludicrous consequences in opposite directions. On the one hand, Luther says, there are "respectable people in Italy nowadays" (was he recalling some scandalous things he had seen when he visited Rome as a young monk in 1510?) who consider it honorable to cohabit with a whore outside of marriage.[17] At the op-

---

[15]*LW* 39:76.
[16]*LW* 39:178.
[17]*LW* 21:84.

posite end of such libertinism, there are legalists who have so tight-
ened the meaning of Jesus' words against lustful gazing that they for-
bid all companionship between men and women, hiding themselves
in monasteries so as to avoid all contact and association with the
world. But Jesus did not call for such sequestration. He distinguished
looking and lusting and allowed "talking, laughing, and having a good
time" with all women. Jesus' words were a call to chastity not just for
a select few but for all of his disciples whom he expected to live in the
real world while resisting its temptations. To drive home his point,
Luther recited the well-known saying from the lives of the fathers: "I
cannot keep a bird from flying over my head. But I can certainly keep
it from nesting in my hair or from biting my nose off."[18]

When news of the controversy about indulgences first reached
Rome, Pope Leo X dismissed it as a mere "monks' quarrel." The
hawker of indulgences, Johannes Tetzel, was a Dominican, and the
protester, Martin Luther, was an Augustinian. The Holy Father expected the whole matter to blow over in a short while, as quarrels
between rival orders usually did. But when he asked the papal court
theologian Sylvester Prierias—another Dominican—to respond to
Luther's Ninety-five Theses, it soon became clear that the distur-
bance in Wittenberg had far-reaching implications. In his *Dialogue
Concerning the Power of the Pope*, Prierias declared that "he who does
not accept the doctrine of the Church of Rome and pontiff of Rome
as an infallible rule of faith, from which the Holy Scriptures, too,
draw their strength and authority, is a heretic."[19] Prierias's assertion
of papal infallibility flew in the face of conciliarist understandings of
authority and anticipated the dogma of papal primacy and infallibility defined by the First Vatican Council in 1870. Prierias made clear

---

[18]*LW* 21:84-88. The saying from the *Vitae patrum* is found in PL 73:940.
[19]Quoted by Heiko A. Oberman, *Luther: Man Between God and the Devil* (New Haven: Yale
University Press, 1982), p. 193. On the exchange between Luther and Prierias, see Scott H.
Hendrix, *Luther and the Papacy: Stages in a Reformation Conflict* (Philadelphia: Fortress,
1981), pp. 44-52.

that the pope was infallible not by virtue of his personal holiness but whenever he made a decision in his capacity as a pope. But he also argued that such authority included not only issues of doctrine but also matters of faith and morals, such as the use of indulgences.

At this point, Luther had not yet rejected the office of the papacy and still spoke with respect of Pope Leo X, referring to him as a shepherd ill-advised in need of better informed advisors. However, his response to Prierias indicated that the Reformation struggle would be defined as a contest between Scripture on the one hand and tradition as interpreted by the pope on the other. Luther answered Prierias's arguments for papal infallibility by quoting two Pauline texts that became central in Protestant arguments against Rome: "Prove all things; hold fast that which is good" (1 Thess 5:21); "Even if an angel descend from heaven and preach a gospel contrary to that you have received, let him be accursed" (Gal 1:8). However, far from relying on "Scripture alone" to defend the supremacy of the Bible, Luther also cited an earlier papal decretal, one by Pope Clement V regulating the practice of indulgences. And, for good measure, he threw in a reference from the early church, a letter of Augustine to Jerome asserting the primacy of Scripture over all other writings, since only the inspired authors of the Bible had been preserved from all error. Thus from the beginning, the controversy with Rome was not simply a matter of Scripture versus tradition. Luther was arguing against tradition from tradition, or better put, he was arguing from a shallower tradition to a profounder one, a tradition that asserted the supremacy of Scripture over all other ecclesial decisions and documents.

In October 1518, Luther was summoned to Augsburg, where he met yet another Dominican theologian, Thomas de Vio, better known to history as Cardinal Cajetan. Speaking in the name of the pope, he demanded that Luther recant. Luther later remembered this meeting as a turning point that led to his final break with Rome. If Cajetan had heard him out, he later recalled, had he been willing to consider scriptural proof rather than simply demanding blind obedience to papal fiat, things might have turned out differently. But at Augsburg, Luther could not bring himself to say those six letters, *revoco*, "I recant." Everyone expected Luther to be arrested following his interview with Cajetan. But Luther was ever the reformer of narrow escapes. Under cover of night, with the stars for his canopy, he was whisked out of town on an unsaddled horse.

For Luther the road from Augsburg to Worms passed through Leipzig, where in 1519 he was *eckt*, "cornered," by Johann Eck into admitting that not only could popes, past and present, fall into error but that also general councils of the church could be and had been mistaken. The condemnation of John Hus at the Council of Constance in 1415 was a case in point. Eck declared Luther a pagan and a

publican for allying himself with a condemned heretic and for repudiating the authority of general councils as well as that of the pope. Luther answered that God's Word is above all human words. A simple layman, he said, armed with Scripture should be believed above a pope or a council without it. In his treatise on the *Babylonian Captivity of the Church* (1520), Luther stated this principle negatively: "What is asserted without the Scriptures or proven revelation may be held as an opinion, but need not be believed."[20]

AETHERNA IPSE SVAE MENTIS SIMVLACHRA LVTHERVS
EXPRIMIT AT VVLTVS GERA LVCAE OCCIDVOS
· M·D·X·X·

Figure 4.1. Luther at age thirty-seven, as portrayed by Lucas Cranach the Elder (1520). Luther appears here as an Augustinian monk with habit and tonsure.

At the Diet of Worms in 1521, Luther was confronted by the high-

---

[20]LW 36:29; WA 6:508: *Nam quod sine scripturis asseritur aut revelatione probata, opinari licet, credi non est necesse.*

est churchly and temporal authorities in the Christian world. There he famously said, "My conscience is captive to the Word of God." In modern depictions of this scene, Luther emerges as the champion of private interpretation, freedom of conscience and modern individualism. However, this popular stereotype of Luther will not bear scrutiny. For how can we understand his concluding remark in the *Disputation Against Scholastic Theology* (1517), repeated in other settings: "In all I wanted to say, we believe we have said nothing that is not in agreement with the Catholic church and the teachers of the church"?[21] In fact, in making his astounding claim at Leipzig, Luther was not saying anything new. Writing nearly a century before, Nicholas de Tudeschis (d. 1445), archbishop of Palermo, had put forth a similar claim: "In matters of faith anyone armed with better reasons and authorities of the New and Old Testaments is to be preferred even to the pope."[22] Even earlier, Henry of Ghent (d. 1293), in commenting on the *Sentences* of Peter Lombard, posed the question of whether Scripture or the church should be believed if they contradict one another. In this hypothetical cleavage, Henry sided with the Scriptures over against that community "which seems to be the church." The true church, he declared, may be found "in a few just people."[23]

During the multipapacy of the Great Schism, the idea of the rem-

---

[21]WA 1:228: *In his nihil dicere volumus nec dixisse nos credimus, quod non sit catholicae ecclesiae et ecclesiasticis doctoribus consentaneum.* LW 32:16. See the exposition of this statement by Otto Hermann Pesch, "Luther and the Catholic Tradition," *Lutheran Theological Seminary Bulletin* (winter 1984): 3-24. In 1519, Luther claimed that his denial of the inerrancy of general councils was in agreement with "all teachers of Scriptures and law" (*WA, Br* 1:472).

[22]The Latin text is cited in Knut-Wolfgang Nörr, *Kirche und Konzil bei Nicolaus de Tudeschis (Panormitanus)* (Köln-Graz: Böhlau, 1964), pp. 104-6. See also Hermann Schuessler, "Sacred Doctrine and the Authority of Scripture," in *Reform and Authority in the Medieval and Reformation Church*, ed. Guy F. Lytle (Washington, D.C.: Catholic University of America Press, 1981), pp. 55-68.

[23]See George H. Tavard, *Holy Writ or Holy Church* (Westport, Conn.: Greenwood Press, 1978), pp. 22-25. Tavard sees an adumbration of reformation views in Henry's "ethereal conception of the Church. She is not necessarily identical with the community of believers. She can be embodied in a small remnant of orthodoxy within an all but universal heresy."

nant church emerged as a major motif in late medieval ecclesiology. The Virgin Mary was seen as the archetype of this remnant church: her faithfulness alone kept the Catholic faith intact during Christ's passion on the cross. When all of the disciples, including Peter, had fled in fear, Mary remained true to Christ and his Word. Her fidelity under the cross showed that the true faith could be preserved in one sole individual, and thus Mary became the mother of the (true remnant) church.

The early reformers retained a stronger degree of Marian devotion than their later followers; even Zwingli defended the use of the "Ave Maria," and Calvin referred to Mary as the "treasurer of grace."[24] But it was Mary's submission to the Word of God and her fidelity to it *contra mundum* that reinforced their own commitment to the primacy of Scripture. Only in this way can we understand Luther's appeal to the "simple layman" at Leipzig or his audacious summary of the events of 1521: "At Worms I was the church!"—a remark that must sound as jarring to Catholics as Pius IX's "I am tradition!" does to Protestants.

RADICAL INSURGENTS

If the mainline reformers found their Catholic opponents guilty of distorting the Scriptures in order to prop up postbiblical institutions such as monasticism and the papacy, it was not long before some of their own radicalized followers were referring to Luther as the Wittenberg pope and to Geneva as the Protestant Rome. The first tremors of the radical reformation took place in Wittenberg under the direction of Luther's senior colleague, Andreas Rudolff Bodenstein von Karlstadt. If the name sounds pretentious, so was he. He held

---

[24]See Timothy George, "Evangelicals and the Mother of God," *First Things*, February, 2007, pp. 20-25. William of Ockham also cited Mary's faithfulness at the crucifixion as an example of how the church *in extremis* could be reduced to just one person. Ockham, *Dialogus de imperio et pontificia potestate*, 1.5.31-35. See John M. Headley, "The Reformation as Crisis in the Understanding of Tradition," *ARG* 78 (1987): 5-23.

three doctorates, one in civil law, one in canon law (both earned in Rome) and one in theology. Trained in Thomistic theology, he was adept in Greek and Hebrew as well as Latin. He presided over the ceremony at which Luther's doctorate was conferred in 1512, and he had been designated as the principal debater against Eck at Leipzig when his understudy Luther stole the show. (Karlstadt's wagon full of books had broken down on the way to Leipzig, an omen of bad things to come.)

His direct conflict with Luther began while Luther was holed up for his own safety in the Wartburg Castle. On the basis of the social implementation of the principle of *sola scriptura*, Karlstadt set forth a "New Order for the City of Wittenberg." In rapid succession, a number of revolutionary changes took place: images in the parish churches were smashed; the first "Protestant communion" was celebrated as Karlstadt, unvested, faced the congregation and distributed both bread and wine to the communicants without requiring prior confession to a priest; the intercession of Mary and the veneration of the saints were condemned; monastic vows, including the vow of celibacy, were repudiated as worthless. Three years before Luther married the runaway nun Katarina von Bora, Karlstadt married sixteen-year-old Anna von Mochau, the daughter of a poor nobleman. To justify his bold actions, Karlstadt appealed not only to the legible word (the Bible) and the audible word (preaching), but especially to the inner word of the Spirit. Karlstadt's pneumatic turn led him sharply to divide Word from Spirit in the experience of the believer. Christ, he said, had called unlearned fisherman to confound the wise and mighty in the days of the apostles, and he has given the same Spirit to his true followers today.

> Are we not to be compared with the apostles? What does Peter say to Cornelius that he had received the Spirit like them? What does Paul say that we must be his imitators? Didn't Christ

promise us his Spirit, as he did to the apostles? Only the Spirit leads us to the recognition of God's words. Therefore, it follows that those who don't hear what God's Spirit says, don't understand God's words, neither are they Christians.[25]

As it turned out, Wittenberg was not large enough to contain both Bible-saturated Luther and Spirit-anointed Karlstadt. "Brüder Andreas," as he came to style himself, left Wittenberg and accepted a pastoral charge in the village church of Orlamünde, where he pushed the Reformation even further in a radical direction. He refused to baptize infants, including two of his own, both of whom died without benefit of the traditional sacrament to the dismay of his young wife. He also denied the real presence of Christ in the Lord's Supper, reconstruing it as a service of remembrance. In his Orlamünde period, Karlstadt even renounced his own academic status and pedigree. Luther recalled how Karlstadt had once come swaggering into Wittenberg in his academic regalia with his double doctorate from Rome. Now he sported instead the simple garments of a peasant farmer. His academic renunciations were short-lived, however, for he spent his final years teaching Hebrew and Old Testament at the University of Basel.[26]

Karlstadt died in the arms of his wife in 1541, but not all leaders of the radical reformation were so fortunate. Thomas Müntzer, the firebrand preacher of the apocalypse, was killed during the Peasants' War and his body drawn and quartered. Melchior Hoffman, a furrier turned seer, predicted the end of the world in 1533, but that was the year he was arrested and imprisoned in Strasbourg. He remained be-

---

[25]Erich Hertzsch, ed., *Karlstadts Schriften aus den Jahren 1523-1525* (Halle: Max Niemeyer, 1956-1967), 2, 17. Quoted by Calvin A. Pater, *Karlstadt as the Father of the Baptist Movements* (Toronto: University of Toronto Press, 1984), p. 21.

[26]On Karlstadt's background in the study of Hebrew, see Hans Peter Rüger, "Karlstadt als Hebraist an der Universität zu Wittenberg," *ARG* 75 (1984): 297-308. On his time in Basel, see Ulrich Bubenheimer, "Andreas Bodenstein von Karlstadt," *OER* 1:178-80.

hind bars for ten years, constantly adjusting his prophecies of the end time to accommodate the nonappearance of Jesus. He died there in 1543, still awaiting the second coming. Balthasar Hubmaier, the most learned of the early Anabaptist leaders, was tortured and burned at the stake in 1528; his wife was drowned in the Danube River.

In commenting on 1 John 2:19, "They went out from us, but they were not of us," Luther recalled his debates with Karlstadt and Müntzer, the "rascals" who came up with a new gospel. "I have often reflected," he said, "whether it would have been better to keep the papacy than to see so many disturbances. But it is better to rescue some from the jaws of the devil than for all to perish."[27] Luther once complained that Karlstadt sounded as though he had swallowed the Holy Ghost, feathers and all! But his problem was not so much with the radicals' appeal to the Spirit as with their detachment of the Spirit from what Calvin would call "the external means or aids by which God invites us into the society of Christ" (*Institutes* 4.1.1). While at table with his students, Luther once said, *sola experientia facit theologum*, "Experience alone makes one a theologian." The context of this remark shows that Luther was not using experience as an independent category of human apperception. He was referring instead to experience with the Scriptures.[28] "Scripture is not understood, unless it is brought home, that is, experienced."[29] What Karlstadt and other radical critics considered Luther's preoccupation with the death-dealing letter of Scripture (his incessant "Bible, bibble, babble"), the reformer saw as an essential medium of the life-giving ministry of the Spirit. Word and Spirit belonged inseparably together.

For when you ask them how one comes by this lofty Spirit, they don't point to the outward gospel, but go up into cloud

---

[27]*LW* 30:254.
[28]*LW* 54:7. Oswald Bayer makes this point in "What Is a Theologian?" in *Martin Luther's Theology: A Contemporary Interpretation* (Grand Rapids: Eerdmans, 2008), pp. 21-22.
[29]WA, TR 3:170: *Die schrifft bersteht keiner, sie kome den einem zu haus, id est, experiatur.*

cuckoo land and say, Ah, you must have the experience of wait-
ing and suddenly, just like that, God will be talking with you.
. . . With the very words "Spirit, Spirit, Spirit," [the devil] kicks
away the very bridge by which the Holy Spirit can come to you,
namely the outward ordinances of God like the bodily sign of
baptism, and the preached Word of God and [he] teaches not
how the Spirit comes to you, but how you come to the Spirit,
so that you may sail up into the sky, however so high, and ride
upon the wind.[30]

SCRIPTURE AND TRADITION

In light of their two-front struggle against the Catholic elevation
of the church above the Bible and the radical distancing of Word
from Spirit, the mainline reformers were forced to clarify their understanding of the relationship between Scripture and tradition.[31]
The principle of *sola scriptura* is found in all of the classic confessions of the Reformation, but nowhere is it more clearly stated than
in the solemn Protestation (from which the word *Protestant* derives) set forth on behalf of the evangelical cause at the Diet of
Speyer in 1529:

> There is, we affirm, no sure preaching or doctrine but that
> which abides by the Word of God. According to God's com-

---

[30]WA 18:137: *Wenn man sie aber fragt, wie kompt man denn zu dem selbigen hohen geyst hyneyn?
So weysen sie dich nicht auffs eusserliche Euangelion sondern ynns schlauraffen land und sagen:
Stehe ynn der lang weyle, wie ich gestanden byn, so wirstu es auch erfaren, Da wirt die hymlische
stymme komen, und Gott selbst mit dyr reden. Wie er dyr mit den worten geyst, geyst, geyst, das
maul auff sperret und doch die weyl, beyde brucken, steg und weg, leytter und alles umbreysst,
dadurch der geyst zu dyr kommen soll, nemlich, die eusserlichen ordnung Gotts ynn der leyplichen
tauffe zeychen und muendlichen wort Gottes und will dich leren, nicht wie der geyst zu dyr,
sondern wie du zum geyst komen sollt, Das du sollt lernen auff den wolcken faren und auff dem
winde reytten.* Quoted by E. G. Rupp, "Word and Spirit in the First Years of the Reformation," *ARG* 49 (1958): 24, and "The Bible in the Age of the Reformation," in *The Church's
Use of the Bible*, ed. D. E. Nineham (London: SPCK, 1963), p. 79.

[31]For a fuller discussion of this theme, see Timothy George, "An Evangelical Reflection on
Scripture and Tradition," *Pro Ecclesia* 9 (2000): 184-207.

mand, no other doctrine should be preached. Each text of the holy and divine Scriptures should be elucidated and explained by other texts. This holy book is in all things necessary for the Christian; it shines clearly in its own light, and is found to enlighten the darkness. We are determined by God's grace and aid to abide in God's Word alone, the holy gospel contained in the biblical books of the Old and New Testaments. This Word alone should be preached, and nothing that is contrary to it. It is the only Truth. It is the sure rule of all Christian doctrine and conduct. It can never fail us or deceive us. Whosoever builds and abides on this foundation shall stand against all the gates of hell while all merely human additions and vanities set up against it must fall before the presence of God.[32]

With such a robust commitment to the authority of the written Word of God, how could the reformers still claim that they were part of the ongoing Catholic tradition, indeed the legitimate bearers of it? To answer this question, it is necessary to see how the Bible functioned as a critical principle in the thought of the reformers. They almost always used the word *tradition* in the plural to refer to those "human traditions instituted to placate God, to merit grace, and to make satisfaction for sins," as the Augsburg Confession puts it.[33] Zwingli was more radical than Luther in his liturgical prunings, eliminating holy days, incense, the burning of candles, the sprinkling of holy water, church art and musical instruments—this "whole rubbish heap of ceremonials" and "hodge-podge of human ordinances" that amounted to nothing but "tom foolery."[34] In both cases, however,

---

[32]On the Diet of Speyer, see E. G. Léonard, *A History of Protestantism* (Indianapolis: Bobbs-Merrill, 1968), 1:122-28.

[33]Philip Schaff, *Creeds of Christendom* (Grand Rapids: Baker, 1977), p. 12.

[34]Edward J. Furcha and H. Wayne Pipkin, eds. and trans., *Huldrych Zwingli: Writings*, vol. 1: *The Defense of the Reformed Faith*, and vol. 2: *In Search of True Religion* (Allison Park, Penn.: Pickwick, 1984), 1:70-71, 73; Z 2:86-90.

the majority use of *traditiones* referred to specific practices and acts believed to be departures from, or distortions of, true worship and sound piety. This negative attitude toward tradition echoed the oft-quoted words of Jesus in Mark 7:8: "You have let go of the commands of God and are holding on to the traditions of men."

The Protestant criticism of "human traditions" was severe at points, but it did not mean the wholesale rejection of all that came before Luther's hammer blows in Wittenberg on October 31, 1517. Indeed, the Reformation appeal to the Bible implied the intrinsic connection between Scripture and tradition in a genuine evangelical sense. This was seen in numerous ways in the writings of the reformers. Here we shall mention only three: their sense of continuity with the church of the preceding centuries; their embrace of the ecumenical orthodoxy of the early church; and their desire to read the Bible in dialogue with the exegetical tradition of the church.

Ecclesial continuity. In their efforts to restore what a noted Puritan of a later age called "the old glorious beautiful face of Christianity," many of the spiritualist and radical reformers denounced the Catholic tradition entirely.[35] Kaspar Schwenckfeld was among the most radical of this lot. He forbade baptism by water, declared a moratorium on the Lord's Supper and announced that the true church was no longer to be found on earth but had ascended to heaven in 1530.[36] In writing against the errors of Schwenckfeld and other radicals, Luther declared, "We do not act as fanatically as the sectarian spirits. We do not reject everything that is under the dominion of the pope. For in that event we should also reject the Christian church.... Much Christian good, nay, all Christian good, is to be found in the papacy

[35]John Owen, *A Vindication of the animadversions on Fiat Lux: Wherein the principles of the Roman Church, as to moderation, unity and truth are examined and sundry important controversies* (1664; reprint, London: Banner of Truth Trust, 1967), p. 207.
[36]See George H. Williams, *Radical Reformation* (Kirksville, Mo.: Sixteenth Century Journal Publishers, 1992), pp. 428-33.

and from there it descended to us."[37] In his 1535 commentary on Galatians, Luther further described the nature of this "descent." Although the Church of Rome is horribly deformed, Luther said, it still is holy because it retains baptism, the Eucharist, "the voice and text of the Gospel, the sacred Scriptures, the ministries, the name of Christ, and the name of God . . . the treasure is still there."[38] Calvin, too, was willing to extend the word *church* to local congregations in Roman obedience so long as the gospel could be discerned in the preaching of the Scriptures and the celebration of the Lord's Supper. Thus the reformers affirmed the tradition of the living Word and believed they could discern it, albeit with difficulty, even within the contemporary Church of Rome.

Ecumenical orthodoxy. The Protestant reformers embraced the trinitarian and christological consensus of the early church, as expressed in the decrees of the first four ecumenical councils (Nicaea, 325; Constantinople I, 381; Ephesus, 431; Chalcedon, 451). They understood these classic statements of Christian doctrine as necessitated by, and congruent with, the teaching of Scripture. Significantly, when Protestants began to publish their own evangelical confessions, they did not, as it were, begin all over again with new statements and original reflections on the person of Christ and the reality of the Trinity. Rather, they accepted the Apostles' Creed, the Nicene Creed and the Athanasian Creed "as the unanimous, catholic, Christian faith," pledging themselves to uphold the doctrine set forth in these historic standards while rejecting "all heresies and teachings which have been introduced into the church of God contrary to them."[39]

This approach was true not only of Lutherans and Calvinists but also of Congregationalists and Baptists, who belonged to the wider

---

[37]Heiko A. Oberman, *The Dawn of the Reformation: Essays in Late Medieval and Early Reformation Thought* (Edinburgh: T & T Clark, 1986), p. 285. *WA* 26:146-47.
[38]*LW* 26:24.
[39]This is from the opening paragraphs of the Formula of Concord. See T. G. Tappert, ed., *The Book of Concord* (Philadelphia: Fortress, 1959), p. 465.

Reformed tradition. Thus, in 1679, long before they had taken up the slogan "No creed but the Bible," Baptists in England published a confession of faith in which they reprinted *en toto* the three historic creeds and commended them as something that "ought early to be received and believed."

> For we believe that they may be proved by most undoubted authority of Holy Scripture and are necessary of all Christians; and to be instructed in the knowledge of them by ministers of Christ, according to the analogy of faith, recorded in sacred Scriptures, upon which these creeds are grounded and catechetically opened and expounded in all Christian families for the edification of young and old which might be a means to prevent heresy and doctrine and practice, these creeds containing all things in a brief manner that are necessary to be known, fundamentally, in order of our salvation.[40]

As this Baptist statement shows, the early councils and creeds were embraced as witnesses and expositions of the faith, as accurate summaries of the Scripture ("an abbreviated word," to use the expression of John Cassian), not as independent authorities alongside of or supplementary to the Bible.[41] While Scripture alone remained the only standard by which all doctrines had to be understood and normed, the early creeds were not mere ad hoc statements that could be used or dispensed with willy-nilly at the whim of an individual theologian or congregation. Rather, they belonged to the unfolding pattern of Christian truth, which could be abandoned only at great peril.[42]

---

[40]Article 38 of "The Orthodox Creed," in *Baptist Confessions, Covenants and Catechisms*, ed. Timothy George and Denise George (Nashville: Broadman & Holman, 1996), pp. 120-21.

[41]John Cassian *On the Incarnation of Christ* 6.4 (PL 50:149 A). Cited by George Tavard, "Scripture and Tradition," *Journal of Ecumenical Studies* 5 (1968): 315.

[42]See the surprisingly strong statement by the Princeton theologian Charles Hodge: "If the

In this sense, tradition served as a kind of guardrail on a dangerous mountain highway keeping the traveler focused on the goal of the
journey by preventing precipitous calamities to the right and the left.
True enough, the reformers did not consider themselves irrevocably
bound to the language and thought forms of the early creeds and
councils, as Luther made clear in his writing against Latomus in
1521: "Even if my soul hated this word *homoousios*, still I would not be
a heretic, if I hold fast to the fact defined by the council on the basis
of Scripture."[43] But when Calvin tried to articulate the doctrine of
the Trinity in biblical language alone, his thoughts were misinterpreted in an antitrinitarian way. Thus he was forced, as Athanasius
had been in the early church, to use nonbiblical language precisely in
order to be faithful to the biblical message.[44]

Exegetical dialogue. In their commentaries on the Bible, the reformers of the sixteenth century revealed a close familiarity with the
preceding exegetical tradition, and they used it respectfully as well as
critically in their expositions of the sacred text. The Bible was seen as
the book given to the church, gathered and guided by the Holy Spirit.
In the early church, Vincent of Lérins set forth as a threefold test of
catholicity, "What has been believed everywhere, always, and by all."
This Vincentian canon, as it came to be called, was restated by Calvin
in his definition of the church as

> A society of all the saints, a society which, spread over the whole
> world, and existing in all ages, and bound together by the doc-

---

Scriptures be a plain book, and the Spirit performs the functions of a teacher to all the
children of God, it follows inevitably that they must agree in all essential matters in their
interpretation of the Bible. And from that fact it follows that for an individual Christian to
dissent from the faith of the universal Church (i.e., the body of true believers), is tanta-
mount to dissenting from the Scriptures themselves." *Systematic Theology* (Grand Rapids:
Eerdmans, 1970), 1:184.

[43]LW 32:244; WA 8:117-18: *Quod si odit anima mea vocem homoousion, et nolim ea uti, non ero
haereticus. Quis enim me coget uti, modo rem teneam, quae in Concilio per scripturas definita
est?*

[44]See Calvin's *Institutes* 1.13.5.

trine and the one Spirit of Christ, cultivates and observes unity of faith, and brotherly concord. With this church we deny that we have any disagreement. Nay, rather, as we revere her as our mother, so we desire to remain in her bosom.[45]

Defined in this way, the visible church had a real, even if relative and subordinate, authority since, as Calvin admitted, "We cannot fly without wings."[46] It was this instrumental authority of the church that Augustine had in mind when he remarked that he would not have believed the Bible unless he had been moved to do so by the church. George Tavard, a modern Catholic scholar, has expressed well the Protestant understanding of the coinherence—though not the coequality—of Scripture and tradition as "a vertical descent of the Third Person upon the members of the church, and a horizontal succession of charismatic transmission by which the Word is handed on."[47]

Is the Bible Clear?

At the heart of Reformation hermeneutics is the claim that, as the original Protestants put it at Speyer in 1529, the Bible "shines clearly in its own light." What could this possibly mean when, on the face of it, the Bible is filled with many puzzling enigmas, mysterious symbols and dark sayings?

The clarity or perspicuity of Scripture presupposes another, equally counterintuitive assertion by the early reformers: Scripture is its own interpreter, *sacra scriptura sui ipsius interpres*. This claim first surfaced in 1520 during Luther's early struggles with the papacy.

---

[45]John C. Olin, ed., *John Calvin and Jacopo Sadoleto: A Reformation Debate* (New York: Harper/Torchbooks, 1966), pp. 61-62.

[46]Ibid., p. 77.

[47]Tavard, "Scripture and Tradition," p. 318. On this issue, see also David C. Steinmetz, "Luther and Calvin on Church and Tradition," in *Luther in Context* (Bloomington: Indiana University Press, 1986), pp. 85-97.

Say for once—if you can—according to which judge, according
to which criterion, can a point of contention be decided when
the opinions of two of the church fathers disagree with one another? In such a case, the decision has to be based on the judgment of Scripture, which cannot happen if we do not give Scripture pride of place. . . . Having said this, the Holy Scripture
itself on its own, to the greatest extent possible, is easy to understand, clearly and plainly, being its own interpreter [*sui ipsius
interpres*], in that it puts all statements of human beings to the
test, judging and enlightening, as is written in Psalm 119[:130]:
"The explanation," or according to its actual meaning in the
Hebrew: the opening or the gate—"of your words enlightens
and gives understanding to youngsters." The Spirit clearly
points here to the enlightenment [of the Scripture] and teaches
that insight is given only by means of the Word of God, as
through an open door or (as those [scholastics] say) through a
first principle [*principium primum*], from which one must start
in order to come to the light and to insight.[48]

At one level, the claim that Scripture interprets itself was nothing
new in the sixteenth century. In book 2 of his hermeneutical handbook, *On Christian Doctrine*, Augustine had established the principle
that the obscure and doubtful passages in Scripture should be understood in light of the clearer and more certain ones.[49] The idea that in
the Bible a clearer place makes known a more difficult one was a staple of both medieval and Reformation exegesis. However, the Protestant reformers used it in a distinctive way: to support their argument

---

[48]WA 7:97 (*Assertio omnium articulorum*, 1520). Cited in Bayer, *Martin Luther's Theology*, p.
74. The principle that "Scripture interprets itself" is also found in Thomas Aquinas (*Summa
Theologiae* 1.1.9). See Otto Weber, *Foundations of Dogmatics* (Grand Rapids: Eerdmans,
1981), 1:281.

[49]Augustine, *On Christian Doctrine*, trans. D. W. Robertson Jr. (Indianapolis: Bobbs-Merrill,
1958), pp. 101-17.

for the primacy of Scripture against the claims of what one scholar has called "the ecclesiastical positivism of the Roman church."[50] In the first work of Protestant theology published in French (1529), Guillaume Farel gave a good summary of this approach:

> It is necessary to discourse upon and convey the Scripture in fear and reverence of God, of whom it speaks, diligently regarding it not in bits and pieces, but entirely, considering that which goes before and that which follows, and to what end it has been written, and for what purpose it says what Scripture contains, regarding the other places, where that which is said in a passage more clearly and openly, comparing one passage of Scripture with the other. For it is written by one and the same Spirit, who speaks more clearly by one than by the other, how that all that which they have said which Scripture contains "has been spoken by the Holy Spirit" (2 Peter 1:20-21). And from this it happens that one place makes known the other.[51]

The declaration of Scripture's inherent clarity, however, involves more than the application of sound philological rules to the reading of a text. It is another way of saying that the Bible cannot be "read like any other book." To read the Bible is to encounter a numinous other. The Bible does not lend itself to being analyzed and mastered as a mere literary artifact from antiquity. As Calvin said, the Bible is "something alive, and full of hidden power which leaves nothing in anyone untouched."[52] John Rogers, a former disciple of William Tyndale, said something similar to Bishop Stephen Gardiner before being consigned to the flames of Smithfield during the reign of Mary

---

[50]Eric W. Gritsch, "Introduction to Church and Ministry," *LW* 39:xvi.

[51]"William Farel's Summary (1529)," in *Reformed Confessions of the Sixteenth and Seventeenth Centuries*, ed. James T. Dennison Jr. (Grand Rapids: Reformation Heritage Books, 2008), 1:65. A facsimile of the 1534 French edition has been provided by Arthur Piaget, *Sommaire et Briefve Declaration* (Paris: E. Droz, 1935).

[52]CNTC 12:51.

Tudor. You can prove nothing by the Scriptures, Gardner said to Rogers, for the Scripture is dead without a living expositor. To which Rogers retorted, "No, the Scripture is alive!"[53] This is how Luther put it: The Spirit "cannot be contained in any letter, it cannot be written with ink, on stone, or in books as the law can be, but it is written only in the heart, a living writing of the Holy Spirit."[54]

The Bible is its own interpreter in the sense that it does its own interpreting: it interprets its readers. The Bible is alive because through it the Spirit convicts of sin, awakens faith in believers and conveys its intended meaning to those who approach it with humility and prayer. This is a very different model of Scripture reading from the one dominant in historical-critical methodologies since the Enlightenment. There the Bible is an object of disinterested inquiry, a thing to be mastered and managed rather than a word of address from the living God. Luther had his own struggles with the Aristotelian academic theology of his day, and the way he admonished his fellow Scripture scholars still rings true today: "It behooves us to let the prophets and apostles stand at the professors' lectern, while we, down below at their feet, listen to what they say. It is not they who must hear what we say."[55]

Luther can also speak of the "soundness" and "simplicity" as well as the lucidity of Scripture.[56] Between 1519 and 1521, Luther was engaged in writing a commentary on the Psalms. He had earlier lectured on the Psalms (1513-1516) prior to the Sturm und Drang of the

---

[53]John Foxe, *Acts and Monuments*, ed. T. Pratt (Philadelphia: J. & J. L. Gihon, 1813), 6:596.

[54]*LW* 39:182-83.

[55]*LW* 34:284. See Bayer's comment: "No one who refers to the reformational 'Scripture principle' should fail to take into account the paradox that lies therein. This Word makes sense only when understood as the description of a conflict—the conflict that academic theology presented at the time of Luther, still presents today, and will continue to present in time to come. Whoever speaks of the 'scriptural principle' can do so only in radical criticism of a concept of academic study that assumes there is a timeless, pure *a priori*" (*Martin Luther's Theology*, pp. 73-74).

[56]*LW* 32:236.

Reformation crisis. These new lectures incorporated his maturing insights about the nature of the Bible, the church and the Christian life. In his second series of lectures on Psalms, Luther's Christ-centered and gospel-centered understanding of justification by faith is clearly on parade. As Luther would later say, Jesus Christ is "the King of Scripture who is the price of my salvation."[57] Jesus Christ is the Alpha and Omega of the Bible; all Scripture must be understood in favor of Christ and not against him. The clear light of Christ radiates through the Old Testament as well as the New, for "all of Scripture has a clear meaning in terms of the Gospel."[58] Luther came to this insight in part through his focus on the single sense of Scripture. In the next chapter we shall consider Luther's engagement with the traditional fourfold sense of Scripture, but here we recognize his emphasis on the one, literal, legitimate, proper, genuine, pure, simple and constant sense of Scripture. This is the sense that "drives home Christ" and manifests the Bible's clear message of salvation to all regardless of social status or academic training. For this reason, Luther can say that "even the humble miller's maid, nay, a child of nine if it has faith," can understand the Bible.[59] The Bible was to be made available to the common people because its basic message was clear and plain for all to see and read.

The debate over the clarity of the Bible was taken to a new level in the exchange between Erasmus and Luther on the bondage of the will. In the opening salvo, Erasmus charged that Luther made too many assertions ignoring the fact that God has left many matters in Scripture veiled in secrecy. There is much obscurity in the Bible,

---

[57]WA 40/1:458. See Paul Althaus, *The Theology of Martin Luther* (Philadelphia: Fortress, 1966), p. 80.

[58]Althaus, *Theology of Martin Luther*, p. 80. See also *LW* 34:112.

[59]*LW* 31:341. See B. A. Gerrish, *The Old Protestantism and the New* (Chicago: University of Chicago Press, 1982), p. 57. See also Siegfried Raeder, "The Exegetical and Hermeneutical Work of Martin Luther," in *Hebrew Bible/Old Testament: The History of Its Interpretation*, vol. 2: *From the Renaissance to the Enlightenment*, ed. Magne Saebo (Göttingen: Vandenhoeck & Ruprecht, 2008), pp. 363-406.

doctrines we should contemplate "in mystic silence" rather than seeking to penetrate with "irreverent inquisitiveness." Which doctrines does Erasmus have in mind? The ones he mentions all have to do with the dogmatic tradition of the church—the divinity and humanity of Christ, the Trinity, the designation of the mother of Jesus as Theotokos, the God-bearer, as well as the controverted doctrine of predestination, the matter at stake in his quarrel with Luther. On all such doctrines, Erasmus insinuates, he would side with the skeptics if he could get away with it, that is, if the church would allow it. However, on other matters, Erasmus concedes, the Scriptures do speak quite plainly. There is no need for controversy when the Bible speaks about behavior and morality, when it sets forth "the precepts for the good life."[60]

Luther responded to Erasmus's tilt toward skepticism by declaring that the Holy Spirit is no skeptic. He also reasserted the need for assertions, "for it is not the mark of a Christian mind to take no delight in assertions; on the contrary, a man must delight in assertions or he will be no Christian. And by assertion . . . I mean a constant adhering, affirming, confessing, maintaining, and an invincible persevering."[61] As to the Scripture, Luther admits that it contains many texts that seem obscure and abstruse. But the problem, he claims, is not with the Bible but with us. It is our blindness, indolence and sin that places a veil over our hearts and minds and prevents us from understanding the clear meaning of the text. Just as a person hidden away in some dark corner of an alley should not blame the sun for shining so clearly in the bright light of day, so those blinded to the truth of the Bible should "stop imputing with blasphemous perversity the darkness and obscurity of their own hearts to the wholly clear Scriptures of God."

---

[60]E. Gordon Rupp and Philip S. Watson, eds., *Luther and Erasmus: Free Will and Salvation* (Philadelphia: Westminster Press, 1969), pp. 37-40.
[61]Ibid., p. 105.

For what still more sublime thing can remain hidden in the Scriptures now that the seals have been broken, the stone rolled from the door of the sepulcher (Mt 27:66; 28:2) and a supreme mystery brought to life, namely, that Christ the Son of God has been made man, that God is three in one, that Christ has suffered for us and is to reign eternally? Are not these things known and sung even in the highways and byways? Take Christ out of the Scriptures and what will you find left in them?[62]

Later in his treatise against Erasmus, Luther makes an important distinction between the outer clarity and the inner clarity of Scripture. The inner clarity is the special gift of the Holy Spirit by which the individual Christian is enlightened. As Susan Schreiner has pointed out, Luther was drawn to "the experiential, affective language of interiority and immediacy" to describe reality of the Spirit's internal work of verifying the truth of Scripture in the heart of the believer. Thus Luther could speak of a "feeling," "tasting," "sweetening" or "experiencing" that resulted from the work of the Holy Spirit within.[63] In his early commentary on the Magnificat, Luther declared that no one "can correctly understand God or his Word unless he has received such understanding immediately from the Holy Spirit. But no one can receive it from the Holy Spirit without experiencing, proving, and feeling it. In such experience, the Holy Spirit instructs us as in his own school."[64] The emphasis on the internal clarity of Scripture became a major axiom of Reformation exegesis. In Zwingli's ser-

---

[62]Ibid., p. 110.

[63]Susan E. Schreiner, " 'The Spiritual Man Judges All Things,' Calvin and the Exegetical Debates About Certainty in the Reformation," in *Biblical Interpretation in the Era of the Reformation: Essays Presented to David C. Steinmetz in Honor of His Sixtieth Birthday*, ed. Richard A. Muller and John L. Thompson (Grand Rapids: Eerdmans, 1996), p. 193.

[64]*LW* 21:299; *WA* 7:546: *Denn es mag niemant got noch gottes wort recht vorstehen, er habs denn on mittel von dem heyligen geyst. Niemant kansz aber von dem heiligenn geist habenn, er erfaresz, vorsuchs und empfinds denn, unnd yn der selben erfarung leret der heylig geyst alsz ynn seiner eygenen schule.*

mon "The Clarity and Certainty of the Word of God," originally preached to cloistered Dominican nuns in 1522, the reformer of Zurich spoke about the "concurrent or prevenient clarity" of the Word of God that "shines on the human understanding," and "enlightens it in such a way that it understands and confesses the Word and knows the certainty of it." This is accomplished in "a gentle and attractive way" so as to bring assurance of the Savior's presence.

> And the gospel gives us a sure message, or answer, or assurance. Christ stands before you with open arms, inviting you and saying (Matthew 11:28): 'Come unto me, all ye that labor and are heavy laden, and I will give you rest." Oh glad news, which brings with it its own light, so that we know and believe that it is true, as we have fully shown above. For the one who says it is a light of the world. He is the way, the truth, and the light. In his Word, we can never go astray. We can never be deluded or confounded or destroyed in his Word. If you think there can be no assurance or certainty for the soul, listen to the certainty of the Word of God.[65]

Calvin echoes this same theme in his teaching about the internal witness of the Holy Spirit. The same Spirit who inspired the writers of Scripture long ago is present whenever believers today open the sacred text to study and learn. The Spirit is the inviolable nexus between inspiration and illumination.[66]

Beyond the internal clarity of Scripture conveyed to the believer by the Spirit, Luther argued for the Bible's external clarity. This objec-

---

[65]LCC 24:73, 75, 84.

[66]*Institutes* 1.7.1-5. According to John Webster, Calvin developed his doctrine of the internal witness of the Holy Spirit as "a pneumatological replacement for the idea of ecclesial approbation." *Holy Scripture: A Dogmatic Sketch* (Cambridge: Cambridge University Press, 2003), p. 62. The contemporary relevance of the Reformation doctrine of the clarity of Scripture is set forth in James P. Callahan's excellent essay, "*Claritas Scripturae*: The Role of Perspicuity in Protestant Hermeneutics," *JETS* 39, no. 3 (September 1996): 353-72.

tive, external clarity was related to the public ministry of the Word and was thus a major concern for preachers and teachers of Scripture. No less than the Catholic tradition, the churches of the Reformation emphasized the necessity of a well-ordered ministry and a program of rigorous theological education for its pastors and teachers. Indeed, the Protestant reformers were pioneers in this effort with the founding of new universities and academies devoted to the study of biblical languages and exegesis. (The establishment of Jesuit seminaries following the Council of Trent did much to close this gap by raising the level of preparation for many priests.) While the reformers found strong scriptural support for their doctrine of the Bible's inner clarity in the words of Paul in 1 Corinthians 2:15, "The spiritual person judges all things, but is himself to be judged by no one," they found an equally compelling justification for their focus on the external clarity of Scripture in the story of Philip and the Ethiopian eunuch in Acts 8:26-38.

"Do you understand what you are reading?" Philip poses to the eunuch the quintessential hermeneutical question. In commenting on this account in Acts, Calvin offers three distinct insights about the right way to read and understand Scripture. First, the Ethiopian scholar had been reading from the book of Isaiah. Calvin surmises that he would surely have been able to grasp many things he was reading in the prophet, his discourse on the goodness and power of God for example. But there were other things hidden from him, obscurities he may have encountered "in every tenth verse or so." Yet the eunuch did not throw away the scroll of Isaiah in frustration or disgust. He kept on reading and pondering even though some of the text's meaning he could not yet fathom. This is a good example for us, Calvin says. "There is no doubt that this is the way we must also read Scripture; we ought to accept eagerly and with a ready mind those things which are clear, and in which God reveals his mind; but it is proper to pass by those things which are still obscure to us, until a clearer light shines."

Second, the Ethiopian seeker displays a proper humility and modesty when he recognizes precisely that he is not able on his own fully to comprehend the mysteries of the text before him. In taking this attitude, the eunuch proves himself teachable. *Docilitas*, teachableness, is one of the marks of a true disciple of Christ, and this man has shown himself to be "one of God's pupils by reading the Scripture." This is far from the idea that one can master the Bible by an act of will or sheer academic brilliance. Calvin comments, "There must certainly be very little hope of a person who is swollen-headed with confidence in his own abilities ever proving himself docile."

And, finally, Calvin uses the example of Philip's witness to the eunuch to argue for the importance of interpreters and teachers in the church. We must make use of all the aids that the Lord has given for the understanding of Scripture including written commentaries and the public preaching of the Word. Yes, Calvin acknowledges, God could have given to the seeker from Ethiopia a direct revelation of the meaning of Isaiah. After all, God chose an angel to direct Philip to his chariot. But, while the sovereign God remains ever free to work in extraordinary ways, we must not disparage the ordinary means he has given to the church through the written Word and the sacraments, baptism in this instance. "It is certainly no ordinary recommendation of outward preaching," Calvin declares, "that the voice of God sounds on the lips of men, while the angels keep silence."[67]

Clarity of Scripture, then, does not obviate the need for careful study and exegesis of the Bible. Nor does it mean that all difficulties are immediately or easily resolved. But this is no reason to withhold the Scriptures from the common people, for in matters related to one's eternal destiny the Bible speaks clearly for all to read and understand. The framers of the Westminster Confession in the seventeenth century set forth this Reformation principle in these classic words:

---

[67]CNTC 6:243-48.

All things in Scripture are not alike plain in themselves, nor alike clear unto all; yet those things which are necessary to be known, believed, and observed, for salvation, are so clearly propounded and opened in some place of Scripture or other, that not only the learned but the unlearned, in a due use of the ordinary means, may attain unto a sufficient understanding of them.[68]

CRANMER'S PREFACE

We close this chapter where it began, with the tumultuous English Reformation and the consequences of putting the Bible into the hands of the common people. Thirteen years after Tyndale's New Testament (1526) had been smuggled back into England from the Continent, King Henry VIII finally gave approval for printing of the first officially sanctioned English Bible. The Great Bible, as it was called, was to be placed in every parish church in England. The title page showed Henry VIII handing copies of the Bible to his two Thomases, Cranmer and Cromwell. They in turn distribute it to the priests and prelates beneath them until it finally reaches the rabble of men and women crowded together at the bottom of the page, all of whom are saying, "Long live the king!" From the mouth of King Henry come the words of Isaiah 55:10-11, "For as the rain and snow come down from heaven . . . so shall my word be that goes out from my mouth; it shall not return to me empty, but it shall accomplish that which I purpose, and shall succeed in the thing for which I sent it." With prepublication sales assured by the crown, it is not surprising that the first print run of the Great Bible in 1539 was soon exhausted. Archbishop Cranmer, the moving force behind the Bible's release, provided a preface for the second edition, which was issued in April 1540.

---

[68]Schaff, *Creeds*, 3:604. See also John Leith, *Assembly at Westminster: Reformed Theology in the Making* (Richmond: John Knox Press, 1973).

Cranmer's preface to the Great Bible was so successful that many people called it Cranmer's Bible. Showing his patristic prowess, Cranmer quoted extensively from John Chrysostom and Gregory of Nazianzus in his defense of making the Bible available in the mother tongue of the common people. Chrysostom had admonished the people in his day to make time for the private reading of the Bible in their homes, and he had no patience for the many excuses he heard.

> Do not let anyone say to me any of those vain words, worthy of a heavy condemnation, "I cannot leave the courthouse, I administer the business of the city, I practice a craft, I have a wife, I am raising children, I am in charge of a household, I am a man of the world; reading the Scriptures is not for me, but for those who have been set apart, who have settled on the mountain tops, who keep this way of life continuously." What are you saying, man? That attending to the Scriptures is not for you, since you are surrounded by multitudes of cares? Rather it is for you more than for them. . . . You need more remedies. Your wife provokes you, for example, your son grieves you, your servant angers you, your enemy plots against you, your friend envies you, your neighbor curses you, your fellow soldier trips you up, often a lawsuit threatens you, poverty troubles you, loss of your property gives you grief, prosperity puffs you up, misfortune depresses you, and many causes and compulsions to discouragement and grief, to conceit and desperation surround us on all sides, and a multitude of missiles fall from everywhere. Therefore we have a continuous need for the full armor of the Scriptures.[69]

Like Calvin and other reformers, Cranmer appealed to the example of Philip and the eunuch from Ethiopia in Acts 8. Cranmer finds

---

[69]Cranmer gives here a paraphrase of Chrysostom's third sermon on Lazarus and the rich man. See John Chrysostom, *On Wealth and Poverty*, trans. Catherine P. Roth (Crestwood, N.Y.: St. Vladimir's Seminary Press, 1984), pp. 58-59.

in the eunuch an example of perseverance in the reading of the Scriptures. Even when no Philip appears to help us understand what we encounter in the text, the Holy Spirit "will be ready and not fail thee if thou do thy diligence accordingly."[70]

If John Chrysostom exhorted his people to read the Bible avidly, Gregory of Nazianzus encouraged them to read it carefully. Nothing in this world is so good that it cannot be abused—even too much honey makes one sick. Cranmer knew that he was involved in a dangerous project. He anticipated that there would be "idle babblers and talkers of the Scripture out of season and all good order." Others afflicted with tongue-itch would use the Bible to sow discord in the commonwealth and bring confusion to the church. Like Luther, Cranmer wanted to make haste slowly. Thus he counseled his readers to approach the sacred text with a reverent spirit and in the fear of God, to treat that which is holy in a holy manner. Such cautions were important, but with them in place, he opened the gates wide for all to come.

> Here may all manner of persons, men, women, young, old, learned, unlearned, rich, poor, priests, laymen, lords, ladies, officers, tenants, and mean men, virgins, wives, widows, lawyers, merchants, artificers, husbandmen, and all manner of persons, of what state or condition soever they be, may in this book learn all things what they ought to believe, what they ought to do, and what they should not do, as well concerning Almighty God, as also concerning themselves and all other. Briefly, to the reading of the Scripture, none can be enemy, but that either be so sick that they love not to hear of any medicine, or else that be so ignorant that they know not Scripture to be the most healthful medicine.[71]

---

[70]Gerald Bray, ed., *Translating the Bible from William Tyndale to King James* (London: The Latimer Trust, 2010), p. 84.
[71]Ibid., p. 85.

F I V E

DOCTOR MARTINUS

What else was Luther than a teacher of the Christian church whom one can hardly
celebrate in any other way but to listen to him, or rather, to listen to
what he himself has heard and therefore said.[1]

KARL BARTH

By PROFESSION, MARTIN LUTHER WAS A SWORN DOCTOR of Scripture. He was, of course, many other things as well: monk, reformer, pastor, publicist, translator, educator, counselor, husband, father, friend. But it was what one scholar has aptly called his *Dokoratsbewusstsein*, his "doctor consciousness," that shaped his life's work as a theologian of the church and a student of the Bible.[2]

How did Luther become a doctor of sacred Scripture? It was not in the cards from the beginning. It was not as though Luther had taken a personality test and chosen the best career path to become a

---

[1] Karl Barth, "Lutherfeier," *Theologisch Existenz heute* 4 (1933), p. 11: *Was ist Luther dann anderes gewesen als ein Lehrer des christlichen Kirche, den man dann schwerlich anders feiern kann als indem man ihn hört. Oder vielmehr: indem man das hört, was es selber gehört und darum zu sagen hat.*

[2] Hermann Steinlein, *Luthers Doktorat* (Leipzig: A. Deichert'sche, 1912). See also B. A. Gerrish, "Doctor Martin Luther: Subjectivity and Doctrine in the Lutheran Reformation," in *Continuing the Reformation* (Chicago: University of Chicago Press, 1993), pp. 38-56.

professor in the university. True enough, Luther was a precocious student, and by 1509 he had already received four academic degrees: his bachelor's degree and the master of arts from the University of Erfurt before he had begun the study of law, to which as a young monk he added the baccalaureate in Bible (from Wittenberg) and the *sententiarius* degree (again from Erfurt). This last degree permitted him to teach on the first two books of Peter Lombard's *Sentences*, the standard theological textbook in all medieval universities, which he did in a series of lectures held from 1509 to 1511.

At this point, Luther may have suffered a kind of academic burn-out compounded by spiritual depression and his still unresolved quest for a gracious God. Luther never forgot the conversation he had with Johann von Staupitz in September 1511, as the two of them sat together under a pear tree in the garden of the Black Cloister in Wittenberg. Staupitz, his mentor and superior in the Augustinian order, directed him to proceed to complete the requirements for his doctorate in theology. Luther was a monk and had taken a vow of obedience. He knew he had to do what he was told, but he was apparently surprised at this command and immediately protested. He gave fifteen reasons why he should not pursue such an arduous task. For one thing, it would surely kill him; he would be dead in three months at the most, he said. Staupitz could have pointed out that Luther was silly to make such an excuse: he was still in his twenties and in vigorous health. He had just returned from Rome, an 850-mile journey of forty days, a strenuous trip he had made across the Alps by foot. Instead, Staupitz calmly replied that, should Luther die prematurely, it would be quite all right: the Lord had need of several good doctors in heaven and he could then give counsel to the Almighty! Through the voice of Staupitz, Luther heard the call of God. Looking back on this event from 1531, he said:

However, I, Doctor Martinus, have been called to this work and

Figure 5.1. *Johannes Cochlaeus, Luther's first Catholic biographer, published at Leipzig (1529) an attack on the Reformer depicting him as a seven-headed monster: Doctor, Martinus, Lutherus, Preacher, Fanatic, Visitant and Barabbas.*

was compelled to become a doctor, without any initiative of my own, but out of pure obedience. Then I had to accept the office of doctor and swear a vow to my most beloved Holy Scriptures that I would preach and teach them faithfully and purely. While engaged in this kind of teaching, the papacy crossed my path and wanted to hinder me in it. How it has fared is obvious to all, and it will fare worse still. It shall not hinder me.[3]

Luther's promotion to the doctorate took place in solemn ceremo-

[3]*LW* 34:103; *WA* 30/3:386.

nies in Wittenberg's Castle Church on October 18 and 19, 1512. On
that occasion, a woolen biretta was placed on Luther's head, a silver
doctor's ring (which still survives) on his finger. He was then presented
with two Bibles, one closed, the other open. He had been appointed for
life *lectura in Biblia* at the University of Wittenberg, succeeding Staupitz
himself. When the academic proceedings were over, the real party
began. The town bell rang out and Luther was carried through the
streets of the town by his fellow students, much as a local football hero
might be celebrated on a college campus or in a small town today.[4]

When the cheering had stopped, Luther was officially elected as a
member of the theological faculty and got down to the serious work
of preparing for his lectures on the Psalms (1513-1515), which were
followed in turn by Romans (1515-1516), Galatians (1516-1517), Hebrews (1517) and again the Psalms (1518-1519). During those years,
Luther moved from being an unknown monk in a backwater university to the center stage of European politics. In the turmoil that followed, he was sustained by a compelling sense of the importance of
his calling as a professor of Scripture. While Luther later renounced
his monastic vows and married a former nun, he clung tenaciously to
his teaching office and to his doctoral degree.

In 1530, when the pressures of his reforming work were beginning to take their toll, Luther again remembered his vocation as a
sworn doctor of Scripture. In his commentary on Psalm 82, Luther
defended himself against the charge that he was a mere local
preacher with no right to challenge the received teaching of the institutional church.

> But perhaps you will say to me, "Why do you, by your books,
> teach throughout the world, when you are only a preacher in
> Wittenberg?" I answer: I have never wanted to do it, and do not

---

[4]This image is that of E. G. Schwiebert, *Luther and His Times* (St. Louis: Concordia Publishing House, 1950), p. 196.

want to do it now. I was forced and driven into this position in the first place, when I had become Doctor of Holy Scripture against my will. Then, as a Doctor in a general, free university, I began at the command of pope and emperor, to do what such a doctor is sworn to do, expounding the Scriptures for all the world and teaching everybody. Once in this position, I have had to stay in it, and I cannot give it up or leave it yet with a good conscience, even though both pope and emperor were to put me under the ban for not doing so. But what I began as a Doctor, made and called at their command, I must truly confess to the end of my life. I cannot keep silent or cease to teach, though I would like to do so and am weary and unhappy because of the great and unendurable ingratitude of the people.[5]

Luther has been interpreted as the supreme subjectivist by both Roman Catholic polemicists (who see this as a fatal flaw) and liberal Protestant enthusiasts (who extol it as a great virtue). Both have misunderstood Luther's deepest concern. Luther's theology was certainly intensely personal, relational and experiential. But this was the antithesis of the kind of theological egocentricity projected back onto him by modern critics. As Luther said in his 1535 commentary on Galatians:

This is the reason why our theology is certain: it snatches us away from ourselves and places us outside ourselves, so that we do not depend on our own strength, conscience, experience, person, or works but depend on that which is outside ourselves, that is, on the promise and truth of God, which cannot deceive.[6]

It was Kierkegaard, not Luther, who was the prophet of introspec-

---

[5]*LW* 13:66; *WA* 31/1:212.
[6]*LW* 26:387; *WA* 40/1:589: *Ideo nostra theologia est certa, quia ponit nos extra nos: non debeo niti in conscientia mea, sensuali persona, opere, sed in promissione divina, veritate, quae non potest fallere.*

tion and sheer inwardness. Luther's Christ did not come into the world in order to calm anxious consciences.

Luther's "conscience" speech at the Diet of Worms is one of several dramatic moments in his life that are frequently equated with the beginning of the Reformation: his famous tower experience when he grasped the true meaning of justification; the posting of the Ninety-five Theses on All Hallows Eve in 1517; his debate with Johann Eck at Leipzig in 1519; his burning of the papal bull and the corpus of canon law at Wittenberg's Elster Gate in 1520. None of these events, however, is understandable apart from the exegetical labors that took place along a seven-year trajectory (1512-1518) during which Luther discovered what Heiko Oberman has called the "theological grammar" of the Scriptures.[7] We might say that Luther's quest for a gracious God coincided with his quest for the grammar of God. His work as a biblical interpreter was not the result of the private probings of an eccentric monk gazing at his own soul. It emerged rather from the single-minded effort of Dr. Martinus, carried out amid much anguish and temptation, no doubt—*tentatio facit theologum!*— to listen afresh to what God had once and for all said in Scripture about what God had once and for all done in Jesus Christ. For Luther, this meant two things: a hermeneutical shift toward a dynamic and christocentric reading of Scripture; and the triumph of biblical theology over scholastic methods and assumptions.[8]

THE EXEGETICAL TRADITION

What was it like to be a student in the classroom of young professor

---

[7]Heiko A. Oberman, "Martin Luther Contra Medieval Monasticism: A Friar in the Lion's Den," in *Ad fontes Lutheri: Toward the Recovery of the Real Luther*, ed. Timothy Maschke et al. (Milwaukee: Marquette University Press, 2001), pp. 183-84. This expression is from Luther, who begins his exposition of Psalm 1 (in his second series of lectures on the Psalms) by saying, *Sed primo grammatica videamus, verum ea theologica*, "First let us look at the matters of grammar [in the text], but let us see them as theological" (*WA* 5:27).

[8]See the still valuable essay by Gerhard Ebeling, "The New Hermeneutics and the Early Luther," *Theology Today* 21 (1964): 34-46.

Luther in Wittenberg? Before listening in to Luther's lectures on the epistle to the Romans, we must look more closely at the two settings—the university and the monastery—that formed the background not only for Luther's personal vocation as a reformer but also for the revival of biblical exegesis in the age of the Reformation. Since the time of the Venerable Bede (d. 735), sometimes called the last of the fathers, serious study of the Bible had taken place primarily in the context of cloistered monasteries. The rule of Saint Benedict brought together *lectio* and *meditatio*, the knowledge of letters and the life of prayer. The liturgy was the medium through which the daily reading of the Bible, especially the Psalms, and the sayings of the church fathers came together in the spiritual formation of the monks.[9] Essential to this understanding was a belief in the unity of the people of God throughout time as well as space, and an awareness that life in this world was a preparation for the beatific vision in the next.

The source of theology was the study of the sacred page (*sacra pagina*); its object was the accumulation of knowledge not for its own sake but for the obtaining of eternal life. For these early monks, the Bible had God for its author, salvation for its end and unadulterated truth for its matter, though they would not have expressed it in such an Aristotelian way. The medieval method of interpreting the Bible owed much to Augustine's *On Christian Doctrine*. In addition to setting forth a series of rules (drawn from an earlier work by Tyconius), Augustine stressed the importance of distinguishing the literal and spiritual or allegorical senses of Scripture. While the literal sense was not disparaged, the allegorical was valued because it enabled the believer to obtain spiritual benefit from the obscure places in the Bible, especially in the Old Testament. For Augustine, as for the monks who followed him, the goal of scriptural exegesis was freighted with

---

[9]See the classic study by Jean Leclercq, *The Love of Learning and the Desire for God* (New York: Fordham University Press, 1961).

eschatological meaning; its purpose was to induce faith, hope and love and so to advance one's pilgrimage toward that city with foundations (see Heb 11:10).

Building on the work of Augustine and other church fathers going back to Origen, medieval exegetes came to understand Scripture as possessed of four possible meanings, the famous *quadriga*. The literal meaning was retained, of course, but the spiritual meaning was now subdivided into three senses: the allegorical, the moral and the anagogical. Medieval exegetes often referred to the four meanings of Scripture in a popular rhyme:

> The letter shows us what God and our fathers did;
> The allegory shows us where our faith is hid;
> The moral meaning gives us rules of daily life;
> The anagogy shows us where we end our strife.[10]

In this schema, the three spiritual meanings of the text correspond to the three theological virtues: faith (allegory), hope (analogy) and love (the moral meaning). It should be noted that this way of approaching the Bible assumed a high doctrine of scriptural inspiration: the multiple meanings inherent in the text had been placed there by the Holy Spirit for the benefit of the people of God. The biblical justification for this method went back to the apostle Paul, who had used the words *allegory* and *type* when applying Old Testament events to believers in Christ (Gal 4:21-31; 1 Cor 10:1-11). The problem with this approach was knowing how to relate each of the four senses to one another and how to prevent Scripture from becoming a nose of wax turned this way and that by various interpreters. As G. R. Evans explains, "Any interpretation which could be put upon the text and was in keeping with the faith and edifying, had the warrant of God

---

[10]A translation of the well-known Latin quatrain: *Littera gesta docet/Quid credas allegoria/ Moralis quid agas/Quo tendas anagogia*. See Robert M. Grant, *A Short History of the Interpretation of the Bible* (New York: Macmillan, 1963), p. 119.

himself, for no human reader had the ingenuity to find more than God had put there."[11]

With the rise of the universities in the eleventh century, theology and the study of Scripture moved from the cloister into the classroom. This does not mean that monks stopped studying the Bible with the advent of the universities, but rather that the new social context of academic theology involved a shift in interpretive method. Scripture and the fathers were still important, but they came to function more as points of reference, footnotes as it were, to the theological questions debated in the schools and brought together in an impressive systematic way in works such as Peter Lombard's *Sentences* and the great scholastic *summae* of the thirteenth century.

Indispensible to the study of the Bible in the later Middle Ages was the *glossa ordinaria*, a collection of exegetical opinions by the church fathers and other commentators. Heiko Oberman summarized the transition from devotion to dialectic in this way: "When, due to the scientific revolution of the twelfth century, Scripture became the *object* of study rather than the *subject* through which God speaks to the student, the difference between the two modes of speaking was investigated in terms of the texts themselves rather than in their relation to the recipients."[12] It was possible, of course, to be both a scholastic theologian and a master of the spiritual life. Meister Eckhart, for example, wrote commentaries on the Old Testament in Latin and works of mystical theology in German, reflecting what had come to be seen as a division of labor between the two. The study of the Bible in the Reformation harked back to the earlier monastic pattern, with its stress on the coinherence of learning and meditation, this despite the Protestant rejection of monasticism.

An increasing focus on the text of Scripture in the later Middle

---

[11]G. R. Evans, *The Language and Logic of the Bible: The Road to Reformation* (Cambridge: Cambridge University Press, 1985), p. 42.

[12]Heiko A. Oberman, *Forerunners of the Reformation* (Philadelphia: Fortress, 1966), p. 284.

Ages led to a revival of interest in its literal sense. The two key figures in this development were Thomas Aquinas (d. 1274) and Nicholas of Lyra (d. 1340). Thomas is best remembered for his *Summa
Theologiae*, but he was also a prolific commentator on the Bible.
Thomas did not abandon the multiple senses of Scripture but declared that all the senses were founded on one—the literal—and
this sense eclipsed allegory as the basis of sacred doctrine. Nicholas
of Lyra was a Franciscan scholar who made use of the Hebrew text
of the Old Testament and quoted liberally from works of Jewish
scholars, especially the learned French rabbi Salomon Rashi (d.
1105). After Aquinas, Lyra was the strongest defender of the literal,
historical meaning of Scripture as the primary basis of theological
disputation. His postils, as his notes were called, were widely circulated in the schools and monasteries and became the first biblical
commentary to be printed in the fifteenth century. More than any
other commentator from the period of high scholasticism, Lyra and
his work were greatly valued by the early reformers. According to an
old Latin pun, *nisi Lyra lyrasset, Lutherus non saltasset*, "If Lyra had
not played its lyre, Luther would not have danced." While Luther
was never an uncritical disciple of any teacher, he did praise Lyra as
a good Hebraist and quoted him more than one hundred times in his
lectures on Genesis, where he declared, "I prefer him to almost all
other interpreters of Scripture."[13]

Luther was passionate about biblical exegesis but showed little
concern for hermeneutics as a separate field of inquiry. Niels Hemmingsen, a Lutheran theologian in Denmark, did write a treatise, *On
Method* (1555), in which he offered a philosophical and theological
framework for the interpretation of Scripture. This was followed by
the *Key to Sacred Scripture* (1567) of Matthias Flacius Illyricus, which
contained some fifty rules for studying the Bible drawn from Scrip-

---

[13]*LW* 2:164.

ture itself.[14] However, hermeneutics as we know it today came of age only in the Enlightenment and should not be backloaded into the Reformation.

It is also true that the word *commentary* did not mean in the sixteenth century what it means for us today. In the dedication to his 1519 study of Galatians, Luther declared that his work was "not so much a commentary as a testimony (*ennaratio*) of my faith in Christ."[15] The word *testimony* here connotes a public witness and points to the fact that for Luther his intense study of the Bible was related to his vocation as a teacher of the church. The modern distinction between the academic and devotional study of Scripture was foreign to Luther as it had been to earlier monks. While he strongly encouraged personal Bible reading, this was meant to take place in the context of the church's regular worship and preaching, not as the centerpiece of one's private quiet time. Luther would have even less sympathy for the so-called scientific study of the Bible that subjects the Scripture to criteria that are foreign to its own nature and message. Though Luther was trained as a scholastic theologian and made ample use of the philological tools of biblical humanism, he remained faithful to the Augustinian notion of Scripture study as an essential ingredient in spiritual formation. He followed the monastic discipline of the sacred page, the day-to-day rhythm of Christian life involving prayer, meditation and temptation. For Luther, biblical exegesis remained "a spiritual exercise performed in service to God and the church, a task for which one was fitted for the Holy Spirit and by living faith, given in baptism."[16]

---

[14]See Kenneth G. Hagen, "'De Exegetica Methodo': Niels Hemmingsen's *De Methodis* (1555)," in *The Bible in the Sixteenth Century*, ed. David C. Steinmetz (Durham: Duke University Press, 1990), pp. 181-96.

[15]Kenneth G. Hagen, "What Did the Term *Commentarius* Mean to Sixteenth-Century Theologians?" in *Théorie et pratique de l'exégèse*, ed. Irena Backus (Geneva: Droz, 1990), pp. 13-38.

[16]Mickey L. Mattox, "Martin Luther," in *Dictionary for Theological Interpretation of the Bible*, ed. Kevin J. Vanhoozer (Grand Rapids: Baker, 2005), p. 472.

LUTHER AT THE LECTERN

We are ready now to take a brief look over the shoulder of Luther the teacher. What was his methodology? What were his sources and style?

We know that Luther's lecture course on Romans took place on Monday and Friday at 6:00 in the morning. As far as we know, they were the first university lectures on the Bible delivered in the German tongue. John Oldecop of Hildesheim, who later became a strong opponent of Luther, matriculated at the University of Wittenberg just as Luther began his course on Romans at Easter in 1515. "The students liked to hear him," he reported, "for no one like him had been heard there who translated so boldly every Latin word."[17] Another student from this same time has left us the following portrait of Luther at the lectern:

> He was a man of middle stature, with a voice which combined sharpness and softness; it was soft in tone; sharp in the enunciation of syllables, words, and sentences. He spoke neither too quickly nor too slowly, but at an even pace, without hesitation very clearly, and in such fitting order that each part flowed naturally out of what went before. . . . His lectures never contained anything that was not pithy or relevant. And, to say something about the spirit of the man: if even the fiercest enemies of the gospel had been among his hearers, they would have confessed from the force of what they heard that they had witnessed, not a man, but a spirit, for he could not teach such amazing things from himself, but only from the influence of some good or evil spirit.[18]

It was an achievement to be so inspiring at 6 a.m. even in 1515!

---

[17]Robert Herndon Fife, *Young Luther* (New York: Macmillan, 1928), p. 185. This and the following section are adapted from Timothy George, "Martin Luther," first published in *Reading Romans through the Centuries*, ed. Jeffrey P. Greenman and Timothy Larsen (Grand Rapids: Baker, 2005), pp. 107-19.

[18]*Reading Romans*, pp. 1xi-1xii.

But what exactly were the students hearing from Luther? Already, in his first course on the Psalms, Luther had developed a style of lecturing that he continued to use with Romans. He had asked the local printer, Johann Grunenberg, to print the Vulgate text of Romans (from the 1509 Froben edition published at Basel) on a special sheet of paper with broad margins and a full centimeter between the lines. The text of Romans printed in this way took up twenty-eight sheets, with fourteen lines on each page. Luther followed closely the medieval exegetical tradition of glossing the text, writing in a small, meticulous hand his own marginal comments in this special edition of the text prepared by Grunenberg. The students were provided with an identical copy of this text and copied down, word for word, Luther's carefully dictated comments. (We know this from several student copies of Luther's lectures that were discovered and published by Johannes Ficker in the Weimar edition.)

In developing his glosses on Romans, Luther drew on the tradition of Christian exegesis we have just described making special use of five sources:

1. The *glossa ordinaria*, the famous anthology of patristic witnesses including Ambrose, Augustine, Gregory the Great, Origen, Chrysostom, Jerome, the Venerable Bede, and others.

2. The *glossa interlinearis*, a somewhat more expansive interpretation of the phrases of the biblical texts, with special emphasis on their spiritual meaning. This important research tool was assembled by the great scholar Anselm of Laon in the early twelfth century.

3. The *postillae perpetuae* of Nicholas of Lyra (d. 1340), a commentary on Scripture that emphasized the literal or historical interpretation of the text. All three of these resources had been made conveniently available in Froben's six-folio volumes of the Bible, an edition with which Luther was thoroughly familiar.

4. Jacques Lefèvre d'Étaples, a French humanist scholar (also known by his Latin name, Faber Stapulensis), whose translation and

commentary on Paul's letters Luther had before him as he developed his lectures.

5. Erasmus. In his comments on the early chapters of Romans, Luther frequently referred to the Greek text in Lorenzo Valla's Greek edition of the New Testament, as well as to Faber's Latin translation, which was based on the Greek. However, from Romans 9 onward, Luther had available, and frequently cited, Erasmus's newly published critical edition of the Greek New Testament.

Even in his glosses, Luther displayed a remarkable freedom in dealing with all of these sources. He appreciated Lyra's focus on the literal meaning of the text, but he did not hesitate to criticize his interpretation of Romans 1:17: "The righteousness of God is revealed from faith to faith." Lyra interpreted that phrase, in typical medieval fashion, to mean "from unformed faith to formed faith." This distinction was well known in scholastic theology, but Luther found it invidious. He claimed that "there is only one faith, the same for the laity as the scholars—and that while there may be growth in saving faith, that 'growth does not make it more real but only gives it greater clarity.'"[19] As for Erasmus, as we have seen, while Luther was appreciative of his philological prowess, there was already a growing disdain for his inability to grasp the gravity of sin and the true dilemma of the human before God. "No one is a wise Christian just because he knows Greek and Hebrew," Luther noted. Between Romans and *Bondage of the Will* ten years later, the theological chasm between Luther and Erasmus would grow deeper and wider.

In addition to his glossing of the text, Luther prepared extensive expository notes that were handwritten on 123 separate sheets of paper. Luther did not present most of this material to the students, but it is precisely here that we can track most clearly his personal struggles with the text and his evolving theology of grace.

---

[19]*Reading Romans*, p. 19.

THE LURE OF BIBLICAL THEOLOGY

Gerhard Ebeling, one of the great Luther scholars of the twentieth century, and James S. Preus, who wrote a groundbreaking dissertation on Luther's hermeneutics, have both found a major shift in Luther's interpretation of the Scriptures in his first lectures on the Psalms, which immediately preceded his commentary on Romans. Ebeling argues that Luther's "new hermeneutics" involved his reducing of the traditional four senses of Scripture to two: Christ himself as the literal sense, and faith in Christ as the moral or tropological sense. Justification by faith was arrived at by merging these two senses—in other words, "faith became Jesus Christ tropologically understood, or what Jesus means *for me*."[20]

Preus presents Luther's hermeneutical shift somewhat differently: instead of seeing Christ speaking directly in the Psalms eliciting personal faith from the believer, Luther "began to appreciate the Psalms as the witness of a historical person, David, who, like himself and other Christians, had to sustain his life by faith in God's Word and promise."[21] Reformation theology thus focused on the promise or the covenant (*pactum*) through which David heard the word of justification in his day, just as we do in ours as we listen to the Word of God in Scripture. *Fides ex auditu*: Faith comes by hearing, as Luther says in his comment on this phrase in Romans 10:17: "The Word is of such a character that unless it is received by hearing and by faith, none can grasp it." In the gloss on this text, Luther quotes several scriptural passages to prove the importance and priority of hearing (Ezek 7; Obad 1; Pss 16; 110; Is 1; Heb 3). Luther's emphasis on hearing the Word of promise led him to exalt preaching above mere reading and study alone. As he would later say, the church is not a

---

[20]Steven E. Ozment, *The Age of the Reform, 1250-1550* (New Haven: Yale University Press, 1980), p. 71. See also Ebeling, "The New Hermeneutics"; James S. Preus, *From Shadow to Promise: Old Testament Interpretation from Augustine to the Young Luther* (Cambridge, Mass.: Harvard University Press, 1964).

[21]Preus, *From Shadow to Promise*, pp. 226-28.

"pen house" but a "mouth house": Christ himself has not written anything, nor has he ordered anything to be written, but rather to be preached by word of mouth. Or, again, "the Word of God shall remain free, to be heard by everyone."[22]

Luther's hermeneutical revolution was carried out within the structures of the medieval exegetical tradition. Throughout his lectures on Romans, Luther still makes use of the fourfold interpretive grid. Even later, when he had abandoned its use as standard exegetical technique, he would sometimes revert to allegorical interpretations. Richard Muller explained the basic Reformation approach in this way: "Both Luther and Calvin strengthen the shift to the letter (increased by the emphasis on textual and philological study), but they then proceeded to find various figures and levels of meaning embedded in the letter itself."[23]

Running throughout the lectures on Romans, however, is a steady critique of scholastic theology—Aristotle and "those fools, the pig theologians," as Luther unkindly referred to some of his predecessors and contemporaries. He speaks against the "quiddities" and "foolish opinions of the philosophers that befog us in metaphysics."[24] Luther was well-trained at Erfurt in nominalist theology (the *via moderna* of the late Middle Ages) and, indeed, in some ways he continued to be a nominalist for the rest of his life. But early on he came to recognize the Pelagian pull in nominalist soteriology. He could sometimes condemn his scholastic masters with faint praise. In October 1516, as he was nearing the end of his series on Romans, Luther wrote to his friend Johannes Lang, who had just been made prior of the Augustin-

---

[22]*LW* 39:22. See Timothy George, *Theology of the Reformers* (Nashville: Broadman & Holman, 1988), p. 91.

[23]Richard A. Muller, *Biblical Interpretation in the Era of the Reformation* (Grand Rapids: Eerdmans, 1996), p. 12.

[24]*Reading Romans*, p. 236. See William S. Campbell, "Martin Luther and Paul's Epistle to the Romans," in *The Bible as Book: The Reformation*, ed. Orlaith Sullivan (London: The British Library and Oak Knoll Press, 2000), pp. 103-14.

ian convent in Erfurt, where Luther had taken his vows. He wrote to Lang about Gabriel Biel, whose works they had both studied and commented on as students: "I know what Biel says and it is all good except when he deals grace, love, hope, faith and virtue."[25] Well, these are quite a few things to get wrong!

Luther went on in this letter to accuse Biel of "pelagianizing" the gospel. Evidently, the students at Wittenberg were voting with their feet. In May 1517, six months after he had completed the course on Romans, Luther wrote, "Our theology and St. Augustine's is progressing well. Lombard's *Sentences* are disdained. No one can expect to have students if he does not lecture on the Bible and St. Augustine."[26] In the same year, Luther wrote his *Disputation Against Scholastic Theology*, in which he said that it was wrong to think that one cannot become a theologian without Aristotle. The truth, he wrote, is that "one cannot become a theologian unless he becomes one without Aristotle, for Aristotle is to the study of theology as darkness is to light."[27] Long before the principle of *sola scriptura* had become a matter of public controversy at Leipzig, Luther was insisting that the true theologian would pay attention to God's distinctive way of speaking (*modus dicendi*) in Scripture. In the Bible, God defines his own terms not in the speculative grammar of scholastic theology, saturated as it was with the definitions of Aristotle, but rather in his direct address to the prophets and apostles, and through them, by his Spirit, to us.

Two Experiences?

Near the end of his life, in 1545, Luther looked back on his early work as a biblical theologian and the difficulty he had had in under-

---

[25]Walther von Loewenich, *Martin Luther: Man and His Work* (Minneapolis: Augsburg, 1986), p. 103.

[26]Ibid. See *LW* 48:42, 19; James Atkinson, ed., *Luther: Early Theological Works* (Philadelphia: Westminster Press, 1962), pp. 269-70.

[27]Atkinson, *Luther*, pp. 269-70.

standing Romans 1:17: "For in the gospel is the righteousness of God revealed."

> I hated the expression "righteousness of God," for through the tradition and practice of all the doctors I had been taught to understand it philosophically, as the so-called "formal"—or, to use another word, "active"—righteousness through which God is just and punishes sinners and the unjust. But I could not love the righteous God, the God who punishes. I hated him. . . . I pondered incessantly, day and night, until I gave heed to the context of the words, namely: "for in the Gospel is the right-eousness of God revealed, as it is written: the just shall live by faith." Then I began to understand the righteousness of God as a righteousness by which a just man lives as by a gift of God, that means by faith. I realized that it was to be understood this way: the righteousness of God is revealed through the Gospel, namely the so-called "passive" righteousness we receive, through which God justifies us by faith through grace and mercy. . . . Here I felt that I was altogether born again and had entered paradise itself through open gates.[28]

The context of this autobiographical reflection makes it clear that this decisive shift occurred when Luther began his second exposition of the Psalms, that is, around 1518-1519. However, many Reforma-tion scholars, finding an evangelical understanding of the gospel in Luther's earlier writings, including Romans, have laid this late dating to an old man's faulty memory. Thus the sharp divide between the young Luther and the mature Luther, between Luther the Augustin-ian monk and Luther the Protestant reformer.

Could it be, however, that we should distinguish two separate ex-

---

[28]WA 54:179-87; LW 34:336-37. For a balanced assessment of this famous and much dis-cussed text, see Bernhard Lohse, *Martin Luther's Theology* (Minneapolis: Fortress, 1999), pp. 85-95.

periences of Luther: one, an initial evangelical awakening prompted by the counsels of Staupitz, dated perhaps prior to or even during his first lectures on the Psalms in 1513-1514; the other, a theological discovery that led to a clear and different understanding of justification, dated around 1518 or 1519, that is, after the controversy about indulgences and before the great treatises of 1520? If this interpretation is correct, then Luther's theology in the lectures on Romans will be transitional: redolent of Reformation motifs yet reflective of a mind and theology in process. This is indeed what we should expect from Luther's own testimony. "I did not learn my theology all at once," he later remarked, "but I followed where my temptations led me. It is not reading, nor writing, nor speculating that makes one a theologian. Nay, it is rather living, dying, and being damned that makes one a theologian."[29] Several themes in the lectures on Romans indicate a theology on the move. Let us see how Luther treats the themes of sin, God's righteousness and humility.

THE CONCEPT OF SIN

Paul has a lot to say about sin in Romans, and Luther devotes many pages of his *scholia* trying to unpack this all too human problem. At the beginning he said, in words that echo the first chapter of Jeremiah,

> The chief purpose of this letter is to break down, to pluck up, and to destroy all wisdom and righteousness of the flesh. This includes all works which in the eyes of people or even in our own eyes may be great works. No matter whether these works are done with a sincere heart and mind, this letter is to affirm and state and magnify sin, no matter how much someone insists that it does not exist, or that it was believed not to exist.[30]

---

[29]WA, TR 1:146: *Jch hab mein theologiam nit auff ein mal gelernt, sonder hab ymmer tieffer vnd tieffer grubeln mussen, da haben mich meine tentationes hin bracht;* WA 5:163: *Vivendo, immo moriendo et damnando fit theologus, non intelligendo, legendo aut speculando.*
[30]*Reading Romans,* p. 135.

How is it that Paul seeks to "magnify" sin, to "establish" sin in Romans? Luther's reading of the human situation disallowed the kind of watered-down, attenuated doctrine of original sin that had come to prevail in nominalist schemes of salvation in the late Middle Ages. For example, in his comment on Romans 5:12-14, Luther opposes those theologians who construe original sin as the mere absence of original righteousness. According to this teaching, original sin means that something is missing. It is deprivation—the original standing Adam had enjoyed with God before the Fall no longer obtains. The human will has been weakened, impaired. This is a serious breach that must be restored initially through sacrament of baptism. And this initial healing must then be supplemented or enhanced through the penitential-eucharistic channels of sacramental grace.

For Luther this schema is totally inadequate. Original sin is not merely the privation of quality in the will or simply the loss of light in the intellect or of strength in the memory, but, in a word, it is the loss of all uprightness and of the power of all our faculties of body and soul and of the whole inner and outer person. Beyond this, original sin produces proneness toward evil; loathing of the good; disdain for light and wisdom; fondness for error and darkness; the avoidance and contempt of good works and an eagerness for doing evil.[31]

Luther describes a person affected by sin as *incurvatus in se*, "curved in on one's self." As the prophet Jeremiah says in Jeremiah 17:9, "The heart of man is crooked and inscrutable; who can know it?" We are so curved in on ourselves that we are not able even to recognize our own spiritual malady. We do not even know that we need help. As the psalmist put it in Psalm 19:12, "Who can discern his errors? Cleanse thou me from my hidden faults!"[32]

Luther did not invent the *curvitas* image; it was a well-worn motif in the Augustinian tradition signifying pride, self-seeking and rebel-

---

[31]Ibid., pp. 167-68.
[32]Ibid., p. 159.

lion against God. But, as Anders Nygren noted, there is a significant difference in the way Augustine and Luther used this image. While Augustine spoke of sinners as bent or crooked, curved and bowed down to the earth, Luther makes the self, not just earthly goods, the supreme object of this deforming curvature.[33] In other words, Luther deepens and radicalizes the Augustinian notion of sin as *amor sui* (love of self).

Luther's understanding of the human person anticipated by more than three centuries the deepest insights of modernity's two great prophets of atheism: Ludwig Feuerbach and Sigmund Freud. In his comment on Romans 1:20, Luther approached Feuerbach's critique of religion when he observed that the root of all idolatry is the proclivity of human beings to "worship God not as he is but as they imagine and think him to be." They think of God as they wish him to be and value God only in terms of the benefits they receive from him.[34] Thus religion itself, the very thing that is meant to help us and connect us with the divine, becomes an expression of our captivity, as we project onto God our own wishes and desires. Rather than "letting God be God," we turn him into "the God who looks like me."

Luther's insight here comes not only from his critique of external religious practice but also from his own tortured quest to find a gracious God. In his struggles with penance and confession, he wrestled with Psalm 19:12, "Clear thou me from hidden faults." Luther's problem was never whether his sins were large ones or small ones but whether in fact he had confessed every single one. What about the sins he could not remember? What about the sins committed in his sleep? Luther anticipated Freud by recognizing a depth-dimension to the human person and by refusing to limit the effects

---

[33] Anders Nygren, *Agape and Eros*, trans. Philip S. Watson (New York Harper & Row, 1953), pp. 713-15. See also the discussion in Gordon Rupp, *The Righteousness of God* (London: Hodder & Stoughton, 1953), pp. 164-67.

[34] *Reading Romans*, pp. 23-25.

of sin to the conscious mind alone. Such a radical reading of the human situation could be answered only with an even more radical doctrine of divine grace.

JUSTIFICATION BY FAITH

Alister McGrath, among others, has pointed to the lectures on Romans as the locus of Luther's decisive break with the theology of justification in which he had been trained as a student of the *via moderna*. Elements of Luther's later view are present already in Romans:

1. an emphasis on God's "alien" righteousness;

2. the utter passivity of humans in their own justification;

3. the abandonment of the idea (earlier embraced by Luther) that by doing one's best—*facere quod in se est*—one could prepare for the reception of grace.

In all our efforts to procure divine favor, Luther says, we are treating God "like a cobbler handles leather."[35] Such a strategy is not only futile but also blasphemous.

All the same, at this point in his theological trajectory, Luther was still working within the framework medieval Augustinian soteriology. From the time of the lectures on Romans in 1515-1516 until his *Preface to Romans* in 1522, Luther abandoned a set of images and ideas inherited from the Augustinian tradition in favor of what he took to be a more purely Pauline approach. Luther later evaluated his definitive position on justification vis-à-vis Augustine in this way: "Augustine got nearer to the meaning of Paul than all the scholastics but he did not reach Paul. In the beginning I devoured Augustine, but when the door into Paul swung open and I knew what justification by faith really was, then it was out with him."[36]

---

[35]Ibid., p. 33.
[36]Quoted in Gordon Rupp, "Patterns of Salvation in the First Age of the Reformation," *ARG* 57 (1966): 52-66. See also David Maxwell, "Luther's Augustinian Understanding of Justi-

Luther's new insight was that the imputation of Christ's alien righteousness was based not on the gradual curing of sin but rather on the complete victory of Christ on the cross. The once-for-allness of justification was emphasized: "If you believe, then you have it!" Nor is there any direct correlation between the state of justification and one's outward works, as Luther made clear in his "Sermon on the Pharisee and the Publican" (1521): "And the publican fulfills all the commandments of God on the spot. He was then and there made holy by grace alone. Who could have foreseen that, under this dirty fellow?"[37]

Luther's doctrine of justification by faith was radical, for it challenged the entire theology of merit that was so central to the sacramental-penitential structure of the church. It is no wonder that the Dominican inquisitor of Cologne, Jacob Hochstraten, regarded it as blasphemy for Luther to describe the union of the soul to Christ as a spiritual marriage based on faith alone. How could Christ be thus joined to a sinner? This was to make the soul "a prostitute and adulteress" and Christ "a pimp and a cowardly patron of her disgrace."[38] Hochstraten was rightly shocked at the import of Luther's message. But Luther found an equally shocking statement in Paul: "God justifies the ungodly."

Does this mean that Luther had no place for good works in the Christian life? He vigorously denied the charge. While we are in no wise justified by works, works do follow faith as its proper fruit. The fruit of justification is faith active in love. Such love is directed in the first instance not toward God in hope of attaining a possible advantage toward salvation but rather toward one's neighbor, for "the Christian lives not in himself, but in Christ and in his neighbor." In his

fication in the Lectures on Romans," *Logia: A Journal of Lutheran Theology* 5 (1996): 9-14.

[37]WA 17/1:404: *Haec fides vera, per quam deus solvitur et datur, quod deo debet. Et hic statim implevit praecepta dei, ibi mera gratia per sanctitatem, wher het sich des stuck versehen unter dem unflat?*

[38]Ozment, *Age of Reform*, p. 150.

1522 preface to *Romans,* Luther described such faith as "a living, busy, active, mighty thing. . . . It is impossible for it not to be doing good works incessantly. It does not ask whether good works are to be done but before the question is asked, it is already done them, and is constantly doing them. Whoever does not do such works, however, is an unbeliever. . . . Thus it is impossible to separate works from faith, quite as impossible as to separate heat and light from fire."[39] Luther's Catholic and Anabaptist opponents would reply that Dr. Martinus's saying so did not make it true. The place of good works in the life of faith would be one of the most debated issues in the sixteenth century and beyond.

HUMILITY

In his lectures on Romans, Luther came close to equating humility and faith. Humility is the predisposition required for the verdict of justification. "Therefore we must keep ourselves humble in all these respects, as if we were still bare, and look for the naked mercy of God that he may reckon us righteous and wise."[40] According to some scholars, it was precisely Luther's break with this humility theology that led to his mature doctrine of justification by faith alone.

It would be a mistake, however, to regard Luther's emphasis on humility in Romans as a mere phase through which he passed. While his emphasis on humility was transformed by his deepened doctrine of justification, it remained a distinctive mark of his spirituality.

Luther's emphasis on humility in Romans was informed by his profound encounter with the mystical tradition. True, Luther has some quite negative comments about mysticism in his lectures on Romans. For example, in commenting on Romans 5:2, he says, "Mystical rapture is not a passageway to God."[41] But as the context shows,

[39]*LW* 35:370-71.
[40]*Reading Romans,* p. 5.
[41]Ibid., p. 156.

Luther was referring here to that stream of Dionysian mysticism with its doctrine of inner darkness, disparagement of the incarnation and illicit desire to hear and contemplate the uncreated Word apart from the cross and the Scriptures. However, just as he was beginning the course on Romans, Luther had a close encounter with another stream of mysticism, a tradition of mystical theology represented in Germany by the Dominican preacher Johannes Tauler. Luther published two editions of sermons from the German mystics (1516, 1518), the famous *Theologia Deutsch*, precisely in the same period that he was wrestling with Paul in Romans.

We can identify two themes in the lectures on Romans that recur throughout Luther's lifelong teaching on humility. The first is the theme of self-abandonment (*Gelassenheit*). In commenting on Romans 8, Luther quotes the voice of the birds from the Song of Solomon, "I am sick with love." He then comments, "We must always take the word love to mean a cross and suffering. Without these the soul becomes languid and tepid. It ceases to long for him and does not thirst for him, the living fountain."[42] Here we see the visible roots of an emerging theology of the cross, an emphasis that will become explicit in Luther's Heidelberg Disputation of 1518. In explaining Paul's depiction of the "groanings" that mark the life of faith, Luther declares that the soul must "suffer or endure God" (*Gott leiden*). Like a field about to be tilled by a farmer, the soul must submit itself to the plow of experience; it must be broken and split open if it is ever to bring forth fruit. Luther will later resort to this theme especially in his letters of spiritual counsel and pastoral advice to individuals who have appealed to him for help in times of grief and personal crisis.

The ultimate form of self-abandonment, of course, is the willingness to be consigned to eternal damnation, a spiritual disposition that the mystics called *resignatio ad infernos*. This topic emerges in

---

[42]Ibid., p. 255.

Luther's discussion of predestination in Romans 9–11. Here he declares that "to be blessed means to seek in everything God's will and His glory, and to want nothing for oneself, neither here nor in the life to come." Indeed, one of the marks of divine election is precisely the willingness to resign oneself to eternal damnation, as Christ did on the cross:

> But the true saints actually achieved this resignation, because their hearts overflow with love, and they do this without great distress. For they are so completely dedicated to God that nothing seems impossible for them to do, not even the suffering of the pains of hell. And because of this very readiness, they escape from such a punishment. Indeed, they do not need to fear that they will be damned because they submit gladly and willingly to damnation for God's sake. But it is those who want to escape from damnation that will be damned.[43]

This paradoxical theology underscores the role of humility in the life of faith. Since God's electing grace was grounded on his eternal decree, there was no room for boasting or self-assertion. But Luther recognized that the gift of resignation to hell was dispensed to the elect briefly and sparingly, most often at the hour of death. More commonly, Luther's advice to those tormented by the question of election was, "Thank God for your torments!" It was characteristic of the elect, he said, not of reprobates, to tremble at the hidden counsel of God. Beyond this, he urged a flat refutation of the devil and a contemplation of Christ.

On April 30, 1531, Luther wrote to a woman named Barbara Lisskirchen, who was distressed that she was not among the elect:

> When such thoughts assail you, you should learn to ask yourself, "If you please, in which Commandment is it written that I

---

[43]Ibid., p. 263.

should think about and deal with this matter?" When it appears that there is no such Commandment, learn to say, "Be gone, wretched devil! You are trying to make me worry about myself. But God declares everywhere that I should let him care for me. . . . " The highest of all God's commands is this, that we should hold up before our eyes the image of his dear son, our Lord Jesus Christ. Every day he should be our excellent mirror wherein we behold how much God loves us and how well, in his infinite goodness, he has cared for us in that he gave his dear Son for us. In this way, I say, and in no other, does one learn how to deal properly with a question of predestination. It will be manifest that you believe in Christ. If you believe, then you are called. And if you are called, then you are most certainly predestinated. Do not let this mirror and throne of grace be torn away from your eyes. . . . Contemplate Christ given for us. Then, God willing, you will feel better.[44]

Here we see the pastoral import of Luther's exegetical work. The counsel Staupitz had once offered him in his own despair Luther now shared with this troubled woman: "Look to the wounds of Jesus and find comfort in Christ."

THE THREE RULES

Luther was acquainted with the spiritual pride connected with the lust of seeing one's name in print, of having one's every utterance published for all the world to see.

If, however, you feel and are inclined to think you have made it, flattering yourself with your own little books, teaching, or writing, because you have done it beautifully and preached excellently; if you are highly pleased when someone praises you in

---

[44]T. G. Tappert, ed., *Luther: Letters of Spiritual Counsel* (Philadelphia: Westminster Press, 1955), p. 116.

the presence of others; if you perhaps look for praise, and would sulk or quit what you were doing if you did not get it—if you are of that stripe, dear friend, then take yourself by the ears, and if you do this in the right way you will find a beautiful pair of big, long, shaggy, donkey ears. Then don't spare any expense! Decorate them with golden bells, so that people will be able to hear you wherever you go, point their fingers at you, and say, "See, see! There goes that clever beast, who can write such exquisite books and preach so remarkably well." That very moment you will be blessed and blessed beyond measure in the kingdom of heaven, that is in that "heaven" where hell fire is ready for the devil and his angels.[45]

Three years after his posting of the Ninety-five Theses, Martin Luther became the first author whose works were assembled into a collected edition at the outset of his career—something that the great Erasmus "dreamt of for his own works as only a posthumous possibility."[46] Luther resisted the idea of the publication of his *opera omnia* for several reasons, including the fear that his writings might be read instead of the Bible when he meant them to be only a guide to understanding the Bible. He would be happy for all his works to perish with him, Luther said, so long as the Scriptures remained in the hands of the people. When printers in Augsburg and Wittenberg urged Luther to allow them to publish his collected works, he replied, "I'll never consent to this proposal of yours. I'd rather that all my books would disappear and the Holy Scriptures alone would be read. Otherwise, we'll rely on such writings and let the Bible go."[47]

Despite his protestations, however, Luther reluctantly agreed to

---

[45]*LW* 34:287-88.
[46]Robert Kolb, *Martin Luther as Prophet, Teacher and Hero* (Grand Rapids: Baker, 1999), pp. 139-40.
[47]*LW* 54:311.

write a preface for a German edition of his writings that appeared in 1539. In this preface, Luther offered counsel for studying the Bible, a pattern of scriptural engagement he found in Psalm 119. Luther's "three rules," prayer, meditation and temptation, harked back to his own monastic formation and underscored the personal, antispeculative thrust of his entire theology.

Oratio. George Spalatin was one of Luther's closest friends and his chief liaison with Frederick the Wise. He wrote to Luther in 1518 asking his advice about the best way of studying Scripture. Luther responded by saying that the first task is to begin with prayer, as it is certain that one cannot penetrate the meaning of the Bible by study and talent alone. "You must ask that the Lord in his great mercy grant you a true understanding of his words . . . for there is no one who can teach the divine words except he who is their author, as it says, 'They shall all be taught by God' (John 6:45)."[48] For Luther, true prayer always brings the believer into the presence of the triune God, though he admits that sincere prayers will be heard no matter which person of the Holy Trinity is called on. "For you cannot call upon one person without calling upon the others, because the one, undivided divine essence exists in all and in each person."[49] True prayer is hard work, Luther says, harder even than preaching, yet all genuine insight into the meaning of Scripture begins with supplication. "But kneel down in your little room (Matthew 6:6) and pray to God with real humility and earnestness, that he through his dear Son may give you his Holy Spirit, who will enlighten you, lead you, and give you understanding."[50]

Luther's recommendation of prayer as essential to the proper study of the Bible is not an excuse for lazy thinking. The true interpretation

---

[48]*LW* 48:53-54.
[49]*WA* 54:69: *Denn du kanst keine Person on die andern anruffen, Sinte mal da ist ein einiges unzertrennets Goettliches wesen, in allen und in einer jglichen personen.*
[50]*LW* 34:285-86.

of Scripture requires arduous labor, as Luther demonstrated in his struggles of how best to translate the Bible into German. He and his colleagues once spent four days trying to complete just three lines from the book of Job.[51] The posture of prayer is a way of recognizing the limits of reason, of cultivating humility and self-mistrust in favor of the Spirit's guidance. In a sermon on the eighth commandment, preached in 1517, Luther stressed the priority of prayer over self-assertion in the study of Scripture.

> Since Holy Writ wants to be dealt with in fear and humility and penetrated more by studying with pious prayer than with keenness of intellect, therefore it is impossible for those who rely only on their intellect and rush into Scripture with dirty feet, like pigs, as those Scripture were merely human knowledge not to harm themselves and others whom they instruct. So utterly do they fail to differentiate; and they move about in Scripture without any reverence. That is why so many dare to be teachers. As soon as they have learned grammar, they profess without any further study, to know theology and say: Oh well, the Bible is an easy matter! Particularly those do this whose bellies have been distended by the husks of those swine, the philosophers.[52]

Meditatio. If Luther's first rule relates to the inner disposition of the heart in seeking divine help in understanding the scriptural text, his second rule, meditation, focuses on something external—the performance of Scripture in repeating and pondering it out loud. So,

---

[51]WA 18:468.

[52]WLS 78; WA 1:507: *Quocirca cum scriptura sancta velit in timore et humilitate tractari et magis studio piae orationis penetrari quam acumine ingenii, impossibile est, quod sine damno sint vel suo proprio vel aliorum quos docent, qui nudo ingenio freti in eam irruunt illotis pedibus sicut porci, tanquam sit humana quaedam scientia: adeo nullo reverentiae discrimine versantur in illa. Inde veniunt tot promptuli ad docendum, qui statim cognita grammatica theologiam sine omni studio profitentur dicentes 'Hem, Biblia res facilis est': maxime autem id faciunt qui distenderunt ventrem suum siliquis illis porcorum, id est philosophorum.*

Luther says that one should meditate not only in the heart but also outwardly, "by actually repeating and comparing oral speech and literal words of the book, reading and rereading them with diligence, attention, and reflection, so that you may see what the Holy Spirit means by them." He further emphasizes that the call to meditation is a lifelong vocation: "And take care that you do not grow weary or think that you have done enough when you have read, heard, and spoken them once or twice, and that you then have complete understanding. You will never be a particularly good theologian if you do that, for you will be like untimely fruit which falls to the ground before it is half ripe."[53]

In his first lecture series on the Psalms, Luther distinguished meditating and thinking by defining the former as "to think carefully, deeply, and diligently . . . to muse in the heart, to stir up in the inside, or to be moved in the innermost self." To be stirred so deeply in this way is not a matter of private musing but rather a rule of life that involves, as the psalmist says, meditating on God's law "day and night." Day and night refer not only to matins and vespers but also to every season of human existence, good times and bad times, times of prosperity and times of adversity, of contemplation and activism, of life and death. In this context, Luther applies the description of the godly woman in Proverbs 31:18 to the ever-present solace of Scripture: "Her lamp does not go out at night," that is, in the time of death.[54] The focus of meditation is always the God-given external word, the inspired text of Scripture, not the innermost recesses of the human psyche. Oswald Bayer has well expressed Luther's concern at this point: "Those who want to search for the Holy Spirit deep inside themselves, in a realm too deep for words to express, will find ghosts, not God."[55]

---

[53]*LW* 34:286; *WA* 50:659.
[54]*LW* 10:17-18.
[55]Oswald Bayer, *Theology the Lutheran Way* (Grand Rapids: Eerdmans, 2007), p. 55.

Thus, in his first two rules, Luther brings together two movements: the yearning of the suppliant heart from within and the taking in of the external word from without. While the mature Luther has no sympathy for Word-less mysticism, he does find a place for silent reflection. It is the place of receptivity where "deep calls unto deep," where prayer and meditation become one.

> [If] an abundance of good thoughts comes to us we should disregard the other prayers, make room for such thoughts, listen in silence, and under no circumstances obstruct them. The Holy Spirit himself is preaching here, and one word of his sermon is far better than a thousand of our prayers. Many times I have learned more from one prayer than I might have learned from much reading and speculation.[56]

Tentatio. "Temptation" is a weak translation of what Luther means by *tentatio* or *Anfechtung* in German. The word *Anfechtung* derives from the world of fencing; a *Fechter* is a fencer or gladiator. A *Fechtboden* is a fencing room. Thus *Anfechtung* refer to spiritual attacks, bouts of dread, despair, assault, anxiety, conflicts that rage both within the soul of every believer and in the great apocalyptic struggle between God and Satan. In a comment made at table in 1531, Luther declared that "experience alone makes one a theologian."[57] His own experience that made him a theologian included severe spiritual trials. These were not limited to his struggles in the monastery but continued throughout his career. Philipp Melanchthon gave this eyewitness account of Luther's *Anfechtungen*:

> On those frequent occasions when he was thinking especially about the wrath of God or about extraordinary instances of retribution, such violent terrors afflicted him that he almost died.

---

[56]*LW* 43:198; *WA* 38:363. Bayer cites this quotation in his analysis of Luther's three rules (*Theology*, p. 59).
[57]*LW* 54:7; *WA* 25:106.

I have seen him, distressed by his concentration on some dispute over doctrine, lie down on a bed in a nearby room and mingle with his prayers this oft-repeated sentence: "He has concluded all under sin so that he may have mercy upon all."[58]

It is significant that in this account Melanchthon related Luther's spiritual tribulation to his wrestling with a particular biblical text. For Luther, the Bible was his mainstay against the insinuations of the Evil One. He persistently reminded the devil of the promises of God, of God's reliability in the face of all adversity. But as the temptation of Christ in the Gospels reveals, the devil himself can quote (and misquote) Scripture. The Bible is an arena of conflict but also the source of consolation. "For as soon as God's Word takes root and grows in you, the Devil will plague you and make a real doctor of you, and by his attacks will teach you to seek and love God's Word."[59]

How does this third rule affect the way Luther read the Bible? He allowed Scripture to interpret him as he read his own temptations in the light of the *Anfechtungen* of God's covenant people. He wrestles with Jacob at the River Jabbock, he stands betrayed with Joseph in the dungeon of Pharaoh, he feels the blows of Job's desolation at the loss of his children, and he weeps with Mary beneath the cross of Christ. Through the prism of Scripture he is able to discern the concealment of God (*Deus absconditus*) in the events of life, especially the inexplicable and imponderable ones. In his comment on Psalm 118:5, "Out of my distress I called on the Lord; the Lord answered me and set me free," Luther wrote doubtless for himself as well as for his readers, "Don't just sit there by yourself or lie on your belly with your head hanging down and let these thoughts bite

---

[58]CR 6, 156-60. Translated by Ian D. Kingston Siggins in *Luther* (New York: Barnes & Noble, 1972), p. 34. See also David C. Steinmetz, "Luther Against Luther," in *Luther in Context* (Bloomington: Indiana University Press, 1986), pp. 1-11.
[59]*LW* 34:286.

into you, and don't get eaten up worrying over them. Get up, you
lazy fellow, and then get down on your knees and hold up your
hands to heaven and pray a psalm with the Lord's Prayer and bring
your complaints to God."[60]

---

[60]WA 31/1:96: *Vnd nicht da sitzen bey dir selbs odder liggen auff der banck, den kopff hengen vnd
schutteln, vnd mit deinen gedancken dich beissen vnd fressen, sorgen vnd suchen, wie du los werd-
est, Vnd nicht anders ansehen, denn wie vbel dirs gehe, wie wehe dir sey, wie ein elender mensch
du seyest, Sondern, Wolauff du fauler schelm, auff die knie gefallen, die hende vnd augen gen
himel gehaben, Ein psalm odder Vater vnser furgenomen, Vnd deine not mit weinen fur Gott
dargelegt, geklagt vnd angeruffen.*

Six

Lutheran Ways

---

*Not everything on the Reformation is in
a shoebox labeled "Luther, M."*

Monsignor Charles Burns,
Librarian, Secret Archives of the Vatican

Would the Reformation have happened without Luther? Historians are wary of "what if" questions, for they invariably yield speculative, counterfactual construals of the past—more like playing Monopoly than Scrabble. Yet the course of the sixteenth century might have turned out quite differently. Had Emperor Maximilian I not died on January 12, 1519, then the pope might have been less inclined to curry favor with Frederick the Wise, Luther's protector, whose vote he needed in the upcoming imperial election. Or if the Fifth Lateran Council, held in Rome from 1512 to 1517, had fulfilled its goal of reforming the church, then perhaps Luther's message may not have struck fire in the way it did and the Council of Trent's lines in the sand may have been preempted by more moderate reforms, as some cardinals at Trent urged at the time. Hans Küng once surmised that had the Church of Rome yielded on three points, the breach with the Protestants would probably not have occurred. Küng's three points were making the Bible available to the people in their own language, allowing the laity to have the cup as well as the bread in the Eucharist, and permitting priests to get married.[1] On another front, think what would have happened had Erasmus openly embraced Luther and the evangelical cause, instead of wriggling on the sidelines. Had he succeeded, would the story of the Reformation and humanism have turned out differently? As late as 1527, Martin Bucer, an early Erasmian turned Protestant ecumenist, was still trying to persuade the Dutch scholar to cast his lot with the reformers. As it was, the fate of Martin Luther and the Reformation became inexorably linked so that now trying to think of the Reformation without Luther is like imagining early Christianity without Paul.[2]

By the early 1520s, the fledgling university of Wittenberg (founded in 1502) had become not only a place to study but also the center of a tumultuous movement. Hundreds of students from all over Europe flocked to Wittenberg to hear the Augustinian monk who had become, almost overnight, the world's most famous theologian. Luther was well aware of the personality cult that was developing around him, and he tried to resist it. "The world will not come to an end when Brother Martin is buried," he said. "God can create many Dr. Martins."[3] (His enemies might have thought that one was quite enough!) He was upset when he learned that the first Protestants in England and France no less than those in Germany were being called Lutherans:

---

[1]Merle Severy, "The World of Luther," *National Geographic*, October 1983, p. 448.

[2]Around 1522 Luther began to style himself after the apostle Paul in his letters shifting from the usual salutation *salutem* to the familiar apostolic greeting, *gratia et pax in domino*. The Saxon preacher had become the apostle to the Germans and eventually to the entire church: "Luther walks consciously in the steps of the Apostle and takes cues not just for theology but for action from him." Timothy J. Wengert, "Martin Luther's Movement toward an Apostolic Self-awareness as Reflected in His Early Letters," *Lutherjahrbuch* (1994): 71-92.

[3]*WA, Br* 2:74. See Karl Holl, "Martin Luther on Luther," in *Interpreters of Luther: Essays in Honor of Wilhelm Pauck*, ed. Jaroslav Pelikan (Philadelphia: Fortress, 1968), p. 19.

The first thing I ask is that people should not make use of my name, and should not call themselves Lutherans but Christians. What is Luther? The teaching is not mine, nor was I crucified for anyone. . . . How did I, poor stinking bag of maggots that I am, come to the point where people call the children of Christ by my evil name?[4]

When Luther made this protest in 1522, one year after his official excommunication by the pope, a community of scholars committed to the cause of reform had already coalesced around him in Wittenberg. They would consolidate and extend the dynamic biblical interpretation Luther had begun. Their work would include the translation and publication of the Luther Bible (completed in 1534), the development of catechisms, confessions, liturgies and church orders, and the emergence of what has been called the Wittenberg school of biblical exegesis.[5]

MASTER PHILIPP

On maps of the former German Democratic Republic (East Germany), the town of Wittenberg appeared as *Lutherstadt*, the city of Luther. It might also have been called *Melanchthonstadt*, for Philipp Melanchthon lived there longer than his more famous colleague and had a more hands-on influence in the enactment of the Lutheran Reformation. His work included shaping the university curriculum, drafting church documents (such as the Augsburg Confession), representing the Lutheran cause in numerous negotiations and corresponding with a host of friends and foes both within and without the Reformation movement. Between 1514 and 1560, Melanchthon wrote more than ten thousand letters, which is more than Luther and

---

[4]WA 8:685: *Tzum ersten bitt ich, man wolt meynes namen geschweygen und sich nit lutherisch, sondern Christen heyssen. Was ist Luther? Ist doch die lere nitt meyn. Szo byn ich auch fur niemant gecreutzigt. . . . Wie keme denn ich armer stinckender madensack datzu, das man die kynder Christi solt mit meynem heyloszen namen nennen?*
[5]See Irena Backus, "Biblical Hermeneutics and Exegesis," *OER* 1:153.

Erasmus put together. Melanchthon's presence is still palpable in Wittenberg today. His impressive tomb in the choir of the Castle Church parallels that of Luther on the other side of the nave; his statue dominates the town square, where he stands on the same level next to Luther; his three-story renaissance-style house with its lovely garden in the back is a favorite tourist attraction on the main street. However, despite his accomplishments, Melanchthon has often been portrayed as Luther's slender shadow, his pale assistant or, to quote the titles of two of his biographies, the quiet reformer and the reformer

VIVENTIS·POTVIT·DVRERIVS·ORA·PHILIPPI
MENTEM·NON·POTVIT·PINGERE·DOCTA
MANVS

Figure 6.1. Albrecht Dürer, a major Renaissance painter in Northern Europe, produced prints and paintings of major humanist scholars including Desiderius Erasmus. This portrait of Phillip Melanchthon shows the reformer as he looked at age twenty-nine (1526).

without honor.[6] Surveying this literature, one scholar has said, "It is almost as if Melanchthon were the Rodney Dangerfield of the Reformation, the man who cannot get respect."[7]

In the history of Protestant theology, Melanchthon has been variously interpreted as the precursor of theological liberalism (Barth), the forerunner of ecumenism (Iserloh), the foil of Calvinism (Dorner) and the formulator of a *via media* more suitable to the Church of England than the Continental Reforma-

---

[6]Clyde Manschreck, *Melanchthon: The Quiet Reformer* (Nashville: Abingdon, 1958); Michael Rogness, *Philip Melanchthon: Reformer Without Honor* (Minneapolis: Augsburg, 1969).

[7]Timothy J. Wengert, "Beyond Stereotypes: The Real Philip Melanchthon," in *Philip Melanchthon: Then and Now (1497-1997)*, ed. Scott H. Hendrix (Columbia, S.C.: Lutheran Theological Southern Seminary, 1999), p. 10.

tion (Franz Hildebrandt). Many of these views are rooted in sixteenth-century controversies over Luther and his legacy in which Melanchthon was scorned as a compromiser (the German word is *Leisetreter,* "pussyfooter") and attacked furiously as an enemy within the camp. When Melanchthon died in 1560, he said he was glad to be delivered from the fury of the theologians. In recent Reformation studies, however, Melanchthon has made a comeback. He is increasingly seen as a reformer in his own right. Neither a cipher for Luther nor an echo of Erasmus, he was a leading interpreter of Scripture and a creative formulator of the Reformation tradition.[8]

Unlike Luther, Melanchthon was neither a monk nor a priest. Nor did he receive a doctorate in theology. He was a lay theologian, if that expression can be used for a church tradition that emphasizes so strongly the priesthood of all believers. What Melanchthon brought to the Reformation was the intellectual energy of an academic prodigy, a scholar well trained in the *via antiqua* and the *via moderna* at the

---

[8]Sheible, "Philip Melanchthon," *OER* 3:44. Heinz Scheible has summarized the results of recent Melanchthon studies in this way: "Melanchthon's historical significance may chiefly be seen in his recognition of the problem of the relation between humanism and the Reformation, (that is the Greco-Roman and biblical heritage in the history of the West), his coming to terms with the problem, and his introduction of the results of his solution into the thought and organization of both ecclesiastical and educational reform in Germany. In so doing, he avoided the twin dangers that either the fledgling reform movement would get sidetracked into an anti-intellectual spiritualism or, at the opposite extreme, philosophy would be imposed upon theology, knowledge upon faith, and reason upon revelation." The harvest of the renaissance in Melanchthon's scholarship includes Michael B. Aune, *To Move the Heart: Rhetoric and Ritual in the Theology of Philip Melanchthon* (San Francisco: Christian University's Press, 1994); John R. Schneider, *Philip Melanchthon's Rhetorical Construal of Biblical Authority,* Oratio Sacra (Lewiston, N.Y.: Edwin Mellen Press, 1990); John Schofield, *Philip Melanchthon and the English Reformation* (Aldershot: Ashgate, 2006); and, in addition to many essays, the following books by Timothy J. Wengert: *Philip Melanchthon's "Annotationes in Johannem" in Relation to Its Predecessors and Contemporaries* (Geneva: Librairie Droz, 1987); *Law and Gospel: Philip Melanchthon's Debate with John Agricola of Eisleben over "Poenitentia"* (Grand Rapids: Baker, 1997); *Human Freedom, Christian Righteousness: Philip Melanchthon's Exegetical Dispute with Erasmus of Rotterdam* (Oxford: Oxford University Press, 1998). Timothy J. Wengert and M. Patrick Graham have also edited an important symposium: *Philip Melanchthon (1497-1560) and the Commentary* (Sheffield: Sheffield Academic Press, 1997).

universities of Heidelberg and Tübingen respectively. In Tübingen he had worked at the print shop of Thomas Anshelm as a copyeditor alongside his friend Johannes Oecolampadius, the future reformer of Basel. Both young men had dropped their vernacular family names, Husschyn (house light) and Schwartzerdt (black earth), for stylish hellenized equivalents, a popular convention among humanist scholars at the time. For a while, even Luther signed his letters "Brother Martin Eleutherius," Luther the free man.

When his great-uncle, the famous Johannes Reuchlin, recommended Master Philipp to the Wittenberg authorities as a candidate for the newly established chair of Greek there, he referred to him as the greatest scholar in Europe, second only to Erasmus. That was high praise for one so young (he was barely twenty-one) even if he was an intellectual wunderkind who had already published a Greek grammar and several plays of Terence. John Schofield is probably right when he speculates that Melanchthon would not likely have made a good first impression in Wittenberg: "He was short in stature, thin and frail looking, rather like the school boy swot who shines in class but looks weedy on the sports field."[9] He also had a slight speech impediment and stammered when he spoke. But Philipp silenced the naysayers and won the heart of Martin Luther by his inaugural address delivered in the Castle Church four days after his arrival in town. In this talk, he lent support to the humanist reform of the curriculum already underway in the university at Wittenberg. He argued that, along with Hebrew, Greek and Latin, the biblical scholar must be trained in the ancient disciplines of dialectic and rhetoric, the purpose of which was "to unleash all the power of language to persuade a truth."[10] With the text of Homer in one hand and Paul's epistle to Titus in the other, Melanchthon began his forty-two-year teaching career at the University of Wittenberg. Out of his lectures would come his *Common Places*, a

[9]Schofield, *Melanchthon and the English Reformation*, p. 9.
[10]Schneider, *Rhetorical Construal*, p. 54.

handbook of theology that evolved out of talks he gave on Paul's letter to the Romans. Over the years Melanchthon also produced a treasury of exegetical works including major commentaries on Romans, Colossians, Proverbs, Daniel and John.[11]

Some scholars have suggested that Melanchthon underwent a vocational crisis in the early 1520s after which his initial enthusiasm for Luther dimmed as he became the Erasmian Trojan horse within the camp of Wittenberg. However, recent scholarship has emphasized continuity in Melanchthon's career grounding his mature theology in his early training in rhetoric, dialectic and the languages. Melanchthon, like Luther, knew how to distinguish. For example, he praised Aristotle's contribution to human learning and called for a fresh engagement with his ideas (as well as a new edition of his writings) while at the same time he opposed the medieval scholastics who has used Aristotle to construct a faulty system of salvation based on a truncated doctrine of grace. He continued to be on friendly terms with Erasmus even after the great man broke with Luther over freedom of the will. Especially after Erasmus's death in 1536, Melanchthon praised the Dutch humanist as a forerunner of the Reformation, the great scholar who had introduced Luther and the other reformers to the Greek New Testament and the writings of the early church fathers. In this way, Melanchthon claimed, Erasmus had paved the way for the recovery of the gospel even if his own theology remained muddled with moralism and an overly optimistic anthropology. As Timothy Wengert has said, "Erasmus's death transformed him into a cipher that Melanchthon could then decipher for his own historical and theological purposes."[12]

Melanchthon himself discovered the heart of the gospel in the

---

[11]See Wengert's survey of Melanchthon's commentary work in "The Biblical Commentaries of Philip Melanchthon," in *Philip Melanchthon (1497-1560) and the Commentary*, ed. Timothy J. Wengert and M. Patrick Graham (Sheffield: Sheffield Academic Press, 1997), pp. 106-48.

[12]Wengert, *Human Freedom*, p. 153.

writings of Paul, especially in his letter to the Romans. Soon after receiving his bachelor's degree in Bible in 1519 (the only theological degree he ever earned), Melanchthon plunged into his work on Paul. In retrospect, it seems providential that the apostle Paul had been chosen as the patron saint of the University of Wittenberg at its founding in 1502. We have seen how Luther's preoccupation with Romans reshaped his understanding of justification by faith. In a sense, Melanchthon picked up where Luther had left off, pursuing the argument in a more deliberate way by means of his dialectical-rhetorical method.

Erasmus had earlier recommended identifying certain major concepts or themes, commonplaces *(loci communes)*, within a given text as a way of organizing its content and grasping more fully its message. Melanchthon pursued this same strategy in his study of Romans, but with a difference. As Scheible puts it: "Whereas Erasmus continued to impose upon the text his own list of *loci communes*, Melanchthon required that the *loci* and their organization arise out of the text itself."[13] Melanchthon believed that careful rhetorical analysis of the text would yield the basic structure and themes for a faithful exposition. With Luther's lecture notes on Romans likely at his disposal, Melanchthon discovered in this letter the fundamental concepts that Paul had intended and Luther had taught, namely, sin, law, grace and forgiveness. Such concepts, however, were not mere theological themes abstracted arbitrarily. Rather, they constituted a

---

[13]Scheible, "Philip Melanchthon," p. 42. Richard A. Muller makes a similar point about Melanchthon's adaptation of the *loci* method: "This approach, moreover, was a result of Melanchthon's firm conviction that the rules of rhetoric were derived from (and not imposed upon) the practice of writing and that, therefore, rhetorical analysis of the forms of a discourse leading to the identification of fundamental topics was the proper method for the exposition of the text." See "'Scimus enim quod lex spiritualis est': Melanchthon and Calvin on the Interpretation of Romans 7:14-23," in *Philip Melanchthon (1497-1560) and the Commentary*, ed. Timothy J. Wengert and M. Patrick Graham (Sheffield: Sheffield Academic Press, 1997), p. 220. On the *methodus Melanchthonis*, see Timothy J. Wengert, "The Rhetorical Paul: Philip Melanchthon's Interpretation of the Pauline Epistles," in *A Companion to Paul in the Reformation*, ed. R. Ward Holder (Leiden: Brill, 2009), pp. 129-64.

framework for understanding the entire history of salvation. Melanchthon came to this insight through his careful rhetorical analysis of Paul's letter that enabled him, as Wengert has put it, to read Paul, and through him the entire Bible, more like a novel than a telephone book.

Basic to Melanchthon's approach is the crucial distinction between law and gospel, a theme already announced by Luther in Thesis 26 of the Heidelberg Disputation (1518): "The law says, 'Do this,' and it is never done. Grace says, 'Believe in this,' and everything is already done."[14] Again, in 1520, Luther wrote, "The entire Holy Scripture is divided into two words, the commandments or law of God and his promise or pledge."[15] For Melanchthon, as for Luther, right understanding of law and gospel was essential for the proper interpretation of Scripture and the right doing of theology. The law accuses, condemns and drives to Christ whereas the gospel is the announcement of forgiveness, pardon and new life based not on any achievements or merits of one's own but solely on the accomplishment of Christ. In the 1540 edition of his commentary on Romans, Melanchthon describes the distinction of law and gospel in terms of two kinds of righteousness:

> The righteousness of the law is to do the law, that is, to render perfect obedience according to the law. So, he says, righteousness is described by Moses when he says "doing them," as though he said: "The righteousness of the law is this very obedience by which the things which the law prescribes are true and wholly done: to glorify God, to burn with love of God with all one's heart, to love the neighbor, to be without concupiscence, to be without any vicious affect, to be without sin." That is the righteousness which the law requires which human na-

---

[14]*LW* 31:41.
[15]*LW* 31:348.

ture is so far from fulfilling that it does not even know what the love of God is. On the other hand, the righteous of faith is not to be righteous on account of fulfilling the law on account of our virtues, but it is to believe that we are righteous, that is, accepted by God, on account of Christ.[16]

The law-gospel schema became a way, then, of reading Romans as Paul intended it to be read, and this became a key to interpreting the entire canon of Scripture. Both Luther and Melanchthon recognized, of course, that "law" had several distinct meanings within the Bible. The "theological" use of the law proclaims God the justifier and savior of sinners, which is the only proper subject of theology according to Luther.[17] There is also a "political" use of the law by which God preserves some semblance of order in an otherwise chaotic world through the divinely sanctioned institutions of marriage, the state and civil society. For the mature Melanchthon, there is also a third use of the law that allows believers, justified by faith alone, to live their lives in accordance with God's moral standard, a view that approaches if it does not exactly match the Reformed position.

Melanchthon and the Lutheran tradition more broadly have been criticized for concentrating so intently on soteriology that other major theological concerns were marginalized. In this view, Melanchthon is seen as the forerunner of Schleiermacher, who allowed reason to triumph over faith and ended up by relegating the entire doctrine of the Trinity to a twelve-page appendix at the end of his major dog-

---

[16]Melanchthon, *Commentary on Romans*, trans. Fred Kramer (St. Louis: Concordia Publishing House, 1992), p. 196. Increasingly, Melanchthon explained justification by faith alone in forensic terms, that is, through the divine imputation of Christ's alien righteousness. The forensic character of justification, which is also present in Luther, became more pronounced in the course of Melanchthon's debate with Andreas Osiander and his doctrine of the infusion of the "essential righteousness" of Christ to the believer. See Gottfried Seebass, "Andreas Osiander," *OER* 3:183-85.

[17]See "Luther's Commentary on Psalm 51," *LW* 12:311.

matic work, *The Christian Faith*. This view is based, in part, on one of Melanchthon's most famous statements, from the first edition of his *Common Places* in 1521: "To know Christ is to know his benefits and not, as they teach, to perceive his natures and the mode of his incarnation." The "they" in this statement refers to medieval scholastics who indulged in theological speculations on the great mysteries of the faith. In his letter to the Romans, Melanchthon asserted, Paul did not philosophize about the mysteries of the Trinity but emphasized instead those realities on which the knowledge of Christ depends: law, sin and grace. However, as Wengert has shown, Melanchthon was lecturing on the Gospel of John in the same time period that he was drafting his *Common Places* and teaching on Romans. "Melanchthon assumes trinitarian doctrine and never explicitly attacks it. He omits much of the traditional discussion of these problems and even some of the verses which clearly raise them. Instead he focuses on the soteriological implications of the text, putting flesh on the famous comment from the *Common Places* that 'to know Christ and to know his benefits.'"

Until trinitarian and christological heresies arose among certain radical reformers, Melanchthon was content to concentrate on "the power, function and benefits of Christ, and not upon his essence or natures."[18] But he always assumed an orthodox trinitarian theology even when his focus was on the distinction of law and gospel or the doctrine of justification. Melanchthon continued to revise his *Common Places* in response to new challenges, especially from Servetus and other antitrinitarian radicals. Thus the 1555 edition opens with an extended statement about the Trinity, the Father, the Son and the Holy Spirit. Melanchthon then explains the importance of this teaching and offers a statement about theological method that should perhaps be read as a retrospective piece of self-criticism: "For if one is

---

[18]Wengert, *Melanchthon's Annotationes in Johannem*, esp. pp. 43-48, 150.

careless about doctrine and omits a few necessary pieces, delusion and error follow in other parts; and if one does not keep the end in view, it is the same as if one undertook a journey and gave no thought to the city to which one desired to go."[19]

Melanchthon's many commentaries on the Bible and his continually expanding *Common Places* had a tremendous influence on biblical exegesis at Wittenberg and far beyond. The *loci* method of identifying major themes in a given text was especially useful to preachers who found Melanchthon's commentaries a rich resource for their pulpit preparations. Melanchthon extended and deepened Luther's presentation of the Christian faith and did so in a way that consolidated and strengthened what Luther achieved. This is nowhere more clearly seen than in his exegetical labors. In January 1544, two years before Luther's death, Melanchthon summarized the enterprise that occupied so much of his life and work. In a letter to Veit Dietrich, one of his former students who was then serving as a preacher in Nuremberg, Melanchthon wrote:

> Although I approve the studies of commenting and writing (for minds must be inspired somehow), nevertheless, all of us who write I view as similar to the boy described by Augustine (as they report), who was sitting by the seashore and digging a channel in the sand with his little fingers. He claimed that he was going to transfer the sea into that channel. We cannot drain the magnitude of things about which God speaks by our expositions. Nevertheless, as I have said, minds must be inspired, some things must be pointed out, human studies must be encouraged; afterward, as John says [1 Jn. 2:27], "the anointing [of God] will teach" [the upright].[20]

---

[19]*Melanchthon on Christian Doctrine: Loci communes 1555*, trans. and ed. Clyde L. Manschreck (Oxford: Oxford University Press, 1965), p. xlvi.
[20]CR 5:290-91; MBW 3431. Quoted by Wengert, *Melanchthon and the Commentary*, p. 8.

A FLOOD OF BIBLES

For all of his learned commentaries and doctrinal writings, it may well be that Melanchthon's greatest contribution to the Reformation took place in December 1521 before he had published any of his own theological works: he persuaded Luther to translate the Bible into German. Some of the most consequential books ever written were penned in periods of confinement. Think of Paul's prison epistles, John Bunyan's *The Pilgrim's Progress* and Adolf Hitler's *Mein Kampf*. Sequestered in the great fortress of the Wartburg, "my Patmos," "this wilderness," "in the land of the birds," as Luther called the place of his seclusion, he was beset by midnight wrestlings with the devil and new bouts of *Anfechtungen*.

Cut off from the company of his friends in Wittenberg, Luther experienced great swings of mood. In the same paragraph of a letter to Melanchthon in May 1521, he could say that his respite from his responsibilities in Wittenberg "brings me great peace of heart" and two lines later add "I would rather burn in live coals than rot here alone, half alive and yet not dead."[21] No doubt his intensive work on the German New Testament helped him face his demons in the Wartburg. Friedrich Nietzsche, who was no friend of orthodox Christianity in any form, accorded high praise to Luther's Bible by calling it not merely "the best German book" but "our only real book thus far, compared with which nearly everything else is only 'literature.'"[22] With Melanchthon's help, Luther's draft was polished and ready for publication in September 1522, just in time for the autumn book fair at Leipzig.

Just as it is doubtful that Paul ever realized that the personal letter he dashed off to his friend Philemon would one day be included in the Bible, so Luther had no idea that his New Testament would be-

---

[21]LCL 2:35. Luther to Melanchthon, May 26, 1521.
[22]Nietzsche, *Musarion* 25, 205-6; 16, 352. In this context, Nietzsche also said, "Unser letztes Ereigniss ist immer noch Luther." Cited in Heinz Bluhm, "Luther's *German Bible*," in *Sevenheaded Luther: Essays in Commemoration of a Quincentenary, 1483-1983*, ed. Peter N. Brooks (Oxford: Clarendon, 1983), p. 178.

come the world's first bestseller and a formative shaper of the German language. Thus when he learned that his friend Johann Lang had begun work on his own translation of the Gospel of Matthew, Luther encouraged him to complete his task. "Oh, that every town had its own translator and that this book might be found in all tongues, hands, eyes, ears, and hearts!"[23] Lang's translation, however, has been long forgotten, as have the other German Bible translations already published when Luther began his work.

Melchior Lotter the Younger, Luther's Wittenberg printer, brought out an initial print run of three thousand copies of Luther's New Testament in September 1522, an amazing feat for the times. To meet the deadline for the fair, several presses ran day and night. The first edition was soon sold out, and a new, slightly revised version appeared in December of the same year. It is estimated that one hundred thousand copies of the New Testament were printed in Wittenberg alone during Luther's lifetime. More than twice that number of the complete Luther Bible were on the market by the time of Luther's death in 1546. In addition to these Wittenberg Bibles, 253 editions are known to have been published elsewhere accounting for one-half million complete Bibles and portions distributed throughout Europe in less than three decades.[24] Luther always considered his translation of the Bible his greatest achievement. Among his other works, he valued highly his treatise against Erasmus on the bondage of the will, and his 1535 commentary on Galatians, which he called affectionately "my Katie von Bora." Yet even these important contributions were only "scaffolding" meant to support the great cathedral of Scripture. That Luther's translation had a transforming effect on the people of his day is beyond dispute. Johann Cochlaeus, one of Luther's harshest adversaries, acknowledged as much. As soon as Luther's New Testament was pub-

---

[23]WA, Br 2:413. Cited in Willem J. Kooiman, *Luther and the Bible*, trans. John Schmidt (Philadelphia: Muhlenberg, 1961), p. 91.
[24]Kooiman, *Luther and the Bible*, p. 178.

lished, he noted, it "was reproduced and distributed in such numbers by the book printers that tailors and shoemakers, yes, even womenfolk and other simple idiots, as many of them who adopted this Lutheran *Evangelium* and who had also learned a little bit of German from off a gingerbread cookie, read it immediately with great fervor and took it to be a source of all truth. Some even carried it around with them in their bosoms and memorized it."[25]

Why was Luther's translation so successful? That he was a genius with words is evident to anyone who reads him today, in either German or English. But his goal to make the Word of God a living reality for the common people was aided by his philosophy of translation. He wanted to put the Scriptures in *Gemeindeutsch*, the common German idiom that one could hear among farm workers in the field, fishmongers at the market and in a mother's chatter with her children. His remarkable success in doing just this was noted by the nineteenth-century German Jewish poet Heinrich Heine, who once said that Luther could scold like a fishwife and whisper like a maiden.[26]

In addition to his intuitive grasp of the common idiom, Luther also had his ear to the ground. For example, while translating Leviticus, he several times visited the Wittenberg slaughterhouse to observe the dissection of a sheep so as better to describe the inner organs of the animal sacrifices in the Bible. On these field trips the learned doctor became the student of the lowly butcher. When he got to Revelation 21, Luther persuaded his friend Spalatin to show him the crown jewels in the palace of the prince to help him find the right German names for the precious stones of the New Jerusalem described in Revelation 21:18-21. He also sought help with the names

---

[25]Cochlaeus, *Historia*, p. 121. Cited in Jane O. Newman, "The Word Made Print: Luther's 1522 *New Testament* in an Age of Mechanical Reproduction," *Representations* 11 (1985): 115.

[26]This is Jaroslav Pelikan's translation of Heine's comment. See Pelikan's *Whose Bible Is It?* (New York: Viking, 2005), p. 172. The original text is, *Derselbe Mann, der wie ein Fischweib schimpfen konnte, er konnte auch weich seyn, wie eine zarte Jungfrau.* Heinrich Heine, *Der Salon* (Hamburg: Hoffmann and Campe, 1834), p. 60.

of the many birds and beasts of the Old Testament. Again he wrote to Spalatin, "I am alright on the birds of the night—owl, ravel, horned owl, tawny owl, screech owl—and on the birds of prey—vulture, kite, hawk, and sparrow hawk. I can handle the stag, roebuck, and chamois, but what in the Devil am I to do with the taragelaphus, pygargus, oryx, and camelopard?"[27] These were Latin names given for Old Testament animals in the Vulgate, and Luther scratched his head to come up with German equivalents.

Though Luther agreed with Melanchthon that Paul's letter to the Romans was "truly the purest Gospel," he held a special affection for the Psalms beyond any other book in the Bible.

> The Psalter ought to be a precious and beloved book, if for no other reason than this: it promises Christ's death and resurrection so clearly—and pictures his kingdom and the condition and nature of all Christendom—that it might well be called a little Bible. In it is comprehended most beautifully and briefly everything that is in the entire Bible. It is really a fine enchiridion or handbook. In fact, I have a notion that the Holy Spirit wanted to take the trouble himself to compile a short Bible and book of examples of all Christendom or all saints, so that anyone who could not read the whole Bible but have here anyway almost an entire summary of it, comprised in one little book.[28]

Luther had lived with the Psalter on a daily basis since his early time in the monastery. He had already given two lecture courses on the Psalms and published a translation and commentary on the seven penitential Psalms before he turned his attention to a translation of the entire book. In 1524 he brought out *Der Psalter deutsch*, his first published edition of the complete Psalter. He continued to revise his

[27]Quoted by Roland H. Bainton, *Here I Stand: A Life of Martin Luther* (New York: Abingdon-Cokesbury, 1950), pp. 327-28.
[28]*LW* 35:365, 254.

translation of the Psalms throughout his lifetime.

Luther had hoped to publish a commentary on the complete Psalter, but his summons to the Diet of Worms in 1521 interrupted his
second lecture course on Psalms at Psalm 22, and he was never able
to finish this work. However, throughout his life, Luther gave special
lectures and many sermons on the Psalms, and some of these were
published as individual works. A treatise on Psalm 68 was completed
during his stay at the Wartburg, and a longer one on Psalm 118 while
he was holed up in the Coburg Castle during the Diet of Augsburg in
1530. We owe Luther's commentary on Psalm 23 to the diligence of
his loyal scribe Georg Rörer, who wrote down the comments Luther
made "one evening after grace at the dinner table" and published
them in 1536. Luther gave a thoroughly christocentric interpretation:
Christ is the good, friendly shepherd, so different from Moses, who
"is harsh and unfriendly toward his sheep." The green pasture with
which Christ feeds his sheep is "the dear Gospel," made audible and
visible through the gifts of preaching and the sacraments by which
the flock is fed. The overflowing cup is the "blessed intoxication" of
the Holy Spirit.

In his discourse on this psalm, Luther reflected on a problem that
by the mid-1530s was becoming a serious concern for the reformers.
Now that more and more people had the Scriptures in their own language, with easily affordable editions at hand, would God's Word
now be taken for granted? Would it be neglected by the people?
Would the Bible come to be held in contempt by reason of its very
familiarity? While Luther knew nothing of the Bible glut so common
in the North American church today, he did lament the beginnings
of this development in his time:

> Thus the saying is true: When something is in common use,
> it is not appreciated but is despised, however precious it may
> really be. Unfortunately such a saying is true, especially true in

the case of our dear Word. Where people have it, they do not want it. But where it is not available, there they would be sincerely glad to have it. Where people have the church, in which God's Word is taught, at their doorstep, there they go strolling along the market place during the sermon and sauntering about the moat. Where they have to go ten, twenty, or more miles for it, there, as we read in Psalm 42:4, they would gladly go with the throng and lead them in procession into the house of God with glad shouts and psalms of thanksgiving.[29]

Erhart von Kunheim, who married one of Luther's daughters, inherited his father-in-law's copy of his 1528 Psalter. He found it filled with the reformer's notations and marginalia.[30] He reported that Luther had this Psalter with him at all times, day and night, even on his journeys outside Wittenberg. In Cranach's paintings of the mature Luther, the reformer is often shown holding this old, well-thumbed book, which was the mainstay for his daily prayers and meditations. As the prayer book of the Bible, the Psalms confronted every reader with the demand and promise of God. It was a present address that required a personal response. The Psalms "are not words to read, but to live," Luther wrote.[31] Every Christian should take the Psalms to heart, memorize them and ponder their meaning.

In short, if you would see the holy Christian church pictured in living color and form, as in the small portrait, pick up the Psal-

---

[29]LW 12:151. For Luther's other comments on Psalm 23, see LW 12:147-79. See also Luther's comment: "God be praised, the Bible itself is now in the hands of the people, together with plenty and useful books of many learned writers. In these a Christian can nourish himself well, as the saying goes 'The cow walks in grass up to the belly.' Just so we, too, are truly well supplied in our time with the rich, full pasture of the divine Word. God grant that we gratefully use it and become fat and strong from it before the drought and punishment for our unthankfulness come. Let us use the Word so that we shall not be obliged to devour stones and thistles again, as we had to heretofore under the papacy, but that we bring forth much fruit and become the Lord's disciples (John 16)" WLS, 2:83.
[30]Some of these notations have been included in WA, DB 4:510-77.
[31]WA 31/1:67.

ter. There you have a fine, bright, and clear mirror that will show you what Christendom is. Yes, you will even find yourself in it, for it is the true 'know yourself' and, above all, God himself and all his creatures.[32]

In Luther's encounter with the Scriptures, the distance between the ancient people of God and the contemporary believer collapsed before the timeless Word of God. Luther once said that the very words of the psalmist present us not with "silent saints" (such as those that might be met, say, in the pages of Jacobus da Voragine's *The Golden Legend*) but with a living communion across the centuries. The words of the psalmists revealed "how they talked and prayed to God, how they are still speaking and praying, so that other legends and examples present us, as compared with the Psalter, with silent saints. The Psalter creates in our minds good sturdy living saints. Why, a silent man compared with a speaking man is the same as dead, there being no more powerful, no nobler gift than speech."[33]

It was a mark of Luther's genius that he knew he could not accomplish the translation of the Bible alone. Even his solo masterpiece, the 1522 New Testament, was thoroughly reviewed and revised by Melanchthon and other friends in Wittenberg. "Translators must never work by themselves," Luther said. "When one is alone, the best and most suitable words do not always occur to him."[34] Luther spent many months revising the various rescensions of his Bible translation that was published over the years. This was a task that required team-

---

[32]*WA*, DB 10/1:105. *Summa, Wiltu die heiligen Christlichen Kirchen gemalet sehen mit lebendiger Der Psalter malet die heilige Kirchen mit jrer rechte farbe. Farbe vnd gestalt, in einem kleinen Bilde gefasset, So nim den Psalter fur dich so hastu einen feinen, hellen, reinen, Spiegel, der dir zeigen wird, was die Christenheit sey. Ja du wirst auch dich selbs drinnen, vnd das rechte Gnotiseauton finden, Da zu Gott selbs vnd alle Creaturn.* See Kooiman, *Luther and the Bible*, p. 156.

[33]*WA*, DB 10/1:100. Quoted by H. G. Haile, *Luther: An Experiment in Biography* (Princeton, N.J.: Princeton University Press, 1983), p. 61.

[34]*WA*, TR 1:961: *Nec translatores debent esse soli, denn eim einigen fallen nicht allzeit gut et propria verba zu.*

work, and he gathered around him his "Sanhedrin," as he called them. This group included, in addition to Melanchthon, Johannes Bugenhagen, Luther's pastor, the primary municipal preacher at Wittenberg; Justus Jonas, dean of Wittenberg's theology faculty; Caspar Cruciger, Melanchthon's ally in the inter-Lutheran disputes and editor of Luther's collected works; and Matthew Aurogallus, professor of Hebrew at Wittenberg. The indefatigable Rörer was also there to take notes and write protocols of the discussions, some of which have survived. These notes give a glimpse of Luther's team at work—the first Protestant Bible translation committee:

> After the Doctor had first looked through the earlier published Bibles and in addition consulted Jews and experts in foreign languages and asked old Germans for proper terms, he used to come to the consistory with his old Latin and new German Bible, always bringing the Hebrew text as well. Master Philip always brought the Greek text along. . . . Everyone had already prepared himself for the text that was to be discussed and had looked through Greek and Latin, as well as Jewish exegetes. Then, as president, he proposed a version and let everyone speak and listened to what everyone had to say with reference to the quality of the language or the exegesis of the old doctors.[35]

In an age of wildcat printing, before either copyrights or royalties were in vogue, Luther was often frustrated by printers who reproduced his works haphazardly with only a quick profit in mind, those "greedy bloodsuckers and thieving reprinters," he called them.[36] He himself received no financial gain from his Bible translations. Luther liked to quote the voice of God speaking in Isaiah 55:11: "The Word

---

[35]This description is from Johannes Mathesius, Luther's first biographer, in a series of sermons on Luther's life first published in 1566. See Heiko A. Oberman, *Luther: Man Between God and the Devil* (New Haven: Yale University Press, 1989), p. 308, and Robert Rosin, "Johannes Mathesius," OER 3:32-33.

[36]Kooiman, *Luther and the Bible*, p. 183.

that goes forth out from my mouth; shall not return to me empty, but it shall accomplish that which I purpose, and shall succeed in the thing for which I sent it."[37] This text re-assured Luther that God's Word would ultimately triumph over all the shenanigans and ploys Satan could devise to thwart it.

Beginning in 1524, Luther had his personal coat of arms, the Luther rose, printed on authorized copies of his Bible translations. In time, this emblem came to represent Luther's entire work as a reformer. Some Lutheran pastors explained its symbolism in terms of the major themes in Luther's theology. According to Andreas Kreuch,

Figure 6.2. The Luther Rose, with its cross-centered heart, was both the Reformer's personal seal and the emblem of the Lutheran Reformation.

> The white rose suggests the comforting promise of God's affirming his gracious aid against sin, death, the devil, and all the enemies of the believer; the red heart represents the confession which believers make from the heart; the cross recall the suffering of the Christian life and points to Christ as the crusader who defeats all the enemies of his people. The cross's color, black, reminds Christians how bitter Christ's suffering was and how bitter theirs is.[38]

Along with the emblem of the Luther rose, later Luther Bibles also carried as a distinctive marking a text from Scripture, *Gottes Wort bleibt ewig*, "God's Word abides forever." On the title page of Luther's first complete Bible in 1534, this verse from Isaiah 40:8 appears at the top of the page below the figure of God, who is shown with a pen

---

[37]*LW* 17:257.
[38]This is Robert Kolb's summary of Kreuch's *Sigillum Lutheri*, published in 1579. See Robert Kolb, *Martin Luther as Prophet, Teacher and Hero* (Grand Rapids: Baker, 1999), p. 82.

in his hand writing the script of this text. In this way, the Lutheran reformation underscored the resilience and indestructibility of the Scriptures, God's written Word, against forces both within and outside of the church that sought to minimalize and marginalize it. In 1934 Lutheran and Reformed representatives from Protestant churches throughout Germany came together to protest the accommodation of the Christian faith to the demands of the Third Reich. The Barmen Declaration they issued has become one of the most famous church documents of modern times. It concludes with Luther's maxim in Latin: *Verbum Dei manet in aeternum*.

BIBLE BATTLES

The politics of the Reformation played a part in the first great battle over the Bible in the sixteenth century. In 1485, when Luther was only two years old, the territory of Saxony was divided into two parts ruled over by two brothers, Ernest and Albert. The new map of Saxony looked something like a jigsaw puzzle so that the ruler of one territory could not get to certain parts of his property without crossing the lands of the other prince. The so-called Leipzig partition, which brought about this geographical and political redistribution of the Saxon lands, would remain in effect more or less until 1918. In the early sixteenth century, an intense rivalry developed between Ernestine and Albertine Saxony. Frederick III, called "the Wise" because of his prudent governance, ruled over electoral or Ernestine Saxony from 1486 to 1525. He is best known for his protection of Luther and his quiet but consistent support for the reform movement. On his deathbed he asked to receive communion in both kinds.

The rival prince of Albertine Saxony was Duke George, who was also called "the Bearded." His control of the University of Leipzig, the oldest such institution in the Saxon lands, prompted Frederick to establish the new University of Wittenberg in 1502. Duke George had a penchant for theology and was once intended for the priesthood himself. Because of this background, he had no reluctance to jump into the doctrinal disputes triggered by the indulgence controversy. At first the duke favored Luther's cause, but after hearing his famous debate with John Eck at Leipzig in 1519, he came to regard Luther as a new John Hus, a destroyer of the church who deserved the same fate as the preacher of Prague. Among the Catholic rulers in Germany, Duke George became the most implacable foe of the Lutheran reformation.

Soon after Luther's 1522 New Testament was published, Duke George forbade its printing and dissemination in his territories. He was especially offended by one of the Cranach woodcuts, which illustrated Revelation 11 by showing the beast from the abyss adorned with the three-tiered crown of the pope. Apparently the duke was not the only one upset by this polemical use of art, for in subsequent printings of the New Testament the papal tiara was taken off the head of the beast. By then, of course, the cat was out of the bag. Luther Bibles were rolling off the presses of Europe right and left, despite the fact that in most places such activity was illegal and dangerous. The first Protestant printer, the first of many, was burned alive at the stake in 1527.

In a classic case of "if you can't beat them, join them," Duke George did an about-face and began to promote the reading of the Bible in the vernacular. The Bible Duke George wanted his subjects to read was a new, Catholic-friendly edition prepared by Hieronymus Emser, the duke's chaplain and official secretary.[39] Emser and Luther shared a relationship that went back to the summer of 1504, when Luther had been a student of Emser in a course he taught at the University of Erfurt.[40] The two shared a friendly relationship for some time. In

---

[39]On Emser, see Agostino Borromeo, "Hieronymus Emser," *OER* 2:42-43, and Kenneth A. Strand, *Reformation Bibles in the Crossfire: The Story of Jerome Emser, His Anti-Lutheran Critique and His Catholic Bible Version* (Ann Arbor: Ann Arbor Publishers, 1961).

[40]This interesting claim was made by Emser himself in his *Quadruplica on Luther's Newest Answer Concerning His Reformation* (Leipzig, 1521): "I will counsel Luther that he go to

1518, Luther was a dinner guest at Emser's home in Dresden. As late as 1519, in a letter to John Lang, he could refer to him as "our Emser."[41] But as with Duke George, the Leipzig debate became a watershed in Emser's opinion of his former student. The thought that the pope and church councils could be wrong and had been wrong—seriously wrong, Luther claimed—was too much for Emser. In 1520, he strongly attacked Luther's treatise "To the Christian Nobility of the German Nation." Luther, who always gave as well as he got, shot back an acerbic response "To the Goat at Leipzig" making sport of Emser's coat of arms, the ibex or wild goat, that appeared on all of his writings. Not to be outdone, Emser replied with "Concerning the Wrathful Reply of the Bull at Wittenberg." Back and forth and on and on it went, the bull versus the goat.

Luther could not have been surprised when in 1523 Emser published a long and strident critique of his German New Testament: "On what Ground and for what Cause Luther's Translation of the New Testament Should Justly Be Forbidden the Common Man." Emser claimed to have found fourteen hundred errors and lies in Luther's work. Luther, he admitted, had concocted this poisonous mixture of truth and heresy "in a more delicate and sweet-sounding way" than earlier German translations of the Bible. But for that very reason, "the common folk are more inclined to read it and to swallow the hook that is hidden beneath the sweet words before they are aware of it."[42] As it turned out, neither Duke George's decree prohibiting vernacular translations in his territory nor Emser's massive polemic against Luther's work could stem the proliferation of German Bibles in Saxony. Recognizing his failed policy, Duke George commissioned Emser to produce a "better" German New Testament, one shorn of

---

school awhile under Emser . . . sixteen years ago he was my student and at Erfurt first heard from me John Reuchlin's comedy *Sergius*" (Strand, *Reformation Bibles*, pp. 23-24).

[41]Strand, *Reformation Bibles*, p. 28.

[42]See Newman, "The Word Made Print," p. 112.

Luther's "mistakes" and doctrinal deviations. Emser's New Testament was published in 1527, the year of his death.

Not wishing to speak ill of the very recently deceased, at least by name, Luther did not mention Emser in his 1530 treatise, "On Translating: An Open Letter." But there was little doubt about the identity of the "Dresden scribbler," the "Master Know-it-all" whom Luther excoriated for having "played the master to my New Testament."[43] In fact, Luther said (and modern scholars agree), Emser had stolen his translation almost word for word. Even worse than this, to Luther's mind, was Emser's deletion of his evangelical glosses and marginal comments and his substitution of another apparatus that led astray the common reader.

In his "Open Letter on Translating," Luther defended his right to interpret the Bible even when his exegetical work led him to challenge the most learned theologians and scholastic teachers of the day. In a piece of pungent rhetoric, he takes on himself the mantel of Paul, who "boasted" of his own standing against the superapostles at Corinth (2 Cor 11:21-33).

> Are they doctors? So am I. Are they learned? So am I. Are they preachers? So am I. Are they theologians? So am I. Are they debaters? So am I. Are they philosophers? So am I. Are they dialecticians? So am I. Are they lecturers? So am I. Do they write books? So do I.[44]

A common complaint of Luther's Catholic opponents was his rendering of Paul's statement in Romans 3:28 that one is justified by faith (*ex fide* in the Vulgate) as *allein durch den Glauben*, only by faith, or by faith alone. It seemed to Emser and other critics that Luther here deliberately added a word not found in either the Greek or Latin text of Scripture in order to shore up his dubious teaching

---

[43]*LW* 35:184.
[44]*LW* 35:186.

about justification by faith alone. Luther countered by claiming that his opponents had missed the meaning of the text by being overly literal. He knows very well, Luther says, that these four letters S-O-L-A are not in the Greek or Latin text. But he does insist that this wording conveys the sense of the text as it should be rendered in German translation. I want to speak German, he retorts, not Latin or Greek. He cites as a parallel expression the example of a farmer who brings to market "only grain and no money" (*allein korn und kein geldt*). A literalist word-for-word method of translating will not render Paul's words in Romans 3:28 into accurate, idiomatic German.

The force of Paul's argument demanded a nonliteral translation: He had to go beyond the word-for-wordness of the text in order to convey the meaning of the text. But Luther insisted that he was no innovator in claiming that faith alone justifies. In the early church, both Ambrose and Augustine had said the same thing. The apostle's words admitted of no other construal. "Paul's words are too strong; they admit of no works, none at all. Now if it is not a work, then it must be faith alone . . . the matter itself in its very core, then, demands that we say, 'faith alone justifies.' "[45]

The battle for the Bible begun by Emser and Luther continued long after both of them were dead. In 1556, the town council of the Swiss city of Zug ordered that all German translations of the Bible,

---

[45]*LW* 35:197. Most modern translations do not follow Luther's rendering of Romans 3:28, but note this comment by Joachim Jeremias: "Martin Luther in his translation of Rom. 3:28, has added one word. He says: 'Therefore we conclude that a man is justified by faith only' ('allein durch den Glauben,' *sola fide*). He has been criticized for this addition, but linguistically he was quite right. For it is a characteristic of the Semitic language (and, for that matter, Paul's epistles, time and again betray his Jewish background) that the word 'only' or 'alone' is usually left out even in places where the Western usage would consider it indispensible (cf. for example, Mark 9:41, 'whoever gives you a cup of water to drink because you bear the name of Christ, will by no means lose his reward' where the sense is: 'Whoever gives you only a cup of water', even this insignificant service will be rewarded). *Sola fide*! Faith is the only way to find God's grace." *The Central Message of the New Testament* (New York: Charles Scribner's Sons, 1965), pp. 55-56.

including those of Emser and Luther as well as others printed in nearby Zurich, be brought to the city hall and publicly burned. A crackling bonfire was the result. This action was prompted by an itinerant evangelist who had come into Zug promoting a doctrine of salvation that seemed to stress the importance of faith at the expense of good works. Such teaching the town council believed, could lead the citizens of Zug to act immorally resulting in a breakdown of public order. The visiting preacher claimed to know nothing of Luther, but he did say, "I can prove my sermon according to the Bible."[46]

Before he published his own version of the New Testament, Emser had called for an officially sanctioned translation produced by an international team of competent scholars and theologians. A step in this direction took place in 1546, when the Council of Trent defined as canonical the books of the Old and New Testaments and the Apocrypha (sometimes called the deuterocanonical writings) that remain normative for Catholics. The fathers of Trent also recognized the text of the Vulgate as supremely authoritative in the life of the church and asked for a definitive edition. A definitive Vulgate text was published in 1592 under Pope Clement VIII. Henceforth, Catholic vernacular versions, such as the famous Douai-Reims Bible in English, were based on this revised Vulgate text. In modern times, the Second Vatican Council, while honoring both the Latin Vulgate and the Greek Septuagint, recognized the importance of vernacular Scriptures, affirming that "access to sacred Scripture ought to be open wide to the Christian faithful. . . . Since the Word of God must be readily available at all times, the Church, with motherly concern, sees to it that suitable and correct translations are made into various languages, especially from the original texts of the sacred books." In this way, the council affirmed, "the children of the Church can familiarize themselves safely and

[46]Newman, "The Word Made Print," pp. 95-97.

profitably with the sacred Scriptures, and become steeped in their spirit."[47]

Among the Protestant reformers, Luther's translation of the Bible had a magisterial influence. It was, as Philip Schaff once put it, "the most important and useful work of his whole life."[48] But this does not mean that Luther's exegetical work was met with unanimous consent. Although Melanchthon defended Luther's *sola fide* rendering of Romans 3:28, he tried to bring justification in James into alignment with justification in Paul in a way that Luther could never quite accept.[49] Likewise, though Zwingli and Calvin stood shoulder to shoulder with Luther in teaching that a right standing before God is based on sheer grace and not human effort or meritorious works, neither of the Swiss reformers was willing to relegate James to a secondary status within the New Testament. Today, followers of Jesus from all denominations who still want to learn from Martin Luther can do no better than heed his own words: "Go to the Scriptures, dear Christians! Go there alone, and let my exposition and that of all other teachers mean no more to you than the scaffolding on a building, so that we might understand the simple, pure Word of God, accept it as our own, and hold it fast."[50]

---

[47]*Vatican Council II: The Conciliar and Postconciliar Documents*, ed. Austin Flannery, DV 22, 25 (Collegeville, Minn.: Liturgical Press, 1980), pp. 762-65.

[48]Schaff, *HCC* 7:341.

[49]Melanchthon, *Commentary on Romans*, pp. 18-21. Luther did not excise James from the New Testament canon, as is often alleged, though he did say on one occasion, in typical Luther overstatement, "Away with James. I almost feel like throwing Jimmy into the stove, as the priest in Kalenberg did"—a reference to a local pastor who used the wooden statues of the apostles for firewood (*LW* 34:317). After 1522, perhaps under Melanchthon's influence, Luther withdrew his characterization of James as "a right strawy epistle" from subsequent editions of his New Testament. See Timothy George, "'A Right Strawy Epistle': Reformation Perspectives on James," *Review and Expositor* 83 (1986): 369-82.

[50]This is from Luther's Advent and Christmas postils. See *LW* 48:237-48, 243.

Seven

Along the Rhine

Do not put yourself at odds with the Word of God.
For truly, truly it will persist as the Rhine follows its course.
One can perhaps dam it up for a while, but it is impossible to stop it.[1]

Huldrych Zwingli

It would be possible to tell the story of the Bible in the age of Reformation by taking a cruise on the Rhine River, one of the most beautiful and historic international waterways in the world. Rising from headstreams high in the Swiss Alps, the Rhine flows north and west for some 820 miles. If we begin our cruise in the Netherlands, where tributaries from the Rhine flow into the North Sea, we find ourselves not far from Rotterdam, the hometown of Erasmus. As a boy Erasmus came into contact with the Brothers and Sisters of the Common Life. These were devout Christians who practiced a life of piety and prayer and daily reading of the Scriptures. They were part of a movement, known as the Modern Devotion, which had been founded in the late fourteenth century by Gerhard Groote, a lay

---

[1]Z 3:488: *Tund umb gots willen sinem wort gheinen drang an; dann warlich, warlich es wirt als gewüss sinen gang haben als der Ryn; den mag man ein zyt wol schwellen, aber nit gstellen.*

preacher and deacon from Deventer. The most famous book to come out of this movement was the *Imitation of Christ* by Thomas à Kempis, a manual of devotion that still has an enduring appeal. At a time when printing was still a novelty, these lay Bible readers became the great scribes and copyists of Europe—Thomas á Kempis is said to have made at least four copies of the entire Bible. They were also the great schoolteachers of Europe, counting among their pupils both Luther and Erasmus. As a movement that stood somewhere between the religious communities of the Middle Ages and the lay congregations of the Reformation, the Brothers and Sisters of the Common Life encouraged the devotional reading of Scripture and contributed to the general rise in literacy.[2]

Continuing our voyage through the lower Rhine region, we pass by the cities of Duisburg and Düsseldorf. Duisburg would have appeared as a small rural town protected by sturdy walls. However, since the high Middle Ages, it had been a member of the famous Hansa, a network of cities in northern Europe that constituted something of a free trade zone at the time. Düsseldorf was a city of impressive spires and domes. Nearby was the military post at Kaiserswerth, where imperial soldiers monitored the traffic on the Rhine and stood ready at the notice of a command to quell peasant rebellions in the countryside or disturbances in the towns.

Soon we arrive at "holy Cologne," as Germany's largest city (with a population of forty thousand) was called because of its many churches and religious orders. Cologne was the leading center of Catholic thought in sixteenth-century Germany and a major citadel of the Counter-Reformation north of the Alps. Luther was publicly condemned by the university here in 1519, and his writings burned in

---

[2]Kaspar Elm has described the Brothers and Sisters of the Common Life as "a spiritual form of life between the cloister and the world, between the Middle Ages and modern times." See his "Die Bruderschaft vom gemeinsamen Leben," *Ons geestelijk erf* 59 (1985): 470-96. See also John Van Engen, "Brothers and Sisters of the Common Life," *OER* 1:217-19.

November 1520. Later in the sixteenth century, it appeared for a brief moment that Cologne might experience a Reformation breakthrough. In 1540, Archbishop Hermann von Wied, known for his evangelical Catholic leanings, invited Martin Bucer to draw up a plan for reform of the city. Bucer drafted the document with the help of Melanchthon, but nothing came of it. Later in the century, a small Protestant community did take root and gained a measure of toleration in Cologne. A Reformed church was founded in 1565, and a Lutheran one ten years later. In the Middle Ages, both Thomas Aquinas and Albert the Great had taught at Cologne, and the Dominican tradition remained strong in the sixteenth century. In the early years of the Reformation, the University of Cologne attracted students from many parts of Europe, including young Heinrich Bullinger from Switzerland, who took his bachelor's degree there.

A printing press had been established at Cologne in 1465, only ten years after the first Gutenberg Bible was printed. Cologne soon became one of the major printing centers in Germany.[3] In 1534, the year the complete Luther Bible was published in Wittenberg, a Catholic version of the Bible in German rolled off the presses of Peter Quentel at Cologne. Like many printers in the sixteenth century, Quentel was more concerned about making money than publishing correct theology, and he offered his services to both sides in the religious quarrel. This probably explains why he took on a secret printing project by the English refugee William Tyndale. There was a thriving business connection between England and a number of the major trading ports of northeast Europe, including Hamburg, Antwerp and Cologne. English cloth and Rhine wine were major commodities in this trade. We know that Tyndale was well connected to a group of London cloth merchants, and he no doubt found friends

---

[3]See Robert W. Scribner, "Cologne," *OER* 1:383-85. See also Scribner's essay, "Why Was There No Reformation in Cologne?" in *Popular Culture and Popular Movements in Germany* (London: The Hamibledon Press, 1987), pp. 217-41.

within the English expatriate community in Cologne. Somehow he was able to contract the services of Quentel, who began the clandestine project of printing the New Testament in English. However, as it happened, Tyndale's work was betrayed to the authorities by Luther's foe Cochlaeus. The project was disrupted early and the presses stopped at Matthew 22. Tyndale and his helper William Roye escaped in the nick of time. They grabbed the remaining materials and took the next boat up the Rhine toward Worms.[4]

Sailing (or being rowed) past vineyards, castles and picturesque turns in the river, Tyndale would have come to the city of Mainz on the west bank of the Rhine opposite its junction with the Main River. Frankfurt, the site of Europe's most popular book fair, lay some thirty kilometers to the east on the Main. Today one can visit the Gutenberg museum in Mainz and purchase a facsimile reprint page of the world's most famous book. Johannes Schöffer, a descendent of Gutenberg's partner in first print shop, kept the business going in the sixteenth century. Already he had published several of Luther's writings in the early 1520s. This was a controversial thing to do because Mainz was the home base of Elector Cardinal Albert of Brandenburg, whose agents had commissioned the hawking of indulgences by Johannes Tetzel. Profits from the indulgence traffic had drastically dropped as a result of the commotion over Luther's Ninety-five Theses. Before long Luther's writings were publicly burned in Mainz as they had been in Cologne.

A short distance upriver from Mainz is the small city of Worms, best remembered for the meeting of the imperial Diet that took place there in 1521. On that occasion Luther had taken his stand and bound his conscience to the Word of God. When Tyndale arrived in Worms five years later, he found there a hospitable setting for the completion of his English New Testament project. Peter Schöffer, a

---

[4]See David Daniell, *William Tyndale: A Biography* (New Haven: Yale University Press, 1994), pp. 108-33.

nephew of Johannes from the same printing dynasty, saw this work through the press early in 1526. As soon as the spring thaw allowed traffic on the river to resume, several thousand copies of Tyndale's masterpiece were making the reverse journey down the Rhine, slipping past Cologne and on to the North Sea, as contraband headed for England. The loose sheets of the printed text were bundled into separate packages and hidden away in bales of cloth and other wares to be reassembled and bound once they had been safely smuggled into England.

Tyndale was an absolute genius with the English language, and this comes through in many of his phrases that have passed into subsequent versions of the English Bible: "A city that is set on a hill cannot be hid . . . but Mary kept all those things and pondered them in her heart . . . let not your heart be troubled . . . and when they were come to the place which is called Calvary, there they crucified him . . . finally, my brethren be strong in the Lord, and the power of his might."[5] Tyndale's influence on the development of the English language has been underrated by most scholars. Without Tyndale would we have had Shakespeare, or Bunyan, or Milton? Clearly we would not have had the King James Version of the Bible, for some 90 percent of the English Bible Tyndale was able to complete before his death was taken over into the Authorized Version of 1611.

Since the Middle Ages, Worms had been the center of a thriving Jewish community. Worms, and many other cities along the Rhine, have also tragically witnessed persecution and pogroms against the Jews from the age of the Crusades through the time of Hitler. Today one can still see in Worms the ruins of a synagogue dating back before the age of the Reformation. It is possible that Tyndale learned, or at least perfected, his knowledge of Hebrew from Jewish rabbis he

---

[5]These and other examples are cited by Daniell, *Tyndale*, pp. 135-39.

met at Worms. In 1530 he published an English translation of the Pentateuch that was printed in Antwerp. His translation of the remaining books of the Old Testament was interrupted by his betrayal and arrest. He was executed in 1536.

Figure 7.1. William Tyndale was first garroted and then his body was burned at Vilvorde Castle near Brussels in 1536. According to John Foxe, the last words he uttered were, "Lord, open the King of England's eyes."

One of the last letters we have from the pen of William Tyndale comes from his imprisonment in Vilvorde Castle near Brussels, where he awaited the final judicial proceedings that would end in his death. This letter is one of the great documents of the Reformation, for it reveals the humanity of a superb scholar, one who was forced to work on the run and who, until the end, was single-mindedly devoted to the one great passion of his life, the translation of the Scriptures into his native tongue. Tyndale wrote these words to the official in charge of the castle where he was kept in his final days:

I beg your lordship, and that by the Lord Jesus, that if I am to remain here through the winter, you will request the commissary to have the kindness to send me, from the goods of mine which he has, a warmer cap; for I suffer greatly from cold in the head, and am afflicted by a perpetual catarrh, which is much increased in this cell; a warmer coat also, for this which I have is very thin; a piece of cloth too to patch my leggings. My overcoat is worn out; my shirts are also worn out. He has a woolen shirt, if he will be good enough to send it. I have also with him leggings of thicker cloth to put on above; he has also warmer nightcaps. And I ask to be allowed to have a lamp in the evening; it is indeed wearisome sitting alone in the dark. But most of all I beg and beseech your clemency to be urgent with the commissary, that he will kindly permit me to have the Hebrew Bible, Hebrew grammar, and Hebrew dictionary, that I may pass the time in that study. In return may you obtain what you most desire, so only that it be for the salvation of your soul. But if any other decision has been taken concerning me, to be carried out before winter, I will be patient, abiding the will of God, to the glory of the grace of my Lord Jesus Christ: whose spirit (I pray) may ever direct your heart. Amen. W. Tindalus.[6]

The Jewish connection in Worms may also have played a role in the translation of the Old Testament prophets published there in 1527 by Hans Denck and Ludwig Hetzer, leaders of the early Anabaptist-Spiritualist movement. Luther criticized "the Worms

---

[6]This is J. F. Mozley's English translation of Tyndale's Latin text as cited in Daniell, *Tyndale*, p. 379. Daniell also gives John Foxe's well-known description of Tyndale's death and his famous last words: "At last, after much reasoning, when no reason would serve, although he deserved no death, he was condemned by virtue of the emperor's decree . . . and, upon the same, brought forth to the place of execution, was there tied to the stake, and then strangled first by the hangman, and afterwards with fire consumed. In the morning at the town of Vilvorde, A.D. 1536: crying thus at the stake with a fervent zeal, and a loud voice, 'Lord! Open the king of England's eyes' " (ibid., pp. 382-83).

Prophets" because of their faulty theology, but their work was re-printed several times. As Luther's translation of the prophets had not yet been completed, the Denck-Hetzer translation became a part of several combined Bibles. The Zurich Bible of 1530 was one of these. With slight adjustments for the Swiss German dialect, it brought together in one binding the first parts of Luther's transla-tion of the Old Testament, Denck and Hetzer's Prophets, a transla-tion of the Apocrypha by Leo Jud and Luther's revised New Testa-ment.[7] A similar composite translation was published in Strasbourg at about the same time.

Strasbourg, a free imperial city since 1262, is located on the Ill River near its entrance into the Rhine. At the time of the Reforma-tion Strasbourg had a population of twenty-five thousand people. Situated on the axis of north-south, east-west trade routes, Stras-bourg was a dominant urban presence in the upper Rhine region commanding the territory between the Vosges Mountains and the Black Forest as well as the surrounding area from below Colmar to the south and beyond Hagenau in the north. Geographically, Stras-bourg was an important border city between France and Germany, but it also straddled the theological boundary between Rome and Wittenberg, and between Lutherans and the Swiss Reformed. Mar-tin Bucer, the city's leading reformer, was indefatigable in his efforts to bring opposing sides together even as the religious divides grew wider. Within the Protestant movement, Bucer played an important mediating role between the Swiss Reformed churches to the south and the Lutheran world to the north, especially in the church-dividing disputes over the Eucharist both before and after the Col-loquy of Marburg in 1529.

---

[7]See John L. Flood, "The Book in Reformation Germany," in *The Reformation and the Book*, ed. Jean-François Gilmont (Aldershot: Ashgate, 1998), pp. 71-72. On Denck and Hetzer, see George H. Williams, *Radical Reformation* (Kirksville, Mo.: Sixteenth Century Journal Publishers, 1992), p. 1243.

How did Strasbourg become a city of the Reformation? In the fall of 1523, Bucer, a former Dominican monk, submitted to the governing authorities a twelve-point statement of Protestant beliefs. He boldly declared that the Bible was "the first and main article of the new theology" and the "singular norm, rule, and guideline" in all matters related to religion and church life.[8] In his appeal to the city council, Bucer presented *sola scriptura* as a unifying platform among all the German reformers—he mentioned Luther, Melanchthon, Karlstadt and Zwingli. However, by the late 1530s, Bucer's early optimistic prognosis of Protestant unity based on the Bible alone looked rather different. Karlstadt had been expelled from Wittenberg. Zwingli had died in battle leaving behind the bitter fruits of his unreconciled differences with Luther over the Lord's Supper. Melanchthon was at the center of an increasingly bitter family quarrel among the Lutherans. Most of the Anabaptists were in disarray, still haunted by the memories of Mühlhausen and Münster.[9] All of these splinters made the evangelical cause even more precarious in the years leading up to the Council of Trent. Bucer and other evangelical reformers soon learned that the establishment of a Bible-based reformation required more than the announcement of a formal principle of scriptural authority. It was necessary to see what the Bible taught and how it could be applied both to the reform of the church and the renewal

---

[8]Bucer's summary of Protestant beliefs is cited by Steven E. Ozment, *The Reformation in the Cities* (New Haven: Yale University Press, 1975), p. 146. The German text is found in *Martin Bucer's Deutsche Scriften*, 1:83.

[9]After breaking with Martin Luther, Thomas Müntzer became the pastor of the Church of Saint Mary in Mühlhausen, a free imperial city in Thuringia with a population of seventy-five hundred people. Seeing himself as Gideon (Judg 6–8) leading the soldiers of the Lord in battle against the enemies of God's people, Müntzer was caught up in the apocalyptic conclusion of the bloody Peasants' War and decapitated outside the walls of Mühlhausen. Münster was a city in northwest Germany where, in 1534, John of Leiden had established by force an Anabaptist kingdom with himself as king. The truly radical nature of this social experiment—forced rebaptisms, the abolition of private property and the practice of polygamy—aroused both Catholic and Protestant rulers who united their armed forces to restore order in 1536, one of the few successful ecumenical endeavors of the sixteenth century!

of civic life. Such a commitment to Scripture required a steady program of preaching, the establishment of institutions of higher learning and the creation of published resources, especially liturgies, catechisms (Bucer wrote three of these) and biblical commentaries.

Bucer arrived in Strasbourg in 1523 as an excommunicated ex-
Dominican. He was unemployed and recently married—like Luther
he took as his wife a runaway nun, Elizabeth Silbereisen. The new-
lyweds lived for a while in the home of Matthias Zell, a priest in the
cathedral parish. In late 1521 Zell began to preach a series of sermons on Paul's letter to the Romans. Zell also publicly defended
Luther and called into question traditional Catholic beliefs about
Mary, purgatory and the saints. For some, his preaching crossed the
line when he moved from these general ideas and began to attack the
immorality and ignorance of the local clergy. But Zell's sermons attracted hundreds of listeners who filled the nave of Strasbourg's cathedral and demanded that their favorite preacher be given access to
the main pulpit. When this was denied, some local carpenters on
their own initiative constructed a wooden pulpit that they wheeled
in and out of the cathedral after every sermon as a preaching station
for Zell.

The agitation around Zell's preaching paved the way for Strasbourg's embrace of the Reformation, although the adoption of Protestant ways was gradual and the Catholic mass continued to be celebrated until 1529. Zell's reforming work was boosted not only by
Bucer but also by the great Hebrew scholar Wolfgang Capito and his
protégé Caspar Hedio, who became the main preacher in the cathedral in late 1523. The Reformation in Strasbourg also attracted the
support of Jakob Sturm, the chief magistrate of the city who, according to one scholar, was "the most remarkable and influential urban
politician of his day in the Holy Roman Empire."[10]

---

[10]Thomas A. Brady Jr., "Jakob Sturm," *OER* 4:121-22.

Matthias Zell did not lack courage. He preached against enforced clerical celibacy and, to back up his words with a deed, presided at the wedding of Anton Firn, one of the first Strasbourg priests to get married. Zell defended his action on the basis of Scripture. When God said that it was not good for man to be alone (Gen 2:18), no exemption was given for those in holy orders. In December 1523, Zell decided to take matters a step further. He himself married Katarina Schütz, the daughter of a master carpenter, perhaps one of those who helped to provide Zell's makeshift pulpit a few months earlier. Zell was a public figure, and his defiant act drew the ire of the local bishop, who threatened to expel him from the ministry. At this point his new bride came to his defense. Katarina published (without her husband's knowledge, she said) a pamphlet that was as much an attack on the bishop as it was a justification of their decision to get married. This little work, *An Apology . . . for Her Husband, Matthias Zell*, revealed a quick mind and a sharp pen. Why had the bishop attacked married clergy with such vehemence? Perhaps it was because he could extract more money from certain monks and priests who were willing to pay a fee for the privilege of keeping a concubine (she used the word *whore*) than he would be able to collect from those who wished to live together properly in marriage? Moreover, she said, the bishops and church leaders "all condemn married priests, but none of them attack the worst sin of all, sodomy, which they have conspired to protect."[11]

Katarina outlived her husband, at whose funeral she spoke along with Bucer in 1548. Over the course of her long life, she proved herself to be a true mother of the church in Strasbourg. She had been converted to the evangelical cause by reading the early writings of Martin Luther and became one of his many correspondents. After the breakdown of the unity talks on the Lord's Supper at the

---

[11]Cited by Paul A. Russell, *Lay Theology and the Reformation: Popular Pamphleteers in Southwest Germany, 1521-1525* (Cambridge: Cambridge University Press, 1986), p. 205.

Colloquy of Marburg, she wrote to Luther and admonished him to open his heart more widely in love for those with whom he differed over the meaning of the sacrament of the altar. She interpreted Paul's expression about "discerning the body" (1 Cor 11:29) as a reference to the love believers should have one for another within the body of Christ. Katarina Zell was a south German counterpart to Luther's own beloved Katarina, another woman who could teach the great doctor a thing or two in matters theological, though perhaps her method of instruction was more indirect than that of Sister Zell of Strasbourg.

Lorna Jane Abray has noted that "Katarina Zell took on all the duties of an early modern pastor's wife: keeping a household; acting as hostess to visiting dignitaries (including, in Zell's case, Johannes Oecolampadius and Huldrych Zwingli); and visiting the sick, the pregnant and newly delivered, and the imprisoned."[12] Beyond these important duties, however, she also maintained a public career unparalleled by any other female Protestant leader in the Reformation. For example, in addition to defending her husband and their marriage against the bishop, she wrote a letter of consolation to women whose husbands were facing persecution because of their evangelical commitment. She spoke out bravely on behalf of the Anabaptists and presided at the funerals of several followers of Schwenckfeld who had been refused this pastoral service by the regular clergy because of their ties to the radical reformer. She was also a great believer in hymn singing and edited a set of four hymnbooks. Singing, she believed, was to be done not only in formal church services but also amid the responsibilities of everyday life:

> [Teach your household] to know that they do not serve human beings but God when they faithfully [in the faith] keep house, obey, cook, wash dishes, wipe up and tend children, and such

---

[12]Lorna Jane Abray, "Katarina Zell," *OER* 4:309.

like work which serves human life, and that (while doing this very work) they can also turn toward God with a voice of song. And teach them that in doing this, they please God much better than any priest, monk, or nun in their incomprehensible choir song.[13]

When criticized for not keeping silent in church matters, as the traditional understanding of Paul's teaching required, she appealed to the text in Joel 2:28 about the gift of prophecy being given to daughters as well as to sons, and she identified herself with Mary Magdalene as a public proclaimer of the risen Christ.

Katarina Zell was an exceptional person in many ways, but her devotion to the Scriptures and to the practical outworking of the Christian faith exemplified the lay theology that thrived in the Reformed cities along the Rhine. Elsie McKee has described how the Bible was appropriated by lay theologians such as Katarina Zell.

Some lay theologians . . . demonstrated considerable skill in using biblical texts as the grounds of intellectually developed and thoughtful presentations. They knew their bibles well enough to fit together the specific text that shaped their ideas into coherent and often very persuasive arguments. Many of these patterns no doubt had their origin in sermons or pamphlets by clergy, but the lay appropriation is rarely wooden. It is

---

[13]Katarina Schütz Zell, *Church Mother: The Writings of a Protestant Reformer in Sixteenth-Century Germany*, ed. Elsie McKee (Chicago: University of Chicago Press, 2006), p. 95. McKee offers this evaluation of Katarina's contribution to Reformation hymnody: "Close examination of Katarina Schütz Zell's hymnbook edition reveals a rather remarkable project for the reform of piety in sixteenth-century Strasbourg, by one imaginative, astute, and determined lay reformer. . . . Her objective was to fill a pressing need for appropriately reformed devotional works. She wanted to displace old unacceptable songs and texts with wholesome, saving knowledge of true biblical teaching conveyed in attractive hymns and melodies, and illumined with notes to aid ordinary Christians in exhorting themselves, their households, and their neighbors." Elsie McKee, "Reforming Popular Piety in Sixteenth-Century Strasbourg: Katarina Schütz Zell and Her Hymnbook," *Studies in Reformed Theology and History* 2 (1994): 61.

sometimes quite creative and usually offers a distinctive lay angle of vision.[14]

"The Freedom of a Christian," one of Luther's early writings read by the young Katarina Schütz even before her marriage to Mathias Zell, set forth the principle of the priesthood of all believers based on 1 Peter 2:9. Martin Bucer, who had become a devoted "Martinian" after first meeting Luther at Heidelberg in 1518, built his own reforming work on this premise. Every Christian should be able to read the Bible and consider its claims. Indeed, every person, Bucer said, should "examine his own faith under the direction of the Scriptures and by the aid of the Spirit, so that all may enjoy fullness of conviction and remain faithful to the Gospel and to the confession of Christ."[15] Yet such unfettered access to the Scriptures did not obviate the need for biblical scholars and learned teachers. The church at Strasbourg was certainly blessed to have a master interpreter of the Bible of Bucer's stature as its guiding spirit. By 1529 Bucer had published commentaries on all four of the Gospels as well as Ephesians, Zephaniah and the Psalms. His commentary on Romans was published in 1536. In the dedicatory epistle to his own commentary on Romans, written while he enjoyed Bucer's company in Strasbourg, Calvin gave this glowing description of his friend's biblical work:

> Bucer has spoken the last word, as it were, by his published expositions. As you know, in addition to his profound learning, abundant knowledge of many subjects, sharpness of intellect, wide reading and many other diverse strengths, in which is surpassed today by hardly anyone and matched by few and excels most, this scholar enjoys the special credit of devoting himself

---

[14]Elsie McKee, "The Emergence of Lay Theologies," in *Reformation Christianity*, ed. Peter Matheson (Minneapolis: Fortress, 2007), p. 226.

[15]*Common Places of Martin Bucer*, ed. David F. Wright (Appleford, U.K.: Sutton Courtenay Press, 1972), p. 76.

to the interpretation of Scripture with more dedicated exactitude than anyone else in our time.

Not to be accused of flattery, however, Calvin added a qualifying note. Bucer, he said, is "too verbose to be read quickly by people preoccupied with other responsibilities, and too sublime to be capable of being easily understood by unpretentious readers lacking concentration. For whatever the subject-matter he sets himself to expound, so many things are suggested to his pen by the incredible fertility of his powerful mind that he does not know how to stop writing."[16]

Why was Bucer so devoted to the detailed exegesis of the Bible? In his Gospel commentaries he gave an answer to this question that could well be applied to the commentary work of most all of the reformers. His aim, Bucer said, was to encourage those new in the faith or inexperienced in sound theology "to understand each of the words and actions of Christ, and in their proper order as far as possible, and to retain an explanation of them in their natural meaning, so that they will not distort God's Word through age-old aberrations or by inept interpretation, but rather, with a faithful comprehension of everything as written by the Spirit of God, they may expound all to the churches, to their firm upbuilding in faith and love."[17] In order to carry out this purpose, on one occasion Bucer engaged in a "pious fraud" (*pius dolus*). He published his commentary on Psalms under a false name, Aretius Felinus. This made-up character presented himself as a humanist scholar from Lyon. So successful was this ruse that even Johann Eck was deceived, for he admitted that he had consulted Felinus in his own study of Psalm 20. But it was hard to keep the cat in the bag, and the 1564 Index, established at the Council of Trent, correctly identified Felinus with Bucer.[18]

---

[16]CNTC 8:2-3, and D. F. Wright, "Martin Bucer," in *Dictionary of Major Biblical Interpreters*, ed. Donald K. McKim (Downers Grove, Ill.: InterVarsity Press, 2007), pp. 248-49.

[17]Wright, "Martin Bucer," p. 250.

[18]The story of the "pious fraud" is told by R. Gerald Hobbs, "How Firm a Foundation: Martin

Of all the mainline reformers, none was more suspicious of allegorical exegesis than Bucer. He recognized, of course, that Paul used the word *allegory* as a way of connecting the New Testament people of God with the prophetic foreshadowings of the gospel in the old covenant (Gal 4:24). But this precedent, Bucer insisted, should not be used by interpreters as a license to turn Scripture into a nose of wax or, to change the metaphor, to squeeze the udder until blood gushes forth instead of milk.[19]

The approach taken to the Bible in Strasbourg by Bucer, Capito and the other reformers there placed a high premium on the Erasmian program of *ad fontes*. In fact, they emphasized Hebrew studies more than Erasmus ever did. Bucer once declared that he could even see the day approaching when Hebrew would be universally spoken as the lingua franca in every Christian city. He based this hope on Isaiah 19:18, "On that day five cities in the land of Egypt will speak the language of Canaan and swear loyalty to the Lord of hosts," a worthy goal based perhaps on a faulty eschatology.

Thus Strasbourg in the 1520s and 1530s witnessed a confluence of two major streams in Reformation thinking about the Bible. On the one hand, the humanist program of sacred philology advanced by Erasmus, Reuchlin, and other scholars became a central tenet for reform in both church and academy. But, at the same time, the bub-

---

Bucer's Historical Exegesis of the Psalms," *Church History* 53 (December 1984): 477-91.

[19]This image, like that of the nose of wax, comes from the Middle Ages in which the peril of excessive allegorizing was recognized by scholars who valued the literal sense of the text, notably Thomas Aquinas and Nicholas of Lyra. See Hobbs, "How Firm a Foundation," p. 483. Above all, Bucer was intent on reading the Scripture, especially the Psalms, within the historical context of its original composition, though he was well aware that there were many figures and types of Christ in the Old Testament. Capito, Bucer's Strasbourg colleague, shared his concern about the danger of over-allegorizing the Bible: "Unless the historical has by the Spirit's help faithfully set the foundations in place, whatsoever reflection is built upon them will collapse and ruin, as it meanders about in uncertain passages making itself a laughing stock with its allegories!" This is from Capito's 1526 *Commentary on Habakkuk*, cited by Hobbs, "How Firm a Foundation," p. 483. See also James Kittelson, *Wolfgang Capito: From Humanist to Reformer* (Leiden: Brill, 1975).

bling up of lay theologies based on the priesthood of all believers made the evangelical message a living option, for common folks as well as for society's movers and shakers. This meant that the Bible would not be the only religious work translated into the vernacular. Commentaries, homilies, liturgies, works of devotion along with

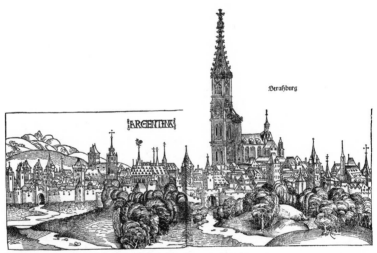

Figure 7.2. The cityscape of Strasbourg at the time of the Reformation, with the prominent Strasbourg Cathedral de Notre-Dame where Mathias Zell preached from a portable pulpit in the 1520s.

theological treatises and collected letters of the major reformers would become a part of an expanding literature evangelical of spiritual life. In this way, the Reformation promoted a new spiritual theology (if not a "new" church) for the newly lettered and the barely literate no less than for the learned elites of church and academy.

Bucer was a strong-willed reformer, and his scriptural interpretations often clashed with those of other colleagues and scholars. But Bucer sincerely wanted to read the Bible in the company of the entire church across the centuries. He could be humble as well as bold. This trait comes through in his desire to set forth a pattern of evangelical exegesis between what Gerald Hobbs has called "the equally unacceptable alternatives of individualism and a papal magisterium." In this statement, Bucer states his belief that Bible study is best done in the context of the entire community of faith.

> Lest I should be peddling my own comments for gifts of God, I wish to have affirmed nothing at all that the common consensus of the orthodox does not receive . . . accordingly I submit whatever I have written in this work [his 1529 commentary on Psalms] to the judgment and censure not only of the leaders of the church, not only of the professors of sacred theology, but precisely of all Christians . . . whatever is such that it conflicts with the Word of God, with the decrees of the holy Church of God, and with the opinions of the orthodox fathers, I wish, I command, I require to be taken as condemned and withdrawn.[20]

Strasbourg became a meeting place and a melting pot for numerous reformers, refugees and dissidents of nearly every stripe in the early Reformation. George H. Williams refers to "the variegated company of sectaries and seekers" who flocked to Strasbourg in the late 1520s and 1530s.[21] We have already met the millennialist prophet Melchior Hoffman, who was imprisoned by the city authorities because they feared that his date setting for the return of Christ based on his interpretation of the book of Revelation could lead to civil unrest. Kaspar Schwenckfeld was a Silesian nobleman by background and found greater acceptance than the hotheaded Hoffman. Schwenckfeld emphasized the invisible church, and the inner workings of the Spirit, more than the externals of water baptism, a physical Eucharist and public preaching. Nonetheless, Schwenckfeld regularly attended services of worship in Strasbourg's great cathedral. He

[20]R. Gerald Hobbs, "Pluriformity of Early Reformation Scriptural Interpretation," in *Hebrew Bible/Old Testament*, ed. Magne Sæbø (Göttingen: Vandenhoeck & Ruprecht, 2008), p. 466.
[21]Williams, *Radical Reformation*, p. 264.

stood directly beneath the pulpit with his hand cupping his ear because he was hard of hearing and did not want to miss a single word of the sermon. Pilgram Marpeck was a mining engineer and found work with the city of Strasbourg while preaching in house churches to a growing number of the city's Anabaptists. The presence of these and other radical reformers made Strasbourg a hotbed of new ideas and public debates.

A refugee of a different stripe was John Calvin. He spent three of the happiest years of his life in Strasbourg following his expulsion from Geneva in 1538. While based there, Calvin preached to a congregation of fellow French-speaking refugees, published his first biblical commentary (on Romans in 1540), taught in the newly-formed academy and participated with Bucer and others in theological conversations with Catholic leaders. He also married Idelette de Bure, the widow of a former Anabaptist convert in his congregation.

In the early sixteenth century, Basel was the center of a kind of Swiss renaissance. Its university attracted students throughout the region including Huldrych Zwingli, who received his master of arts degree there in 1506. Renowned artists such as Hans Holbein the Younger made Basel their home, as did some of the best-known publishing houses in Europe—Amerbach, Petri and Froben. Above all, Basel was the adopted hometown of Erasmus, who came here in 1514 to work on his Greek New Testament and became a permanent resident in 1521. Around the Dutch humanist gathered a cadre of brilliant scholars, proofreaders and illustrators. Chief among this group were Johannes Reuchlin, Beatus Rhenanus, Ulrich von Hutten, Wolfgang Capito and Heinricus Glareanus.

Also closely connected to Erasmus was Melanchthon's friend from their student days at Tübingen, Johannes Oecolampadius. Erasmus was a great scholar but a poor proofreader, and Oecolampadius saved him from a number of errors in the first edition of the Greek New Testament. Oecolampadius also had a hand in the critical notes and commentary to the New Testament, as well as Erasmus's nine-volume edition of Jerome's writings. The next phase in the career of Oecolampadius is somewhat mysterious, or at least it came as a surprise to many of his friends. After accepting the post of cathedral preacher in Augsburg, Oecolampadius suddenly withdrew from public life and entered the Birgitten Monastery at Altenmünster in 1520. Robert C. Walton has suggested that "the reason for his decision was his intellectual turmoil caused by the radicalization of the younger members of the humanist movement and the early impact of Luther's writings. Oecomlampadius sought a quiet retreat to read the church fathers and Luther."[22] In the 1520s, Oecolampadius resurfaced again in Basel and soon became the leading evangelical minister in the city.

For a number of years, historians have recognized that the Reformation in the cities of southern Germany and Switzerland had their own "urban agenda," which resulted in a different shape and pace of religious change than one sees in the Lutheran territories in the north.[23] The city reformers in the south were able to tap into "a late medieval corporate identity that led these towns to see themselves as Christian communes." The evangelical movement was often met with a friendly response by the local guilds and town councils, which were seeking to expand their freedoms against the established authorities of emperor, king and bishop. The reformation in Basel was shaped by similar developments, though there the support of the city magistrates for religious change was reluctant and halting, one might al-

---

[22]Robert C. Walton, "Johannes Oecomlampadius," *OER* 3:170.

[23]The expression "urban agenda" comes from Scott H. Hendrix, *Recultivating the Vineyard: The Reformation Agendas of Christianization* (Louisville, Ky.: Westminster John Knox, 2004). There is a vast literature on the Reformation and the cities, but of seminal importance are these studies: Bernd Moeller, *Imperial Cities and the Reformation: Three Essays*, ed. and trans. H. C. Erik Midelfort and Mark U. Edwards Jr. (Philadelphia: Fortress, 1972); Steven E. Ozment, *The Reformation in the Cities: The Appeal of Protestantism through Sixteenth-Century Germany and Switzerland* (New Haven: Yale University Press, 1975); Berndt Hamm, "The Urban Reformation in the Holy Roman Empire," in *Handbook of European History, 1400-1600*, ed. Thomas A. Brady Jr., Heiko A. Oberman and James D. Tracy (Grand Rapids: Eerdmans, 1996), 2:193-227.

most say Erasmian. This is a different pattern from the one that one sees, for example, in Zurich, where the governing authorities early on became major promoters of Zwingli and the evangelical insurgents. In an attempt to tone down the religious rhetoric in the city, the town council issued a mandate in 1523 requiring that all preachers "proclaim the Gospel according to the Scriptures" while avoiding discussion about other doctrines.[24] While this injunction has a evangelical ring to it, it represents a more cautious approach to church reform, and a different understanding of the role of the Bible in that process, than the more committed evangelicals in Basel were hoping for.

Their view was well summarized in the first two articles of "The Ten Conclusions of Bern," from a disputation in 1528 in which both Zwingli and Oecolampadius took part:

1. The holy Christian church, whose only head is Christ, is born of the Word of God, and abides in the same, and listens not to the voice of a stranger.

2. The church of Christ makes no laws or commandments apart from the Word of God; hence all human traditions are not binding upon us accept so far as they are grounded upon or prescribed in the Word of God.[25]

The difference between the Bern statement and the proposal of the Basel council might be compared with the Golden Rule as given by Jesus, "Do unto others as you would have them do unto you," and the more common variant of this maxim found in other ancient texts, "Do not do to others what you would not have them do to you." The advocates of a hot-gospel reform of the church in Basel had little sympathy with the more measured, halting approach advocated by the city fathers.

---

[24]Amy Nelson Burnett, "Basel," *OER* 1:125.
[25]"The Ten Conclusions of Bern," in *Creeds of the Churches*, ed. John H. Leith (Atlanta: John Knox Press, 1982), pp. 129-30.

In the meantime, a growing sector of Basel's population began to agitate for immediate change. The result was urban revolution on a scale not yet seen in any other Swiss city. The Catholics on the city council were ousted from office, the mass was abolished, the university was closed (it would reopen as a Protestant institution in 1532), the canons of the cathedral chapter were sent packing. These major changes were triggered by a dramatic event that took place on February 9, 1529. On that day, some two hundred Basel residents attacked the cathedral and then other parish churches in the city. With axes and hammers in hand, they destroyed the most visible symbols of Catholic devotion. Altarpieces and rood screens were dismantled, statues of venerated saints were smashed to pieces, and crucifixes, reliquaries, chalices and other sacred objects were desecrated.[26] Iconoclasm was a common phenomenon in the early years of the Reformation, though it took a more violent turn in Basel than elsewhere. In Zurich, for example, the images in the churches were removed in an orderly way behind closed doors, and the colorful religious paintings on the church walls were whitewashed at the behest of the local authorities.

What was behind such acts? The preachers and their supporters who believed that the churches should be "cleansed" of the visual symbols of medieval Catholicism appealed to the Bible's prohibition of images in Exodus 4:6 and Leviticus 5:8-10. The "graven images" forbidden in the Ten Commandments were no different, they believed, from the statues and sacred objects so prominent in the most of the churches of Europe. Oecolampadius, Zwingli and later Calvin all argued that such objects were in fact treated by the common people as though they were "little gods" (*götzen*) or idols. In the years

---

[26]Lee Palmer Wandel has placed the rampage in Basel in the context of other iconoclastic episodes associated with the Reformation. See his *Voracious Idols and Violent Hands: Iconoclasm in Reformation Zurich, Strasbourg, and Basel* (Cambridge: Cambridge University Press, 1994), esp. pp. 148-89. See also Carlos M. N. Eire, "Iconoclasm," *OER* 2:302-6.

leading up to the Basel revolution, Oecolampadius gave a series of lectures on the book of Isaiah that was published as a commentary in 1525. Drawing on his knowledge of both the Hebrew text and the Greek Septuagint, Oecolampadius joined his voice with that of the ancient prophet in decrying idolatry as the great sin of humanity. Zwingli had made a similar protest against images and other forms of ceremonial piety prevalent in the church at Zurich.

What was the upshot of all this? The removal of paintings, statues and even musical instruments, including the organs, must have had a profound impact on those who worshipped in the church week after week. The sanctuary was turned into an auditorium, a space more attuned to the ear than the eye, more suited for listening to talks than for contemplating mysteries. Johann Eck spoke for many Catholics, and no doubt for some Protestants as well, when he said of the Swiss reformers: "They no longer have churches but rather stables."[27] However, in his *Commentary on Isaiah*, first published in 1550, Calvin echoed the themes of Oecolampadius and laid bare the deepest Protestant concern about images. In his exposition of Isaiah 44:10, "Who is the maker of God?" Calvin wrote of the folly of trying to "manufacture gods" that those who set up images in the churches do despite their protest to the contrary.

> They will say that this never entered into anyone's mind, and that injustice is done to them when they are accused of so great madness; just as the papists in the present day say that we slander them, when we employ these arguments of the prophet against them. But in vain do they rely on their sophistical reasonings for avoiding this charge. What the prophet says is most true, that they are so mad as to think that they "make God"; for as soon as the stone or wood has been carved or polished, they

---

[27]Samuel M. Jackson, ed., *The Latin Works of Huldreich Zwingli* (New York: Knickerbocker Press, 1912), 2:66.

ascribe to it divinity, run to it, make prayers, call upon it, and prostrate themselves before it, and in short, ascribe to it those things which they know belong to God alone.[28]

Nearly all of the leaders of the Reformed communities had been disciples of Erasmus. Their fear of placing too much trust in things external owed something to the great humanist's contempt for the unreasonable, the ritualistic and the superstitious. But Erasmus had an aversion to disturbances of any kind, and he must have felt increasingly isolated and forlorn living at Basel in the 1520s as the moderate middle way of reform he preferred gave way to a more radical outcome than he could abide. He once described his life as "an Iliad of calamities, a chain of misfortunes. How can anyone envy *me?*"[29] Like an aged Ulysses seeking shelter from the storms of life, Erasmus made plans to seek refuge at Freiburg im Breisgau, a Rhineland city still in Catholic hands between Basel and Strasbourg. He and Oecolampadius said farewell with a handshake. A crowd of admirers turned out to see him off at the Rhine Bridge. Erasmus came back to Basel once more, this time to die there in 1536. He lies buried in the cathedral that was rocked by the image smashers of 1529.

At about 70 kilometers upstream from Basel, at an important ford in the Rhine, one comes to the town of Waldshut. At the time of the Reformation, Waldshut was in Hapsburg hands under the jurisdiction of Ferdinand, archduke of Austria, though it aspired to join the Swiss Confederation across the river. When I visited Waldshut several years ago, I noticed that one of the major public buildings was decorated with a large painting of a leather shoe, the kind that was typically worn by peasants in the late Middle Ages. This symbol recalled the fact that Waldshut was an important center of the *Bund-*

---

[28]CC 8:370.
[29]Johann Huizinga, *Erasmus and the Age of Reformation* (New York: Harper & Row, 1924), p. 125.

schuh, the League of the Shoe, an association of peasants and urban dissidents that turned the long-brewing cauldron of social unrest into an open revolt in the German Peasants' War (1524-1526).

In Waldshut one can also visit today a German Baptist church. Contemporary German Baptists trace their rise to the mission work of Johann Gerhard Oncken, a Baptist pastor and church planter in the nineteenth century. However, there are similarities if not a genetic connection between Baptists today and the Anabaptist movement during the Reformation. For example, the Baptist church in Waldshut today practices baptism by immersion, a ritual reserved for those who make a public confession of their faith in Christ. They also believe in religious freedom and deny that the state has authority to impose religious conformity of any kind on its citizens. They also teach that the local congregation should have the right to choose its own pastor. This last point was also made in the first of the Twelve Articles circulated among the peasants in their uprising of 1525. Because of its geography and social context, Waldshut was ripe for the ministry of Balthasar Hubmaier, who led the Waldshuters to embrace the Reformation just as the Peasants' War was entering its most violent phase.

Hubmaier has been called "the Doctor of Anabaptism" because he was the only leader of the movement who was also a scholastically trained theologian. Hubmaier became a doctor of theology at the University of Ingolstadt in 1512, the same year Brother Martin was made Dr. Luther at Wittenberg. A protégé of Eck, Hubmaier began to read Luther's writings and later embraced many of Zwingli's ideas. In his *Christian Catechism* (1526), one of the first such documents of the Reformation, Hubmaier pointed out that his high training in scholastic theology had failed to equip him to be a teacher of God's Word.

In order to confess my own ignorance with my own blushes, I

say without subterfuge, and God knows I am not lying, that I
became a doctor in the holy scriptures (as this sophistry was
called), and still did not understand the Christian articles contained here in this booklet. Yes, and at that time I had never
read a Gospel, or an epistle by Paul, from beginning to end.
What kind of a Holy Word could I then teach others or preach
to them? Of course: Thomas, Scotus, Gabriel, Occam, decree,
decretals, legends of the saints and other scholastics. These
were previously our hellish scriptures.[30]

From his base at Waldshut, Hubmaier traveled to Basel on several
occasions and met with Erasmus and Oecomlampadius, both of
whom influenced his changing views, especially about the sacraments. He later claimed that on one occasion Zwingli had even expressed agreement with his view that baptism should be administered
only to those who had repented of their sins and made a personal
commitment to follow Christ, though Zwingli said that Hubmaier
had misunderstood what he meant. In his debate with Hubmaier
over baptism, Zwingli resorted to the standard argument that the
baptism of infants was nowhere forbidden in the Scriptures and thus
should continue to be practiced in keeping with the longstanding tradition of the church. Hubmaier thought little of this argument and
replied, "But that it is not written explicitly: 'Do not baptize them,' to
this I answer: Then I may also baptize my dog and my donkey."[31] In
the Great Commission in Matthew 28:19-20, Jesus instructed his
disciples to go into all the world and make disciples, to baptize them
in the name of the triune God and to instruct them in all the teach-

---

[30]H. Wayne Pipkin and John H. Yoder, trans. and eds., *Balthasar Hubmaier: Theologian of
Anabaptism* (Scottdale, Penn.: Herald Press, 1989), p. 343. Pipkin has reviewed recent
scholarly work on Hubmaier in *Scholar, Pastor, Martyr: The Life and Ministry of Balthasar
Hubmaier ca. 1480-1528* (Prague: International Baptist Theological Seminary, 2008). See
also James M. Stayer, "Balthasar Hubmaier," *OER* 2:260-63.
[31]Pipkin and Yoder, *Hubmaier*, p. 136.

ings of Christ. In giving these marching orders to the church, Hubmaier contended, Jesus not only had told his followers what to do but also had also given a prioritized ordering in which these things should be done: first, evangelize; second, baptize; and, third, catechize.

Even before he became an Anabaptist, Hubmaier devised an alternative service of infant dedication for the parents of the newly born in Waldshut. He thought that the postponement of baptism would be more in keeping with the Protestant principle of justification by faith alone. In a letter to Oecolampadius, he described his infant dedication ritual, though at this point he was still willing to baptize the child if the parents insisted:

> Instead of baptism, I have the church come together, bring the infant in, explain in German the Gospel, "they brought little children" (Matthew 19:13). When a name is given it, the whole church prays for the child on bended knees and commends it to Christ, that he will be gracious and intercede for it. But if the parents are still weak, and positively wish that the child be baptized, then I baptize it; and I am weak with the weak for the time being until they can be better instructed. As to the Word, however, I do not yield to them in the least point.[32]

As Hubmaier's ideas on baptism and church life continued to evolve, several radical disciples of Zwingli, led by Conrad Grebel and Felix Mantz, were moving in a similar direction. They became convinced that the baptism they had received as infants was invalid and, when Zwingli could not be won over to their views, they decided to restore true baptism to believers only. This took place on January 21, 1525, as a small group of these Swiss Brethren, as they came to be called, met in the home of Mantz on Neustadtgasse, in the shadow of the Great Minster itself. Following prayer, they baptized one another,

---

[32]Cited in Williams, *Radical Reformation*, p. 230.

launching a revival movement that soon spread to Zollikon and other Swiss cities.

Wilhelm Reublin, a Zurich Anabaptist, who had established a base of ministry near Schaffhausen, brought the message of repentance, the new birth and adult baptism to Waldshut. On Easter Sunday, April 15, 1525, Reublin baptized Hubmaier and sixty other adult believers in Waldshut. In the following days, Hubmaier baptized another three hundred citizens of the city including a majority of the members of the town council. This meant that more than one-third of the city's entire population of one thousand embraced the Anabaptist reform under Hubmaier's direction. Hubmaier performed his baptisms in the town church and with the approval of the governing authorities, though, significantly, he did not use the baptismal font but rather a milk bucket he had filled with water from the fountain in the city's marketplace.

Following the mass Anabaptist baptism, Hubmaier led his congregation in celebrating the Lord's Supper. Assuming the role of Jesus, he girded himself with a towel and washed the feet of the new baptized believers before distributing the simple elements of bread and wine. Even prior to the baptism events in the spring of 1525, Hubmaier had described the Lord's Supper in words that approached Zwingli's views of the sacred meal. It was a memorial, a memorial sign, a symbol, a visible or outward emblem.[33] He gave little attention to Jesus' most-debated words about the Eucharist, "This is my body." Instead, he emphasized the sacrament of communion as an expression of Christian unity, an event that draws brothers and sisters in Christ together to proclaim the meaning of the Savior's sacrifice on the cross: "As one little kernel does not keep its own flour, but shares it with others, and a single grape does not keep its juice for itself, but shares it with others, so should we Christians also act—for we eat

---

[33]Hubmaier, "Several Theses Concerning the Mass," in Pipkin and Yoder, *Hubmaier*, pp. 72-73.

and drink unworthily from the table of Christ."[34]

The Reformation in Waldshut was intense but short-lived. Caught up in the violence of the Peasants' War, Waldshut was overrun by the Austrian armies. The mass was reinstituted and evangelical worship suppressed. By that time, Hubmaier had fled to Zurich, where he had hoped to find some succor from his old friend Zwingli. But Hubmaier's treatise, "On the Christian Baptism of Believers" published in July 1525, and his public debates with Zwingli on this subject, led to his arrest by the Zurich authorities, who were trying to keep the lid on radical violence in their city. After being tortured on the rack, Hubmaier recanted his views on baptism, was released and fled the city. The first Anabaptist execution in Zurich took place in January 1527, when Felix Mantz was drowned in the icy waters of the Limmat River. After a productive ministry in Moravia, Hubmaier was arrested by the Catholic authorities and taken in chains to Vienna, where he was burned alive at the stake on March 10, 1528. His wife, Elsbeth, whom he had met in Waldshut, stood faithfully by his side through this ordeal. Three days later she was thrown into the Danube River with a stone tied around her neck. The Hubmaiers became one of many martyr couples of the Reformation. While still in Waldshut, Hubmaier had written one of the most effective pleas for religious liberty published in the sixteenth century, "On Heretics and Those Who Burn Them." Hubmaier concluded that "the burning of heretics is an invention of the devil. Truth is unkillable."[35]

---

[34]Ibid., p. 75.

[35]Stayer, "Balthasar Hubmaier," p. 261. Hubmaier's favorite epigram, *Die wahrheit ist vntödtlich*, appeared on all of his writings. In the English translation of Hubmaier's writings prepared by Pipkin and Yoder for the Classics of the Radical Reformation series, this phrase is consistently rendered "truth is unkillable." This was Yoder's preferred translation, and it does seem to convey something significant about Hubmaier's steadfastness and courage through a life of suffering that ended in martyrdom. However, through his careful research of sixteenth-century printed and handwritten sources, Pipkin found no rendering of *vntödtlich* as "unkillable." He also points out that Hubmaier rendered this expression in Latin as *veritas est immortalis*. See the discussion in Pipkin, *Scholar, Pastor, Martyr*, pp. 103-7.

EIGHT

PREACH THE WORD

Faith cometh by hearing the word preached, then I reason thus:
No preaching, no faith; no faith, no Christ; no Christ, no eternal life. . . .
If we will have heaven, we must have Christ. If we will have Christ, we must have faith.
If we will have faith, we must have the Word preached. Then I conclude that
preaching...is of absolute necessity into eternal life.

ARTHUR DENT

T HE REFORMATION WAS A MOVEMENT OF APPLIED theology and lived Christianity. It was not anti-intellectual, but it was antiabstractionist. For the reformers, ecclesiology was never a matter of mere speculation even for those who, like Zwingli and Melanchthon, were more attuned to the modes of philosophical thought. In their exegesis and theology, they aimed to glorify God, not argue for his existence. Because truth mattered to the reformers, dogmatics could never be completely divorced from polemics, but their overriding concern was always constructive. They were more interested in edifying the faithful than in conquering the naysayers, though sometimes they found it necessary to do the latter in order to accomplish the former.

The reformers were concerned that the Bible take deep root in the lives of the people they were called to serve. The Word of God was meant to be not only read, studied, translated, memorized and meditated on. It was also to be embodied in the life and worship of the church. The embodiment of the Bible was most clearly expressed in the ministry of preaching, which was given a new prominence in the worship and theology of the Reformation traditions.

THE PRIORITY OF PREACHING

Contrary to a popular view, preaching was not invented by the Reformation. The late Middle Ages was marked by an immense appetite for the divine. New forms of lay piety, renewed interest in relics, pilgrimages and saints, popular religious movements—the Lollards in England, the Hussites in Bohemia, the Waldensians and Spiritual Franciscans in Italy and France—all testify to a steady growth in the power and depth of religious feelings right up to the time of the Reformation. Popular preaching in the vernacular languages was a part of this resurgence. Mendicant friars, especially the Dominicans and Franciscans, traveled widely throughout Europe preaching on special festivals, saints' days and days of indulgence. Frequently a convoy of confessors traveled in their company offering the ministrations of the church to those who were moved by the sermons they heard.

Bernadino of Siena was, after Saint Francis himself, the most popular Franciscan preacher of this period. He called on his listeners to repent, confess their sins and go to mass. He also encouraged a devotion to the holy name of Jesus, especially to his written name in the form of the monogram IHS. Closer in time to the Reformation was Girolamo Savonarola, a Dominican friar known for his apocalyptic sermons and his many bonfires of "vanities" in the piazzas of Florence. Savanarola was excommunicated by Pope Alexander VI, a frequent target of his tirades, and publicly executed in 1498. He and two of his associates were hanged on a single cross and their bodies roasted over an open fire. Today one can visit the site of his martyrdom in the

Piazza della Signoria in Florence. On his way to the Diet of Worms, Luther carried with him a picture of Savanarola, a reminder of what could happen to him.[1]

Other less famous mendicants preached in village churches or local chapels offering special sermons during the seasons of Advent and Lent. Other sources of popular preaching were pilgrimage sites devoted to the Virgin Mary and other saints. Thousands of pilgrims came to such places to hear sermons, say the rosary and pray for miracles. Before coming to Zurich, Zwingli preached at such a place, the Shrine of the Black Madonna in Einsiedeln, which is still one of the most popular pilgrimage sites for Catholics in Switzerland today. Yet another outlet for preaching at the time of the Reformation was endowed preacherships attached to a major city church or cathedral and often funded by wealthy merchants or guilds. Johann Geiler von Kaisersberg, the most popular preacher in Germany prior to the Reformation, held such a post in the city of Strasbourg, and Zwingli was called to one in Zurich in 1519.

The reformers challenged the medieval pattern of preaching in two important respects. First, they made the sermon the centerpiece of the regular worship of the church. Prior to the Reformation, the sermon was mostly an ad hoc event reserved for special occasions or seasons of the liturgical cycle, especially Christmas and Eastertide. Mass could be said without the sermon and usually was; hence the proliferation of private masses and mass priests. Bernardino and Savonarola were great outdoors preachers and delivered most of their sermons in town squares or open fields. The reformers brought the sermon back inside the church and gave it an honored place in the weekly liturgical hap-

---

[1]On the story of Luther's receiving a picture of Savanarola on his journey to Worms, see Martin Brecht, *Martin Luther: His Road to Reformation, 1483-1521*, trans. James L. Schaaf (Philadelphia: Fortress, 1985), p. 448. On Savonarola's appeal to the Bible and his allegorical reading of the Old Testament in his preaching, see Michael O'Connor, "The Ark and the Temple in Savanarola's Teaching," in *The Bible in the Renaissance*, ed. Richard Griffith (Aldershot: Ashgate, 2001), pp. 9-27.

pening of the gathered community. (Wesley would take the sermon back outdoors again, but that is another story.)

In many church buildings the new prominence given to the place of preaching in worship can be seen in the way the pulpit was raised to a higher elevation. In a famous painting of the interior of Temple de Paradis, a French Protestant church in Lyon, the pastor is shown delivering his sermon while the congregation is seated below, around the elevated pulpit. In keeping with the social conventions of the time, men are separated from women, and those with higher social status are seated on a slightly raised platform. Children are included in the congregation and sit in their designated pews with their Bible or catechism book opened. Even a stray dog appears to be listening intently to the sermon. Everything is focused on the preacher and the pulpit in the center of the room. Seated just below the pulpit is a couple who will be married at the end of the sermon. We also see preparations being made for the baptism of an infant. In the Reformed tradition, both of these traditional rites of passage were incorporated into the regular worship of the church. Both were accompanied by the preaching of the Word.

Second, the reformers introduced a new theology of preaching. Preaching in the Middle Ages was attached to the sacrament of penance. Preaching itself was not considered a sacrament, but it was, we might say, a vestibule to the sacrament of penance. Preachers were supposed to encourage sinners who heard the sermon to feel contrition for their sins, confess their sins to a priest and complete the penitential cycle by receiving absolution and performing an act of satisfaction. Ian Siggins has studied the kinds of sermons Luther would have heard from the Dominican and Franciscan friars who preached at Eisenach when he was a student there in the 1490s. Such preaching, he argues, intensified the anxieties of the listeners by emphasizing the impending reality of death, ever a sudden and unexpected possibility, and the need to seek forgiveness through contrition and confession.[2] With sermons like these ringing in his ears, Luther responded to the crisis in the thunderstorm and entered the monastery at Erfurt seeking release from his guilt and peace with God.

Steven Ozment has studied vernacular confessional manuals published in the late fifteenth century. These popular handbooks for confessors provided set questions to be posed to penitents who came to make confession. A series of piercing questions was attached to each of the Ten Commandments:

> Have you questioned God's power and goodness when you lost a game? Have you muttered against God because of bad weather, illness, poverty, the death of a child or friend? Have you murmured against God because the wicked prosper and the righteous perish? Have you committed perjury in a court of law? Have you sworn in the name of God or a saint that you will do something you had no intention of doing?—These are sins against the second commandment.
>
> Have you skipped mass on Sundays and holidays without a good excuse? Have you conducted business on Sundays rather than reflecting on your sins, seeking indulgence, counting your blessings, meditating on death, hell and its penalties, and heaven and its joys? Have you dressed proudly, sung and danced lustily, committed adultery, girl-watched, or exchanged adulterous glances in church or while walking on Sundays?—These are sins against the third commandment.[3]

---

[2]Ian Siggins, *Luther and His Mother* (Philadelphia: Fortress, 1981), pp. 53-70. Thomas Worcester, while acknowledging the force of Siggins's argument, points out that such guilt-inducing sermons as Luther may have heard in his youth were not "the sole genre of Catholic preaching" on the eve of the Protestant Reformation. He cites as a counterexample the more salubrious sermons of Pelbart of Temesvar, a Hungarian Observant Franciscan, who published a volume of sermons on the Virgin Mary giving thanks for her intercession and expressing special affection for her aid. See his "Catholic Sermons," in *Preachers and People in the Reformations and Early Modern Period*, ed. Larissa Taylor (Brill: Leiden, 2001), pp. 7-9.
[3]Steven E. Ozment, *The Reformation in the Cities: The Appeal of Protestantism through Sixteenth-Century Germany and Switzerland* (New Haven: Yale University Press, 1975), p. 24.

Each of the Ten Commandments had a set of similar questions. From what we know of Luther's case, such questions would have been superfluous, for he came to the confessional already well endowed with a robust sense of guilt. Only when Staupitz directed him away from himself to the wounds of Jesus on the cross did he find the forgiveness he had sought in vain through the prescribed path of penance. Luther's 1519 "Sermon on the Sacrament of Penance" was an assault not only on the confessional but also on the kind of preachers who "try to frighten people into going frequently to confession." It was the job of preachers, he said, to announce the promise of forgiveness through the unmerited grace of God. With an eye to his own experience, he advised those plagued by doubt and anxiety about meeting the standards of the confessional:

> You should not be debating . . . whether or not your contrition is sufficient. Rather you should be assured that after all your efforts your contrition is not sufficient. This is why you must cast yourself upon the grace of God, hear his sufficiently sure word in the sacrament, accepted in free and joyful faith, and never doubt that you have come to grace.[4]

Luther himself took up the task of preaching only reluctantly at the behest of Staupitz, who assigned him to preach to the Augustinian monks and in the town church of Wittenberg. It was his concern for the care of souls in his charge, as much as his scholarly work as a university professor, that propelled Luther to take a public stand on indulgences. Even when Bugenhagen took over the primary preaching responsibilities at St. Mary's Church in the 1520s, Luther continued to preach prodigiously. More than two thousand of his sermons are extant, filling twenty-two volumes in the Weimar edition of his works.

---

[4]Ibid, p. 50. Luther's "Sermon on the Sacrament of Penance" is found in *LW* 35:9-22.

For Luther, the public preaching of God's Word was an indispensible means of grace and a sure sign of the true church. The call to the preaching office was a sacred trust, he thought, and should not be used for selfish purposes, for "Christ did not establish the ministry of proclamation to provide us with money, property, popularity, honor, or friendship."[5] Preachers should be wary of listeners who are too complimentary of their sermons, for flattery can have a sinister outcome. Puffed-up preachers are likely to think to themselves: "This you have done, this is your work, you are first-rate man, the real master." Such conceit is not even worth throwing to the dogs, Luther said. Faithful preachers should teach only the Word of God and seek only his honor and praise. "Likewise, the hearers should also say: 'I do not believe in my pastor, but he tells me of another Lord whose name is Christ; him he shows me.'"[6]

Luther was often discouraged by the lack of "visible results" in his preaching ministry. His confidence to carry on came from his belief that God would surely honor his word. Sometimes he felt like a wandering minstrel singing alone in the woods with only his echo responding. But then he remembered that he had been given a message to deliver, and he heard God saying to him:

> Just go on preaching. Don't worry about who will listen; let me worry about that. The world will be against you, don't let that trouble you. Nevertheless, others will be there who will listen to you and follow. You do not know them now, but I know them already. You preach and let me manage.[7]

---

[5]*LW* 21:9.
[6]*LW* 51:388.
[7]Cited in John W. Doberstein, "Introduction," *LW* 51:xx-xxi. Fred W. Meuser has collected a number of Luther's statements on preaching. See his *Luther the Preacher* (Minneapolis: Augsburg, 1983). See also Beth Kreitzer, "The Lutheran Sermon," in *Preachers and People in the Reformations and Early Modern Period*, ed. Larissa Taylor (Brill: Leiden, 2001), pp. 35-63.

Because he had walked through the valley of discouragement, Luther knew how to give advice to younger preachers overcome by self-doubts. On one occasion he said to such a young struggler:

> If Peter and Paul were here, they would scold you because you
> wish right off to be as accomplished as they. Crawling is something, even if one is unable to walk. Do your best. If you can't
> preach an hour, then preach a half hour or a quarter of an hour.
> Do not try to imitate other people. Center on the shortest and
> simplest points, which are the very heart of the matter and leave
> the rest to God. Look solely to his honor and not to applause.
> Pray that God will give you a mouth into your audience's ear.[8]

How does one learn to preach? The proper training of preachers was an enormous challenge for the Protestant reformers who were intent on reshaping the life of the church through the ministry of preaching. A partial response was the printing of books of model sermons beginning with Luther's postils (*Kirchenpostille*). These were sermon digests distributed to those who were new to the Protestant faith or just learning how to preach. Bullinger's *Hausbuch*, called the *Decades* in English, served the same purpose as did printed collections of Calvin's sermons (more than twenty volumes in his lifetime), and, in its own way, the Anglican Book of Homilies. None of the sermons in these books was intended to be read word for word from the pulpit. Rather, they were designed "as a temporary expedient to tide the church over until such time as there should be an instructed and spiritual ministry."[9] Still, some pastors were so ill-prepared that they were reduced to repeating by rote the published sermons of others. Thomas Becon in England complained about such preachers who only had a

---

[8]Kreitzer, "The Lutheran Sermon," p. 58. Also cited in Roland H. Bainton, *Here I Stand: A Life of Martin Luther* (New York: Abingdon-Cokesbury, 1950), p. 350.
[9]Philip E. Hughes, *Theology of the English Reformers* (Grand Rapids: Baker, 1980), pp. 122-23.

ministry of "bare reading." He called them dumb dogs that could not bark.[10] Luther especially emphasized that the church was a "mouth house" not a "pen house." There could be no substitute for the living voice of the gospel. In his comment on Malachi 2:7, "The lips of a priest guard knowledge," Luther made this bold assertion:

> The Word is the channel through which the Holy Spirit is given. This is a passage against those who hold the spoken word in contempt. The lips are the public reservoirs of the church. In them alone is kept the Word of God. You see, unless the word is preached publicly, it slips away. The more it is preached, the more firmly it is retained. Reading it is not as profitable as hearing it, for the live voice teaches, exhorts, defends, and resists the spirit of error. Satan does not care a hoot for the written Word of God, but he flees at the speaking of the Word. You see this penetrates hearts and leads back those who stray.[11]

In the Reformed tradition, preaching was no less important. When one visits the famous Great Minster Church in Zurich today, the following inscription can be read over the portal: "The Reformation of Huldrych Zwingli began here on January 1, 1519." That date, no less than October 31, 1517, can be given as an answer to the question, When did the Reformation begin?

Figure 8.1. Huldrych Zwingli began his duties as "people's priest" at the Grossminster in Zurich on January 1, 1519. His systematic expositional preaching of the Bible influenced the pattern of preaching in the Reformed tradition.

On that first day in January, which happened to be Zwingli's birthday, the new "people's priest" of Zurich began his preaching ministry by announcing his intention to dispense with the prescribed texts of the traditional lectionary. He would follow a new paradigm: preaching expositional sermons, chapter by chapter, starting with the Gospel of Matthew. Why Matthew? Hughes Oliphant Old has suggested that Zwingli was likely imitating the example of Chrysostom, the famous preacher of the early church, whose verse-by-verse sermons on the Gospel of Matthew he had just received in a new edition from Froben in Basel.[12] The decision to begin with the Gospels gave priority to the words and deeds of Jesus. The great invitation of Jesus in Matthew 11:28, "Come to me, all who labor and are heavy laden, and I will give you rest," became one of Zwingli's favorite sermon texts. After completing Matthew, which occupied his first year at the Great Minster, Zwingli resumed the same *lectio continua* method by taking up Acts, then the epistles to Timothy, then Galatians, 1 and 2 Peter, Hebrews, the Gospel of John, and the other Pauline letters. Next he turned to the Old Testament beginning with the Psalms, then the Pentateuch and the historical books.

What was Zwingli like as a preacher? Only a few of his sermons were published in his lifetime and much that remains is in the form of incomplete notes. But we do have several reports of his preaching that would seem to justify our calling him, in the words of Lee Palmer Wandel, "one of the most charismatic and effective preachers of an age of preachers."[13] We have already met one of our witnesses, Thomas Platter, who became a well-known printer and school teacher. When he first came to Zurich as a young man in the early 1520s, he tells of hearing a sermon by Zwingli that was "expounded so powerfully that I felt as if someone was pulling me up by my hair."[14]

---

[12]See Hughes Oliphant Old, *The Patristic Roots of Reformed Worship* (Zurich: Theologischer Verlag Zurich, 1975), pp. 195-207. See also Old's *The Reading and Preaching of the Scriptures in the Worship of the Christian Church*, vol. 4: *The Age of the Reformation* (Grand Rapids: Eerdmans, 2002), pp. 46-48.

[13]Lee Palmer Wandel, "Switzerland," in *Preachers and People in the Reformations and Early Modern Period*, ed. Larissa Taylor (Leiden: Brill, 2001), p. 229.

[14]Theodore K. Rabb, *Renaissance Lives: Portraits of an Age* (New York: Pantheon, 1993), p. 82.

Heinrich Bullinger, who succeeded Zwingli as the leader of the Reformation in Zurich, gave this report about the preaching of his friend and its impact on those who heard him:

> In his sermons he was most eloquent, simple, and understandable, so that many heard him willingly, and there was a great rush of people to his sermons. . . . His speech was graceful and sweet, for he spoke idiomatically and was unwilling to use the usual pious chatter, the confusion thrown down from the pulpit, or unnecessary words. . . . There was soon a rush of all sorts of people, in particular the common man, to these evangelical sermons of Zwingli's, in which he praised God the Father, and taught all people to place their trust in God's son, Jesus Christ, as the single Savior.[15]

The greatest contribution of the Zurich reformers to the tradition of preaching was the institution of the "Prophecy." When Zwingli inaugurated the pattern of preaching in sequence through various books of the Bible rather than following the tradition of prescribed texts based on the liturgical cycle, he made preaching rather than the liturgy the main focus of weekly worship. In medieval times, it was common to speak of going to church to hear mass. Soon Protestants began to refer to their worship gatherings as preaching events. French Huguenots would ask, "Have you been to the *prêche*, the preaching, today?" But if preaching were to become a standard part of every service of worship, as the reformers proposed, and if the model of *lectio continua* were to become the method of choice for proclaiming the Word, then an intentional program of preparing preachers for their task had to be devised. The Prophecy met this need.

Starting in July 1525, at 7:00 in the morning in summer (8:00 in winter), on every day except Fridays and Sundays, all of the ministers

---

[15]Wandel, "Switzerland," p. 229.

and theological students in Zurich gathered into the choir of the Great Minster to engage in an hour of intense exegesis and interpretation of Scripture. Zwingli opened the meeting with prayer:

> Almighty, eternal and merciful God, whose Word is a lamp unto our feet and a light unto our path, open and illuminate our minds, that we may purely and perfectly understand thy Word and that our lives may be conformed to what we have rightly understood, that in nothing we may be displeasing unto thy majesty, through Jesus Christ our Lord. Amen.[16]

The text chosen for exposition that day would then be read in Latin, Greek and Hebrew, followed by appropriate textual or exegetical comments. This part of the exercise sounds very much like a modern scholarly seminar on some passage of Scripture. Drawing on the resources of biblical humanism, the Zurich scholars would probe the original setting of the text, what the words meant in the classical literature of antiquity, how the passage had been interpreted in the history of the church, with special deference given to the opinions of the church fathers. In other words, they did the kind of spade work that went into Kittel's *Theological Dictionary of the New Testament* and other contemporary tools of biblical research. When this part of the morning's work was completed, Zwingli or another of the ministers delivered a sermon on the passage in German. By that time, the Great Minster had begun to fill up with townspeople on their way to work who had stopped by to take in the sermon. In this way, the influence of the Prophecy reached beyond the circle of pastors and theologians to the wider lay community in Zurich.

The name Prophecy was taken from 1 Corinthians 14, where Paul

---

[16]Fritz Schmidt-Clausing, "Das Prophezeigebet," *Zwingliana* 12 (1964): 10-34. This is the translation given by Locher, *Zwingli's Thought: New Perspectives* (Leiden: Brill, 1981), p. 28.

referred to the gift of prophesying or the telling forth of the Word of God for the edification of the church. The influence of the Zurich Prophecy was enormous. It was a kind of theological seminary where ministers, preachers and teachers received a thorough grounding in the Scriptures. This in turn became a model for Reformed academies and seminaries throughout Europe. Its influence extended to the founding of Emmanuel College at Cambridge in 1584. Emmanuel became a hotbed for Puritan preachers, including John Harvard and other scholars who brought the Zurich model of Reformed preaching to the New World.

It would be a mistake, however, to think that the kind of scholarly training provided by the Prophecy and its counterparts elsewhere was sufficient to prepare adequate preachers of God's Word. Zwingli believed that it was the Holy Spirit who enlightened the reader of the biblical text and gave unction to the one charged to proclaim it. Scripture was self-authenticating in the sense that the same Spirit who had inspired the prophets and apostles to write the Scriptures long ago had to be present to confirm and persuade believers of its truth today.

Zwingli thus brought together two affirmations that would be even more closely conjoined by Calvin: the supremacy of Scripture over human tradition and the inward illumination of the contemporary reader by the Holy Spirit. Thus he could say, "I understand Scripture only in the way it interprets itself by the Spirit of God. It does not require any human opinion."[17] The preaching of the church fathers and the doctrinal decisions of the early councils were to be studied and embraced with this proviso: all of these had to be subjected to the testing stone of Scripture. If they displayed Christ, they were genuine, of the Spirit of God. In this case, however, there was no need to cry "fathers," "councils," "customs" and "tradition"; these

---

[17]Z 1:559: *Ich verston die geschrifft nit anders, dann wie sy sich selbst durch den geist gottes usslagt; bdarff keins menschlichen urteils.*

merely reflected the truth contained in the God-inspired Scriptures and made known by the Holy Spirit.

Zwingli's preaching meant a great deal to Calvin, perhaps more than he ever acknowledged. When Calvin was compelled through the dreadful adjuration of Guillaume Farel ("If you refuse to join us here, God will condemn you!") to take up the work of reform in Geneva in 1536, he came to a city that had already formally embraced the Protestant cause. Earlier that year, an assembly of citizens had gathered near the cathedral of St. Pierre and voted unanimously to "live henceforth according to the law of the Gospel and the Word of God, and to abolish all papal abuses."[18] But very little reforming work had been done. Looking back on the situation many years later, Calvin remembered that "everything was in upheaval."[19] Young Calvin threw himself into his work as a minister of the divine Word or, as he referred to himself, "Reader in Holy Scripture to the Church in Geneva."

Following the pattern established by Zwingli and Bullinger in Zurich, Calvin adopted the discipline of the *lectio continua*: week after week he marched through the various books of the Bible preaching expositional sermons chapter by chapter, verse by verse. In 1554-1555, he preached 159 sermons on Job; in 1555-1556, there were 200 sermons on Deuteronomy; in 1558-1559, 48 sermons on Ephesians, followed the next year by 65 sermons on Synoptic Gospels; 1561-1563 brought 194 sermons on 1 and 2 Samuel.[20] W. A. Criswell, a well-known Baptist pastor of the twentieth century, pursued this same preaching strategy in his Texas congregation. The people in his congregation became so used to following Criswell through the Bible that they began to mark time in their families by the progress of his preaching schedule: "Remember Tommy was born in Deuteronomy,"

---

[18]This is from Calvin's deathbed speech to the Genevan Company of Pastors, cited by William Monter, *Calvin's Geneva* (New York: John Wiley & Sons, 1957), p. 56.

[19]Ibid., p. 94.

[20]A full listing of Calvin's sermons by year is given in Bernard Cottret, *Calvin: A Biography*, trans. M. Wallace McDonald (Grand Rapids: Eerdmans, 2000), pp. 354-55.

Figure 8.2. John Calvin at work in his library. He would go
directly from his study to the pulpit in the Cathedral de St.
Pierre where he preached extemporaneously from the Hebrew
and Greek texts of the Bible.

they would say. Or, "Aunt Sally got married in Lamentations." "The
tornado hit in 2 Corinthians." One wonders if the citizens of Geneva
marked the seasons of their lives by Calvin's expositions. We do know
that Calvin was so committed to sequential, text-driven preaching
that on the first Sunday of his return to the pulpit of Saint Pierre in
1541 following his exile in Strasbourg, he began the sermon where he
had left off three years before, at the very chapter and verse of whatever book of the Bible (we do not know which one) he had been
preaching at the time. The point he was making by this gesture was

clear. The Reformation was not about Calvin or any other personality. Much less was it about the ups and downs of church politics by which the church is ever beset. No, the Reformation was about the Word of God, which was to be proclaimed faithfully and conscientiously to the people of God. Calvin held himself to a high standard and demanded no less of others called to the office of preaching. The true pastor, he said, must be marked by "ruthless persistence" (*importunitas*).[21] Pastors are not granted the luxury of choosing their own times of service, or suiting their ministry to their own convenience or preaching "sugar stick" sermons removed from their biblical context. "When passages of Scripture are taken up at random, and no attention is paid to the context," Calvin lamented, "it is no wonder that mistakes arise all over the place."[22]

Hughes Oliphant Old has asked why Calvin was so highly regarded as a preacher. Why did people listen to him?

> Calvin did not have the warm personality of Luther. One does not find in Calvin the oratorical elegance of Gregory of Nazianzus, nor the lively imagination of Origen. He was hardly the dramatic public speaker that John Chrysostom was, nor did he have the magnetic personality of Bernard of Clairvaux. Gregory the Great was a natural-born leader, as was Ambrose of Milan, but that was not a gift Calvin had.[23]

To Old's litany we might add that neither did Calvin have the military bearing of Zwingli, who died on the battlefield of Kappel wielding a double-edged sword, or the irenic disposition of Bucer, whose schemes for Christian unity never quite convinced Calvin; nor was he blessed with the longevity of Bullinger, who died at age

---

[21]The phrase "ruthless persistence" is from Calvin's commentary on 2 Timothy 4:2. See CNTC 10:333.

[22]CO 36:277; CC 7:442.

[23]Old, *Reading and Preaching*, 4:128-29.

seventy-one after a long life of service as a reformer and "architect of Reformation."[24]

What was the secret of Calvin's success? Among many answers that might be given, the following have merit. His preaching was informed by his superb exegetical studies and the many commentaries he wrote on nearly every book of the Bible. He was a brilliant public speaker who could express ideas, including very complex ones, with clarity and precision. Calvin knew the Bible so well that he breathed its air, conversed with its characters and inhabited its pages. He always preached from the Greek or Hebrew text without notes or manuscript. He was a master of the French language and had an influence on its development comparable to that of Luther on German.[25] All of this is true, but Old's conclusion as to why so many people listened to Calvin's sermons with such interest touches a deeper chord:

> Surely the fundamental answer is not to be found in their oratorical form but rather in their religious content. Calvin drew out of the Scriptures aspects of Christian teaching which the church had not heard for centuries. This was above all the case with the doctrine of grace. The promise of salvation was presented to all who would believe it. Calvin preached justification by faith, as all the reformers did. More than some, perhaps, he also preached sanctification by faith. The lives of those who believed the Word of God would be transformed by that Word. Holiness was the fruit of faith. To believe the Word was to live by the Word, and that life lived according to the Word of God was blessed, both in this world and in the world to come.[26]

Calvin's preaching was also marked by a practical bent. He was

---

[24]See Bruce Gordon and Emidio Campi, eds., *Architect of Reformation: An Introduction to Heinrich Bullinger, 1504-1575* (Grand Rapids: Baker Academic, 2004).

[25]See Francis Higman, *The Style of John Calvin in His French Polemical Treatises* (Oxford: Oxford University Press, 1967).

[26]Old, *Reading and Preaching*, 4:130.

concerned with applying the sermon to the situations of his listeners. For example, during the 1550s Geneva was flooded with numerous refugees who sought safety within its walls. Calvin never forgot that he himself had fled persecution in France, and he offered warm hospitality to the refugees, most of whom played a constructive role in the city's reformation. Some of the refugee families, however, were troublesome and disruptive. Calvin did not hesitate to address them directly from the pulpit:

> There are households where husband and wife are like cat and dog; there are some who try to "heighten" their own importance and imitate the lords without reason, and have given themselves to pomp and worldly superfluity. Others become so "delicate" that they don't know how to work anymore, and are no longer content with any foods. There are some gossipers and "bad mouthers" who would find something to say against the angel of paradise; and in spite of the fact they are "bursting" with vices, they want to put all their "holiness" into controlling ("blessing") their neighbors. Nevertheless, it seems to them all that God must be pleased with the fact that they have made the voyage to Geneva, as if it would not have been better for them to stay on their manure than to come to commit such scandalous acts in the church of God.[27]

In the course of his ministry at Geneva, Calvin delivered more than four thousand sermons. His home was just a short walk from the cathedral, and he would go directly from his study into the pulpit of St. Pierre. Though he preached extemporaneously, he did not simply "open his mouth and expect the Lord to fill it." No preacher can

---

[27]CO 8:422. This is from Calvin's sermon "Treating Matters of Great Usefulness for Our Times." The translation is that of John H. Leith, "Calvin's Doctrine of the Proclamation of the Word and Its Significance for Today," in *John Calvin and the Church: A Prism of Reform*, ed. Timothy George (Louisville, Ky.: Westminster/John Knox, 1990), p. 216.

faithfully present God's Word to the congregation without doing the hard work of serious Bible study. As Calvin put it,

> If I should enter the pulpit without deigning to look at a book and should frivolously think to myself, "Oh well, when I preach, God will give me enough to say," and come here without troubling to read or think what I ought to declare, and do not carefully consider how I must apply Holy Scripture to the edification of the people, then I should be an arrogant upstart.[28]

Reinhold Niebuhr once said that as a young minister he determined not to become a pretty preacher. Calvin, too, avoided the pomp and embellishment, not to say the showmanship, that marked much pulpit work in his day no less than in ours. "What is required is not nearly a voluble tongue, for we see many whose easy fluency contains nothing that can edify," he wrote.[29] The purpose of preaching is edification. The pastor must not "fly about among the subtleties of frivolous curiosity." The pastor must not be a "questionnairian." Preaching that builds up the people of God not only must be doctrinally sound but also must seek the "solid advantage" of the church, that is, it must be practical, applicable, discriminating.

In his preaching, as in his commentary work, Calvin usually avoided mystical and allegorical approaches to the text. For example, in his sermons on the whirlwind speech in Job 38, Calvin refused to allegorize the great beasts Behemoth and Leviathan as Satan, though this might have been justified given the role of Satan at the beginning of the book. Calvin offers instead a naturalistic reading of Behemoth as simply an elephant and Leviathan as only a whale. As Susan Schreiner has pointed out, this interpretive strategy permitted Cal-

---

[28]This is from Calvin's sermon on Deuteronomy 6:13-15. See Leith, "Calvin's Doctrine of Proclamation," p. 218.
[29]CNTC 10:225.

Figure 8.3. Calvin preaching in the Cathedral to the throngs who crowded in to hear him expound the Scriptures according to the lectio continua method.

vin to lessen the role of Satan in the book of Job so that "the power struggle depicted in chapters 40-41 was not between God and Satan but, rather, between God and Job. . . . Calvin's Job did not have to withstand the power and cleverness of the devil so much as he had to find a way to stand before God, especially now that he had learned about 'the master with whom he had to deal.'"[30]

Calvin strongly emphasized the unity of the Old and New Testa-

---

[30]CO 35:353. See Susan Schreiner, "Calvin as an Interpreter of Job," in *Calvin and the Bible*, ed. Donald K. McKim (Cambridge: Cambridge University Press, 2006), pp. 76-77.

ments and the continuity of God's people through the ages. For Calvin and the Reformed tradition generally, there are not two separate ages of salvation with divergent covenants but rather only one covenant in two dispensations. Calvin's commitment to see the Bible as an integral history led him to tone down some of the traditional christological readings of the Old Testament in favor of a vision of salvation history that emphasizes the kingly rule of God and his providential care for the elect. Some critics, in his day as well as later, accused Calvin of "Judaizing" tendencies because he emphasized so strongly the grammatical reading of the text and was more cautious about the explicitly christological exegesis so loved by Luther and much of the tradition before him. But, as Sujin Pak has shown, Calvin did want to maintain the centrality of Christ in his teaching and preaching on the Old Testament but did so in a way that connected Christology with the doctrine of providence. For Calvin, "the Christological reading must have a clear and intimate tie with the basic plain, historical reading of the text, hence rendering the typological or figural readings deeply tied to the literal sense."[31]

Along with his commentaries, Calvin intended for his *Institutes* to serve as the handbook to the Scriptures, a useful aid for the preparation of sermons. What the Prophecy was in Zurich, the *congrégations* became in Geneva. These were weekly meetings sponsored by the Company of Pastors in which Calvin or other ministers offered intensive biblical instruction for those called to the preaching ministry. These meetings took place every Friday with around sixty or more in attendance at the *Auditoire*, a small building adjacent to the cathedral of Saint Pierre. This is the same site where John Knox and English-speaking refugees met for worship during the Marian exile. Today it still houses an English-speaking congregation of the Church of Scotland. Transplanted to England in the early days of Queen Elizabeth,

---

[31]G. Sujin Pak, *The Judaizing Calvin: Sixteenth-Century Debates Over the Messianic Psalms* (Oxford: Oxford University Press, 2010), p. 138.

this pattern of nascent seminary training called the "prophesyings" became training centers for future preachers and leaders of the Puritan movement.

Calvin's high doctrine of the preached Word has sometimes been interpreted as evidence for his alleged intellectualism, dualism and disparagement of all things corporeal. But the image of Calvin as a body-despising, fun-killing, proto-puritan of the most somber kind who loved to fill his listeners' ears with wordy sermons divorced from the stuff of real life is inaccurate. Calvin's approach to worship and preaching belies such stereotypes. Of central importance is the fact that Calvin believed that the preaching of the Word should be accompanied by the weekly celebration of the Lord's Supper. Despite the fact that the city council of Geneva would only allow four eucharistic services per year, Calvin's insistence on the coinherence of pulpit and table points to the wider sacramental context in which he believed the preaching of the Word should take place.

Apart from predestination, Calvin wrote more about the doctrine of the Lord's Supper than any other controversial issue in the Reformation. It is significant that he was a post-Marburg theologian—he entered the ranks of the reformers after the famous colloquy of 1529 had left Luther and Zwingli at an impasse on the question of the nature of the real presence of Christ in the Supper. In his own eucharistic theology, Calvin tried to steer a middle course between Zwingli, whom he felt had too little regard for the outward signs of bread and wine, and Luther, who extolled them immoderately, thus obscuring the mystery itself. Calvin agreed with Zwingli that Christ was locally present at the right hand of the Father in heaven and should not be thought of as "attached to the element of the bread," to be touched by the hands, chewed by the teeth and swallowed by the mouth. But he agreed with Luther that the Supper was not an empty symbol—"the truth of the thing signified is surely present there"—but rather a

means of "true participation" in Christ.[32] Recent Calvin scholarship
has emphasized the theme of participation as crucial to both his understanding of the Lord's Supper and his emphasis on the proclamation of the Word.

In his essay "Believing Is Seeing: Proclamation and Manifestation
in the Reformed Tradition," Randall Zachman points out that the
contemplation, feeling and enjoyment of God experienced by Adam
and Eve before the Fall is restored to redeemed humanity through
what Calvin calls the "spectacles" of Scripture. Hearing the Word of
God proclaimed in the power of the Spirit does not merely inform
the mind; it heals the eyes, clearing away the bleariness produced by
sin and making contemplation possible and fruitful for the believer.
Put otherwise, preaching gives sight as well as insight. Zachman argues that Calvin never replaces the language of manifestation and
contemplation with the language of proclamation and hearing, but
that he brings the two together in a mutually reinforcing relationship.
Thus "when the church does not attend to the vivid representation of
Christ in its preaching, sacraments, and ceremonies, it is hindering
genuine Christian transformation no matter how much it may be
preaching and teaching sound doctrine."[33]

Thomas J. Davis has also emphasized both the cognitive and affective dimensions of preaching for Calvin. The preaching of the gospel "must not only penetrate the mind but also take deep root in the
heart, so that in both preaching and the sacraments, grace is offered
in the here and now, through the instruments God has chosen to pre-

---

[32]See Calvin's succinct explanation of the Reformation positions on the Lord's Supper in the *Institutes* 4.17.10-12. One of the best expositions of Calvin's views is B. A. Gerrish, *Grace and Gratitude: The Eucharistic Theology of John Calvin* (Minneapolis: Fortress, 1993).
[33]Randall Zachman, "Believing Is Seeing: Proclamation and Manifestation in the Reformed Tradition," public lecture presented at the Institute for Reformed Theology, http://reformedtheology.org/SiteFiles/PublicLectures/ZachmanPL.html. See also Zachman's study, *Image and Word in the Theology of John Calvin* (Notre Dame: University of Notre Dame Press, 2007), and J. Todd Billings, *Calvin, Participation and the Gift: The Activity of Believers in Union with Christ* (Oxford: Oxford University Press, 2007).

sent and to make present the new life in Christ."[34] In an early essay from 1961, Heiko Oberman set forth the distinctive marks of Reformation preaching in terms of three interrelated aspects. First, the sermon is an apocalyptic event, not quite in the sense of Savanarola's preaching of impending doom to the people of Florence, but in the sense that the sermon unveils and makes present the final judgment here and now. Without demythologizing the coming of Christ in the future, it existentializes the final will of God for every hearer by calling for a decisive response. "In the sermon, Christ and the Devil are revealed, Creator and creature, love and wrath, essence and existence, 'Yes' and 'No.'"[35]

Second, as we have seen with respect to Calvin, the sermon is not meant to be an isolated speaking part in an otherwise sterile liturgy. The sermon was a vital and integral part of corporate worship. Praying, singing (the repertoire was limited to the psalms in Reformed worship), confession of sins, declaration of grace, baptisms, weddings, the congregation gathered around the Lord's table to receive in faith the body and blood of Jesus Christ, "in with and under" for Luther, and "exhibited by" for Calvin, the earthly elements of bread and wine—all of these activities presuppose and are supported by the lively preaching of the Word of God. Woven into the texture of the complete worship event by the dynamic operation of the Holy Spirit, the Reformation sermon is "not legalistic but redemptive, not only directed to individual souls but especially to the corporate existence of the congregation, not elevating but mobilizing, not a refuge but a starting point and, finally, not holy and vertical, but secular and horizontal: time, space, and dust."[36]

With this in mind, we are able to hear again the startling an-

---

[34]Thomas J. Davis, *This Is My Body: The Presence of Christ in Reformation Thought* (Grand Rapids: Baker Academic, 2008), p. 100.

[35]Heiko A. Oberman, "Preaching of the Word in Reformation," *Theology Today* 18 (1961): 19.

[36]Ibid., p. 24.

nouncement of Bullinger in the Second Helvetic Confession of 1566: "The preaching of the Word of God *is* the Word of God." This means that the event of preaching, not unlike the Eucharist in medieval Catholic theology, has an utterly objective character that transcends even the weak and sinful status of the preacher. God truly speaks and is truly present in judgment and grace whenever his Word is proclaimed. Despite the deep and divisive differences between Lutheran and Reformed theologians over the Lord's Supper in the sixteenth century, they found common ground in "the *ex opere operato* presence of God's Word in the preached Word."[37] Davis has expressed well the importance of this insight in Calvin's thought: "God has chosen preaching, and God invigorates the preaching of ministers by the power of God's Spirit so that Christ truly comes in the spoken Word to reside with his people; or to reverse the direction as Calvin so liked to do, preaching lifted the congregation to Christ, to participate in Christ and thus gain all the benefits he offers."[38]

The recovery of the themes of presence and participation in Calvin's doctrine of proclamation is a welcome corrective to other views that stress the cognitive and rationalist aspects of his theology at the expense of the affective and experiential. But we must be careful not to make Calvin the advocate of an overly realized eschatology. Calvin preached to a congregation besieged by both physical and spiritual enemies. He trained and sent forth hundreds of pastors to plant churches and preach the gospel in difficult and dangerous places. His life's work was the repair of Christ's church, which to his mind was in dire straights—"tossed on a turbulent sea, and almost sunk in the waves."[39] It was the fate of the gospel, he said, "to be preached in the world amid great contention."[40]

---

[37]Ibid., p. 26.

[38]Davis, *This Is My Body*, p. 102.

[39]CC 2:463-64.

[40]John Calvin, *Tracts and Treatises*, trans. Henry Beveridge (Grand Rapids: Eerdmans, 1958), 1:186.

Calvin's disciples were remarkably successful in overthrowing kingdoms, decapitating rulers and controlling the forces of government in many sixteenth- and seventeenth-century European societies. But Calvin does not read well as an establishment theologian. Herman Selderhuis has reminded us of Calvin's words, "We are always on the road."[41] Calvin was a displaced person, and he never felt completely at home even in Geneva, where he became a citizen only in 1559 near the end of his life. Calvin preached and wrote for sojourners, refugees and emigrants, for pilgrims who like Abraham and Sarah of old were looking for a city whose builder and maker was God. That city was not Rome, but neither was it Geneva or Wittenberg, or Zurich, or Strasbourg, or Waldshut, nor any of the other places we have visited in this book. "There will be no inheritance for us in heaven," Calvin wrote, "unless we are pilgrims on earth."[42] This theme permeates Calvin's theology, his preaching and his prayers.

> Since You promised us rest nowhere but in your heavenly kingdom, so grant, Almighty God, that on our earthly pilgrimage we may consent not to have an abiding city but to be driven here and there, and despite all that, still call upon you with a quiet spirit. Permit us to carry on our warfare, which you have designed to train and to test us, that we may be firm and steadfast in this warfare until at last we arrive at that rest which has been obtained for us by the blood of your only-begotten Son. Amen.[43]

---

[41]Herman J. Selderhuis, *John Calvin: A Pilgrim's Life* (Downer's Grove, Ill.: InterVarsity Press, 2009).

[42]CNTC 12:171.

[43]Cited by Heiko A. Oberman, *The Two Reformations: The Journey from the Last Days to the New World* (New Haven: Yale University Press, 2003), p. 119.

CONCLUSION

Wнen the team of translators who had been assembled by King James I to produce an authorized version of the Bible in their mother tongue presented their work, they provided a preface that contained a dedicatory letter to their royal patron. They defended their new translation against certain "popish persons at home or abroad" who disapproved of Bible translations in general. They also took a swipe at certain "self-conceited brethren, who run their own ways, and give liking unto nothing, but what is framed by themselves, and hammered on their anvil." This comment was directed against the Puritans, who much preferred the Geneva Bible with its illustrations, maps and Calvinist-tinged theological notes. The King James Version had few notes and maps and included the Apocrypha as a separate section between the two Testaments. The translators said of their new translation that they had "great hopes that the Church of England shall reap good fruit thereby."[1]

In addition to addressing the king, the translators also wrote a lengthy preface to "the gentle reader." Here they placed their new

---

[1]Gerald Bray, ed., *Translating the Bible from William Tyndale to King James* (London: The Latimer Trust, 2010), pp. 202-3.

translation in the context of the transmission of the Scriptures through the ages with numerous quotations from the church fathers, especially Jerome, Chrysostom and Augustine, and with due acknowledgment of the work of more recent scholars such as Valla and Erasmus. Tyndale, whose translation they had largely absorbed, is nowhere mentioned by name, though they do commend those translators "that travailed before us" as deserving "to be had of us posterity in everlasting remembrance."[2] One might have thought that such deserved to be mentioned by name! Translators of the King James Version admonished their gentle readers to read, search, study and love the sacred Scriptures, calling on Jerome and Augustine to support their admonition.

> But now what piety without truth? What truth (what saving truth) without the Word of God? What Word of God (whereof we may be sure) without the Scripture? The Scriptures we are commanded to search. They are commended that searched and studied them. They are reproved that were unskilled in them, or slow to believe them. They can make us wise unto salvation. If we be ignorant, they will instruct us; if out of the way, they will bring us home; if out of order, they will reform us; if in heaviness, comfort us; if dull, quicken us; if cold, inflame us. *Tolle, lege; tolle, lege, 'Take up and read; take up and read'* the Scriptures, (for unto them was the direction) it was said unto St. Augustine by a supernatural voice. 'Whatsoever is in the Scriptures, believe me,' saith the same St. Augustine, 'is high and divine; there is verily truth and a doctrine most fit for the refreshing and renewing of men's minds, and truly so tempered that everyone may draw from thence that which is sufficient for him, if he come to draw with a devout and pious mind, as true religion requireth.' Thus St. Augustine. And St. Jerome: *Ama*

---

[2]Ibid., p. 220.

scripturas et amabit te sapientia, etc. ('Love the Scriptures and wisdom will love thee.').[3]

The King James Version was published in 1611, a full century after Luther had received his doctorate in theology in Wittenberg. The Reformation began with an Augustinian monk poring over the text of Scripture discovering therein the meaning of the gospel—that sinful men and women are put to rights by God through the outpouring of his mercy in Jesus Christ, and not by strivings and good works of their own. The doctrine of justification by faith alone became, as later Protestants would say, the article by which the church either stands or falls.

For the reformers it was impossible to separate the core message of the gospel from the written Word of God in which they found it expressed with compelling clarity. For them, the Bible was precious, not as a handbook for happy living or as a primer of metaphysics about God, but because they found there "the swaddling clothes in which Christ lies."[4] As we have seen throughout this book, the principle of *sola scriptura* did not mean that the study of the Bible should be divorced from interaction with its other readers and interpreters across the ages. But the new understanding of the place of the Bible in the life of the church did mean the rejection of the particular synthesis of Scripture, tradition and papal authority that had come to prevail in the western church during the late Middle Ages.

On the fiftieth anniversary of the Augsburg Confession, the Lutheran movement found a new confessional unity in the Book of Concord of 1580. This definitive collection of Lutheran confessions contained seven Reformation-era statements, all of which had originated within German-speaking territorial churches. These *Landeskirchen*,

---

[3]Ibid., p. 208.
[4]LW 35:236. Study the Scriptures, Jesus said, "so that in it you discover Me, Me" (*WA* 51:2): *Und also inn der Schrifft studivet, das ihr Mich, Mich drinnen findet.*

as they were called, together with their Scandinavian sister churches, constituted the heartland of the Lutheran movement well into modern times. Elsewhere in Europe, other Protestant communities had begun to identify themselves as "Reformed, in accordance with the Word of God." The Reformed tradition took root in the city-states of southern Germany and Switzerland, with Zurich and Geneva in the lead, but it soon became a widespread international movement. In the sixteenth century, Reformed confessions of faith were published in Switzerland, Germany, France, Belgium, Scotland, England, Ireland, Hungary, Poland, Bohemia and the Netherlands.

The Reformed churches proved to be remarkably adaptable to different social and political contexts, and no one church or confession was identical with another. The differences between Reformed and Lutheran churches in the sixteenth century were exacerbated by the fact that the 1555 settlement of the Peace of Augsburg, which allowed secular rulers to determine the religious affiliation of their subjects, excluded the Reformed churches from this settlement. The history of theology in the late Reformation, which scholars call the age of confessionalization, is marked by intensifying doctrinal disputes and church polemics. But the post-Reformation period of Protestant orthodoxy was also a time of cultural flourishing and spiritual fecundity. It gave us, to name only two of the giants, John Milton and Johann Sebastian Bach. The work of neither is comprehensible apart from the renaissance of biblical studies in the Reformation.

Several years ago, I was asked to endorse a book titled *Is the Reformation Over?* by Carolyn Nystrom and my friend Mark Noll. In answer to the book's title, I said that the Reformation was over only in the sense that to some extent it had succeeded. One of the most evident signs of that success is the spread of the Bible around the globe in numerous languages and dialects of the world's peoples. While debates about the Bible continue to divide Christians one from another, the Bible has also brought many Christians together.

In the Scriptures they have found a common hope in Christ and a common ground on which to stand in a world fraught with danger and despair. It is not uncommon to see Catholic and evangelical young people today who have come together to pray and study God's Word. The written Word of God is still alive and powerful, for it points us to Jesus Christ, the living Word, the true head of the church that is his body.

In my office at Beeson Divinity School, two paintings stand facing one another on opposite walls. One is a painting of William Tyndale shown in his scholarly garb holding a copy of the Bible in one hand and pointing at it with the index finger of his other hand. The other painting is the famous depiction of the crucifixion by Mathias Grünewald from the Isenheim Altarpiece, a painting originally designed to be placed in a sixteenth-century hospice. The death agonies of Jesus are graphically shown with the nails driven through his hands and his fingers pointing like spikes against the darkened sky. Next to the figure of Christ stands John the Baptist holding a book in one hand and pointing with the other to Jesus on the cross. These two paintings depict the two poles of Reformation theology. Our task is to point men and women both to the written Word in Scripture and to the living Word Jesus Christ.

IMAGE CREDITS

Figure 2.1. The Ecumenical Holy Encyclopedia/www.heiligenlexikon.de/BiographienA/Argula_von_Grumbach.html

Figure 2.2. Used with permission. SPL / Photo Researchers, Inc.

Figure 3.1. "Divine Mill" by Melchior Ramminger, 1521/http://academic.reed.edu/Humanities/Hum210/syllabi/fall04/week11/detail.np/detail-01.html.

Figure 4.1. Martin Luther (1483-1546) (engraving) by Lucas Cranach the Elder. Used with permission. Erich Lessing/Art Resource, NY

Figure 5.1. Anti-Reformatorical caricature showing Martin Luther with seven heads, by Johannes Cochlaeus, printed by Valentin Schumann, Leipzig 1529 (woodcut) by Hans Brosamer (c. 1495-c.1554). Used with permission. Deutsches Historisches Museum, Berlin, Germany/©DHM/The Bridgeman Art Library

Figure 6.1. Philipp Melancthon (1497-1560) by Albrecht Duerer (1471-1528) (engraving). Used with permission. bpk, Berlin/(Kupferstichkabinett, Staatliche Museen)/Art Resource, NY

Figure 6.2. Luther's seal or Luther's rose/http://cyberbrethren.com/2010/11/07/the-story-of-the-luther-seal-or-luther-rose/

Figure 7.1. Used with permission. Hulton Archive/Getty Images

Figure 7.2. View of Strasbourg in France, around 1490, published 1493 in Hartmann Schedel's *Weltchronik*. Wikimedia Commons

Figure 8.1. Woodcut based on a 1549 portrait of Ulrich Zwingli by Hans Asper. Wikimedia Commons

Figure 8.2. Used with permission. Time Life Pictures/Getty Images

Figure 8.3. John Calvin (1509-64) (engraving) (see also 80412) by Johannes & Mortier Covens, Cornelis (fl. c. 1700). Used with permission. Société de l'Histoire du Protestantisme Français, Paris/Archives Charmet/The Bridgeman Art Library

Author Index

Subject Index

Scripture Index

Reformation Commentary on Scripture

Timothy George (General Editor)
and Scott Manetsch (Associate General Editor)

RETRIEVED FOR THE SAKE OF RENEWAL

"Although it will be of use to students of the Reformation, this series is far from being an esoteric study of largely forgotten voices; this collection of reforming comments, comprehending every verse and provided with topical headings, will serve contemporary pastors and preachers very well."

ELSIE ANNE MCKEE, Princeton Theological Seminary

"This commentary series is a godsend!"

RICHARD J. MOUW, president, Fuller Theological Seminary

"Why was this not done before? The publication of the Reformation Commentary on Scripture should be greeted with enthusiasm by every believing Christian—but especially by those who will preach and teach the Word of God."

R. ALBERT MOHLER JR., president, The Southern Baptist Theological Seminary

"This series will strengthen our understanding of the period of the Reformation and enable us to apply its insights to our own day and its challenges to the church."

ROBERT KOLB, Concordia Theological Seminary

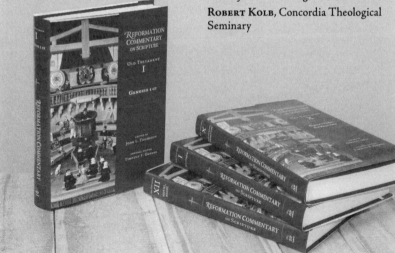